* * * * * *

ENJOY OFTEN ! ! !

* * * * * * * * *

REFLECTIONS OF FORGOTTEN JOYS LOST IN THE SANDS OF TIME DURING OUR QUESTING FOR THE GOOD LIFE

30 SHORT STORIES, ODES, ESSAYS, AND RAMBLINGS BY

JOHN F. HARNISH

* * * * * *

ENJOY

OFTEN ! ! !

JOHN F. HARNISH

ISBN 0-7414-0079-0

Cover design by Cathi A. Wong

Published by:

INFINITY
PUBLISHING.COM

Infinity Publishing.com
519 West Lancaster Avenue
Haverford, PA 19041-1413
Info@buybooksontheweb.com
www.buybooksontheweb.com
Toll-free (877) BUY BOOK
Local Phone (610) 520-2500
Fax (610) 519-0261

Printed in the United States of America

Printed on Recycled Paper

Published March-1999

To my son, my friend,
the much younger more handsome

John Franklin Harnish

Thank you for being the kind of son
I could never seem to be for my father,
and I hope I'm the kind of father
that you'll want to be.

Waste not, want not!!!   --Ben Franklin

ACKNOWLEDGEMENTS

ACKNOWLEDGEMENTS & INFLUENCES & THANKS

Many thanks to a host of lots of helpful folks!!!

WOW...I'd like to thank everyone for helping to make this book possible. All those friends and associates I've known along my path so far and those I've yet to meet. I'd like to again thank my high school English teacher Mrs. Helm for telling me to stick with only doing artwork because I'd never make it as a writer. Sometimes being told you can't do something is a very positive incentive to try to do it even better.

I'd like to thank my long ago friend Nancy Jackson, aka Mason, for all she taught me back in the '70's while editing my first book *COMING....* To Jane Bloom, my literary agent back then, you taught me well about the ways of publishing, and this time I've published without needing an agent to make a good deal. To John Irving, Anne Rice, Tom Clancy, Toni Morrison, Stephen King, John Sandford, Clive Cussler and all the other writers who've shared their wordsmithing crafts with me along the way. Also, all those fine folks who took the time to help put writer's conferences together, especially the Breadloaf Writer's Conference in Vermont and the Cape Cod Writer's Conference.

Thanks to George Carlin for joining with me in helping to make *fuck* a more acceptable and properly used word. Regrets over all the trouble Lenny Bruce got into for using *fuck* in his nightclub act way back when. I'm thankful for the way he opened the door for looking at lots of stuff that needed looking at for a very long time. Also thanks to George Burns for sharing his own very special style of humor, and for buying lunch!!!

A most special thanks to my friend and editor Marta Lewis for her many tireless wordrighting efforts in editing my rambles into a much more acceptable form. Marta was marvelous with her challenging task of trying to edit my creative flows while retaining my unique style of writing, as she says she never worked on a fun book like this one where I change style frequently.

ACKNOWLEDGEMENTS

A very special thanks to my dear wife Linda, for her ongoing encouragement and sincerely supportive ways in giving me the space I needed to ponder thoughts through and to be a sounding board when needed, and for not getting bent out of shape when I did it my way anyhow. Also, for carefully reading through every piece checking for typos and stuff that everyone else might have missed. Thanks too for your kind understanding in putting up with my long hours of working to spin this book into reality.

Thanks to Barb, my NTT Ding friend, who gave me objective reads from a teacher's point of view on every piece and made suggestions along the way, and didn't ding me out when I didn't follow some of her suggestions. Also, a big thanks to all the AOL Name That Tune players and online friends who took the time to give me feedback on many of my early drafts, especially Trixie, May, Shelly, Donna, Laure, JR, Lana, Tee, Adell, Frankie, Stella, Jilly, Mari, Cynthia, Franny, Kelly, Kate, Phylis, Dee, Barbara, Dev 'n Blu, Ronne, Noodles, Patty, MaryJo, Tara, Jean, Terry, Janet, Traci, Nony, Lisa, Karen, Melissa, Jez, Debi, Ellie, Andee, Connie, Suzie, Meri, Joan, Sharon, Sharry 'n Jim, Mad, Boomer, Chris, Bev, Val, Susan, Carol, and Regina for their comments and help with some of the tune stuff, etc, et al.

A special thanks to my friend and mentor Bill Smeltzer for his ongoing positive encouragement to make this book really happen and for his continuing friendship. Thanks to my friend and attorney Susan Pendery for doing her best to keep my ass covered and keep me out of harm's way. A special thank you muchly to my good friend Julia Stahler for sharing her special gift of the garden of the heart concept with me, and for her understanding about my modifications on her concept to adapt her garden of the heart for use in several of my pieces.

Thanks to Mother Earth for silently sharing some of her natural flowing secrets with me, and for the invigorating energy of her not-so-quiet rumbling thunderstorms. At times I've found ideas being birthed in your spectacular sunsets, giving way to twilight skies with a host of stars twinkling into sight. And although weary, I've appreciated your gentle ways of breaking the dawn of a new day into being with refreshing points of view on pondered thoughts that I'd been toiling into words.

Thanks to Father Time for your kindness to me. I've appreciated my ability to reach back into those far way places of my yesteryears to recall events to be honed into some of these sharings, and sifting through the sands of times for gains of happenings worthy of wordsmithing. Thanks too for the ways your mild abrasive sands have smoothed away some of the harsher happenings in the passages of life. Time does indeed heal all wounds by polishing them to a reflective smoothness that's so fluid, they just eventually flow away through the portals of time into the garden pool of reflections.

An eternal thanks to all my students and teachers. When I was a student, I wish I'd paid more attention to the course work which doesn't seem so coarse now. When I was teaching, I hope my students were learning as much from me as I was learning from them. I'm grateful for the students who took the time to let me know that I helped to make learning fun for them. For in truth, all of us are both students and teachers in an endless cycle of learning and sharing what we think we have learned.

I greatly appreciate the influences of several groups and organizations. The YMCA for teaching me how to swim, and for the opportunity to learn how to shoot pool—I still love to swim, but my pool game continues to be just about average. The American Red Cross, for teaching me how to teach swimming and life saving skills—most folks drown when they get in over their head and lose their heads!!! The Boy Scouts of America, for helping me to learn to appreciate the many beauties of nature, and about the gift of making a camp fire with a single match and without a match. The Civil Air Patrol for the opportunity to learn the principles of flight and for many hours of stick time in the squadron's L-16—the precision drill team stuff was a bit much, and to this day I have an aversion of parades. The First Reformed Church, for expelling me from confirmation classes for asking too many questions—yes, I'm still working on the questions that ring true for me and those ding donging bells just don't do it.

ACKNOWLEDGEMENTS

All the participating companies who make the Junior Achievement program possible for teaching youth about the formation and ways of conducting business. The USAF, for putting up with me and for making college possible, also for the chance to meet some great aviators, and for teaching me about the role of a prepared military in maintaining peace during the *cold war*—and for the opportunity of learning to adapt with the ever changing weather flows of Oklahoma. The Lancaster and Pennsylvania Jaycees, for teaching leadership skills for life, the merits of delegation, and for some really great parties and long time friendships, and especially, for giving me the opportunity to successfully turn their traditionally sedate 'summer lawn social' into a weekend long 1969 Age of Aquarius fun party, and for the efforts of many committee members who made all the enjoying possible. Toastmaster's International who helped to teach various ways for taking the fear out of public speaking—ah, they count 'ah's' to help do away with those nervous pauses. The Salvation Army folks who help homeless folks in need without any fanfare or strings attached—they have a positive ring in their bells that tries to give them a helping hand up. The Philadelphia Direct Mail Club, guess these days it's the Philadelphia Direct Marketing Association, for their efforts in promoting the positive and creative applications of direct marketing techniques. The efforts of Planned Parenthood, for their work in keeping family planning within the immediate family and for expanding the scope of responsible birth control to include men. The American Heart Association teaching the public about ways to keep the heart pumping blood. The early efforts of environmental groups to get the public involved in recycling, before recycling became politically correct and a big business—this book has been printed on recycled paper. The Amish, for the merits in their applied concept of shunning people who have done them harmful hurts—there is none of that revenge stuff, no eye-for-an-eye done in payback, 'tis the consequences of the wrongdoers actions that has caused them to be totally avoided, and they cease to part of any future interactions. My friends in Wicca, who follow the olden ways of do no harm as thy will be done—'tis sad, how the path they travel is so often misunderstood and perceived as being something that it isn't.

ACKNOWLEDGEMENTS

My sincere appreciation and deepest respect for the entire population of Iceland, for their Viking determination to cling to their unique national heritage and language, while maintaining a high standard of living—and for enjoying those hot natural springs and for having the smarts to make positive use of their bank of thermodynamic energy. Iceland is also a nation of avid writers and readers, with one of the highest national levels of literacy in the world—more books per household than anywhere else in the world. I'm also grateful for the *Island* souvenir that my mailman Henry brought me when he returned from a recent vacation to Iceland. He shares a similar appreciation for Iceland.

I've also benefited greatly from the various influences of Ben Franklin. Not as a Franklin scholar, but as a living descendant of Ben Franklin, and hearing my father's mother, my grandmother—better known as Nanny, rattle off a litany of her favorite Franklin proverbs that covered a wide variety of situations. I was in my teens when I made the discovery that all the Harnish males had the middle name Franklin, and my grandfather's older brother was named Benjamin Franklin Harnish. Oh, I did forget to mention that my grandfather was also an old letterpress printer, in a long family line of printers. I remember seeing some old printed copies of *Poor Richard's Almanac* and some other Franklin stuff that Pappy had hidden away in an old strongbox, but I don't know whatever became of that old box. Hopefully, Ben's papers have made their way into a museum collection somewhere.

I'm also most grateful for all the folks who have bought my book and for taking the time to read my offerings. I'd enjoy hearing from you via email at: EnjoyOften@aol.com

Take care, my friends, and enjoy often . . . John

A penny saved, is a penny earned!!! --Ben Franklin

TABLE OF CONTENTS

TABLE OF CONTENTS

TABLE OF CONTENTS

Early to bed, early to rise,
makes a man healthy, wealthy, and wise!!!

Ben Franklin

Style and Usage . . . an introduction

Folks familiar with my writing, my creative work, and me in person, are laughing at the concept of my having any kind of affiliation with style and usage in any remote form. Perhaps thinking *style & usage* and *me,* is a really oxymoronic term!!! Because my form of writing changes from ramblings, to odes, to essays, to short stories and into whatever—depending on the topic and my creative mood, thusly, my wordsmithing efforts do take great liberties with word usage and words relational meanings to topics. Much of what I write breaks, or seriously bends, many of the rules and guidelines followed closely by other writers, editors, proofreaders, and writing teachers religiously using all those accepted standards found in *style and usage* handbooks.

I'm most grateful to have benefited from the *wordrighting* skills of a marvelous editor, Marta Lewis, who kept my breaking of rules and bending of those style and usage guidelines within an agreeable scope. Indeed she'd take me to tasks for missing corrections and suggestions she'd made and I'd miss. At times, details do have a way of escaping me, especially commas!!! Thusly, any glaring wordsmithing errors are all my fault, and were not caused by my friend Marta missing them. Sometimes I'd have a most valid reason for structuring my approach in certain ways that are unique to my creative style of writing.

I'm not thumbing my nose at these guidelines, at times some of them can be real helpful to a writer expressing thoughts in a crisp, clean, clear manner. At other times, guidelines may sway writers away from expressing what they are trying to create with their written words. True, applied style standards do provide a sense of continuity to the meaning and arrangements of written words—cuts down on what editors and critics love to call *purple prose.* I enjoy writings with bursts of purple word flows. Purple passions are both pleasing to the eye and gently tug on the mind to come out and play. I love to provoke the reader's mind to stretch a wee bit with my words in play, creating a beautiful rainbow of colors—and even including those colors the eye can't see—until you read between the lines.

I also write in midnight blue—one of my favorite colors, and I love Melissa Manchester singing that song. Sadly, some people have badly stained certain words and phrases with restrictive blues--such as religious, *blue laws*, and the rare second full moon, in a calendar month, is the *blue moon*. Painting the use of certain words as being *vulgar* and *off-color* or even *tasteless* hinders truthful expression. *Shit!!! Don't matter none at all, how much blue paint you're gonna put on shit, shit is still shit.* Shit is happening in real life all the time, and painting over shit or trying to avoid it, doesn't make the shit less real. *Serious writers* don't use such nasty gutter words. At least the educated opinion contends, a professional writer has such an expanded vocabulary that they don't need to sink into foul vulgarisms to write expressively. I believe that all words being utilized effectively, create more realistic interactions with the readers. However, the true color of a word is the perceived association readers attach to word usage. The reader's mind puts the spins upon these words, with hopefully resounding alignments with the word-spinner spinning the words into a yarn. The interactive reverberation makes usage acceptable or not—regardless of the color coding.

I write with all colors of words. I'm color blind to worn out prejudices surrounding words, and I'm color blind to the pigmentation of a person's skin too—although I do avoid nasty people with cold dark hearts. I believe any word is acceptable for use, as long as the word is producing open-minded rethinking by mature readers. In some situations, those society tainted *blue words* are the only correct words to be used to reproduce the *true blue* essence of what's being expressed by the writer. Hopefully you'll discover *true blue* is completely free of the uptight pompous pronouncements frequently rendered by those people who presume they are of *blue blood!!!* Also, I'm not into singing *the blues* and those *somebody-done-somebody-wrong-songs* that are overflowing with all kinds of negative thoughts and demeaning feelings. From my point of view, *blue* is a very versatile color and adapts well to any situation.

One such *blue* word is *fuck*. The use of the word *fuck* doesn't lessen the quality of what's being expressed or render the body of the work worthless. There's nothing foul about the word *fuck*. The foulness is in the narrow gutter minds of those who have to put a dirty meaning on words—dumping their shameful guilty ways on others who say the *four-letter-word*. There is an earthy reality when, *'Oh, fuck!!!'* is used to express extreme frustration. The true depth of disappointment pales when written in the phony niceness of a plastic, *'Oh, foul!!!'*. The impact of knowing the full empathy of those totally *fucked-up* frustration isn't captured with the *foul!!!* There are oftentimes when only *fuck*, or a variation of the word *fuck*, will do. I see nothing harmful with using *fuck* in properly expressive ways—I do see grave distortions when piss poor substitutions are employed as an ill conceived end run around the valid use of any word. My much earlier copyrighted essay, *'The Immortalization of Fuck'* is included in my collection of work in Enjoy Often!!!

Some folks feel a need to shield young ones from words like *fuck* and *blue moon* concepts, thereby, avoiding the need to discuss *touchy topics* and dodging probing questions so as not to go there. Then later, they bemoan their offspring's dumbness and irresponsible behavior in these same *touchy* areas, when those young shielded ones try to mature into adulthood. However, their younger adult years may be very trying as they seek to join the ageless raging battle of the sexes, carrying with them, their heavy burden of false expectations and lots of unanswered questions that were always avoided.

They eventually do enter the playing field with a sexual handicap of disinformation and imposed negative conditioning. Harmfully ordained conditions have the disabling ability to take the joy out of sexual enjoying, and spin into dangerously ugly perverse interactions, often very abusive to themselves and their partners. Some of my reflections touch upon sexual games that get played with the power to take erotic enjoying away. I'm not trying to be rude and crude, but perhaps a bit ludicrous at times, hopefully in positive ways and especially earthy while getting into the *fact of life* that in reality shit happens. I sincerely hope my various mind flows will bring you a few mind-blossoming laughs, and leave you with some positive after-thoughts.

My writing style changes with topics, and you'll see similar chords of core concepts woven in words of different colors and going in a variety of spinning directions. The direction I follow is my path, as I continue to enjoy a most blissful life long love affair with the entire creative process. I do relish joyful opportunities to engage in flows of conjectured solutions to fix-up challenging problems that are perhaps repairable, and for the wisdom to know when something is done an gone. The waxing and waning of cycles, as the wheel goes turning along the path of life, are what makes up the rocking and rolling and bumping into experiences of assorted colors that has become the sum of what's shared here.

The variety of colors felt from life learnings are always changing into new colorful arrays of kaleidoscopic patterns with each turn of the wheel. Some colors are so very joyful, sparkling points of light upon a field of beautiful midnight blues of erotic cosmic enriching alignments. Other hues are felt as reflections of attempts to impose influences of murky blue-green-brownish mucking zaps—those horrid colors of greedy bummers, bumping energies into misalignments from dinging dinks dinging away. At other times, stumbling into bountiful thoughts of blissful blue, flowing free of the murk and into a crystal clear azure blue sky. Slimy green flows slowly transcend to nourish fresh growing plant buds, soon to bring forth blooming blossoms. Shitty brown shades fall away to refresh a yearning mother earth, hungry for the riches of naturally dark brown humus, where bitter and sweet chocolates meet. Where the cold jaded of green melts away the jagged greens of greed, envy, and jealousy, to grow the sweet green grasses of a rebirthing spring. Transcending the ridges of regal purple with an uplifting purple haze upon the winging words of purple prose in delightful flow, thusly, you'll find my discourse follows a variety of wordsmithing ways. Oh my, at times I do get wordy, but hopefully in good ways.

I also need to do a disclaimer with regard to all that legal shit—ah, legal stuff. My words are from a *layman's point of view*, meaning I'm looking from the bottom up, and not from the high lofty peaks of those professionals looking down from ivy covered towers and frowning at what they believe they are seeing. Ergo, my reflections are for the enjoyment of the reader, and no liability is assumed if the reader sees attributes of themselves captured within my observations of life and up close and personal interactions. I'm not presenting the ways and beliefs of any group, sect, or body. However, my beliefs are akin to natural druid ways from olden times of long ago. Yes indeed, I have drawn freely upon those basic foundations and you'll see some druidisms reflected in my writing.

This book isn't being written for fame and fortune—the income from the book will truly be most helpful to me and greatly appreciated. Having been briefly touched by the cold fleeting light of fame, I found fame to be grossly over-rated, way too demanding of time and talents, inflated with ass-kissing, and all those plastic put-ons aren't my cup of tea. Fame blows!!! Also, having been comfortably affluent from earned efforts, and at other times poorer than a field mouse—I know being dirt poor blows big time too. Those money riches of wealth are a yucky trap that will pull you in and drain you dry. These days, my enjoying would sure be enhanced with a bit of earned prosperity, and being clear of all my debts would be fantastic. Oh, but of course, I'd certainly appreciate a few missing creature comforts too—and a long visit to those fun hot springs in Iceland—hear tell of delightful nude bathing places there in those naturally warm bubbling waters—yes, in beautiful Iceland!!!

This book is being published through an arrangement with a writer's self-publishing service. They are very different from traditional mainstream publishing houses in ways that are positive to the writer and fair to the publisher. This book will never go out of print, and may be ordered directly from the publisher at any time in the future when you might want to share a copy of Enjoy Often!!! with your friends. Within days of receiving a book order, they produce a copy of the book and send it out directly to the person who placed the order.

I have retained full creative direction over my book, as long as I adhere to normal print production requirements. No publishing house editorial staff, agents, editorial review boards, or formulated mass media blitzes are involved, and no one to answer to about editorial content, which is a very nice creative freedom for an author. I'm solely responsible for the entire content of this book. My writing has not been slanted to get *acclaimed reviews* from *literary* critics—I mostly disagree with critics anyhow, nor are my stories crafted in stock plots designed to capture mass book market sales, with those marketing bean-counters always keeping the alluring bottom-line potential in mind. I'm sure not trying for some kind of a scholarly dissertation about the ills of society based on smoothed over statistical analysis. Often, dissertations only seek to find the expected truth, and pay no mind to whatever else there is beyond the hypothesis they're trying to prove. I've tried to bring about a creative approach for looking at *whatever* there is to be found. But most importantly, I've tried to write with my focus on the reader's enjoyment. My efforts will be fulfilled if *you* enjoy several rushes of loud laughter while reading, and perhaps the warm tingles of some delighting thought-flows worthy of your kind consideration as lingering mind seeds. I really do wish for your enjoyment when I say, *enjoy often!!!*

Some may find this a hard book to read, not because of my wordsmithing or the presentation of the content, but because of the mirror of themselves the words might be reflecting. Sharing my take on comparable places . . . godsparks reflecting . . . the truth of self be known by the person in the mirrored glass—only you know what the truth is for you. Self-truths can be very scary at times. Truth rings clear and bright with light, free of imposed pondering that ding with dull doubts, dinging away in the darkness of untruths, getting lost in those tricky questions for pondering the meaning of life. Alas, 'tis a far more joyful quest to explore the question: *'What is the difference between orange???'* The preceding question is correct and is typo free, just in case you thought that might have been a glaring error. Perhaps you'll find the answer within these thought flows—perhaps not. There are no guarantees about finding answers herein, but the odds are in your favor, that you'll find some smiles of enjoying here!!!

Several friends who have read a sampling of these pieces as *works-in-progress* via email, have told me they've printed out copies to go back and read again—to cull a few more thought harvests from my wordsmithing. I do appreciate the honor they do my humble efforts, and it feels good to have shared some worthwhile thoughts that ring for them as well. Hopefully, being printed in book form makes this an easy collection of work to come back to and revisit from time to time.

I need to make this very clear, I don't have the answers other folks are looking for. The truth of the matter for me is that in many ways I'm still looking for answers that work for me, and in lots of ways I'm still working on figuring out the questions for myself!!! *The 'between orange' question is an easy one.* The uniqueness of humankind is such that there are lots of different questions and answers for everyone, because each person is unique. Life is NOT a one-size-fits-all situation, and the flows of life are such that changes are always happening. Such is life!!! Those changes bring into being a whole new bunch of questions and possible answers for pondering consideration. Sometimes aged answers waxed with the wisdom from a variety of life experiences that might help to provide expanded understanding for new questions.

Sadly, almost all of my earlier work was destroyed in the raging ravishes of my second marriage, which ended more than a decade and a half-ago in 1984. I lost several major pieces of artwork too, but escaped with my life. Anyhow, life goes on, change is constant, and I'm grateful for my life free of that strife filled time!!! Big time karma lessons from that taxing time!!!

Many of my friends have helped to influence the content of this collection with positive suggestions, with no offense being taken if their suggestions aren't followed by me or when their concepts were reshaped differently than what they had originally intended. Alas, I'm grateful for the positive reception of my renewed writing efforts. I'm most appreciative of my wife, Linda, and several helpful friends who have taken a special interest in my recent writings and have urged me to explore publication again. Several online *ezines* editors—Kelly, *Laffirmations* and *Night Shift;* Kate, *The Daily Meditations;* and Phylis, *ESsence;* who happened upon some of my shared ramblings online, have taken the time to request permission to include a few of my pieces in their online publications. *Ezines* are small publications that are sent via *email* to a controlled list of subscribers who have requested these unique electronic publication. Hearing from many of their readers via email about some especially meaningful expressions they had discovered in my shared writings has been most gratifying and very encouraging in helping me to birth this book into being. Please feel free to email your comments to me at: EnjoyOften@aol.com

Yes, I'm inclined to ramble on and on, being way wordy at times. At times tangents will happen and I go with the writing flows when those tangents are inclined to enhance the topic, and I do hope you find my tangents were done with a positive purpose. I have a mentor friend, Bill Smeltzer, who will read this and most likely say, "Only John turns a brief introduction into an epistle!!!"

Hehehee...and Bill's right about that!!!

Take care, my friends, enjoy often . . . John

Light & Love & Peace . . .
An Introduction of Such

Perhaps some of you reading my offered ramblings in book form, might have read my seasonal gifting shared with folks online and republished in several online magazines. This was written to try to fulfill the Yuletide wish for *world peace*, asked for by a dear friend. My extended hope was for folks who aligned with these resounding thoughts, to kindly involve themselves by sending this shared gifting on to their friends, etc. I've appreciated hearing from a variety of folks who took the time to let me know they have shared, by sending my *Light & Love & Peace* gifting onto their friends and family.

Light & Love & Peace was written in December of 1997. I started writing the initial draft on a Delta flight westward, to celebrate my son's 25th birthday on December 21st, in Sacramento, CA. The final draft was finished, being wordsmithed together on a sunny chilly Christmas Day, in my daughter-in-law and son's apartment. They were the first to read my gifting, before we went off to see the recently opened action movie *Jackie Brown,* while a fine Yuletide dinner was doing a slow cooking.

WOW, what a sharp contrast between the harsh real life world and my tender thoughts of *Light & Love & Peace...*!!! With about 15 minutes of the movie remaining, I noticed lots of people getting up and leaving the theater. I'm thinking this movie wasn't all that great—some of the sex scenes were funny, but I didn't see any reason to get up and leave before the movie was over. Besides, I still had popcorn left!!! Liz had gotten up out of her seat, and was climbing over the seats toward the back of the theater. She is tall and has nice long thin legs—she is also smart, she showed her streetwise moxie by heading for the exit!!! I'm eating popcorn and watching the movie. Now my son Jon is standing up, pulling on my arm, and saying in a loud whisper, *"Dad, get up, we have to leave right now!!!"* I explained to him, stating the obvious, that the movie wasn't over, wondering why we had to leave *right now???*

Pulling me up out of my aisle seat by my arm, my son whispers again that there's a gang fight happening, and we must leave *right now, Dad!!!* Different *colors* were having a melee in the front section of seats in the theater, and I quickly agreed we'd better leave right now. With fighting happening, now seemed like the right time to go. I didn't see much of the *colors* mixing it up in confrontation with each other, but I also knew it was the right time for us to leave when a flood of police and security guards started to surge into the auditorium as we were quickly walking out. Ah, some things are certainly best left for the trained professionals to deal with.

Of course I took the remaining half a bucket of buttered popcorn with me—*waste not, want not*, as Ben Franklin would have said. Ben was very into ways for peaceful enjoying. As the wretched fighting events were happening in real life, it was enough of a waste not seeing the end of the movie, and finding out if Jackie got to keep the stashed money!!! Was there another funny sex scene with Jackie and the older bail bondsman dude or whoever at the end of the movie???

As we were walking to my son's jeep, I told my son that I thought all those street gangs had some kind of unspoken truce not to do any dumb head banging on Christmas Day. You know, that was supposed to be a mutually respected day of peace. My son laughed loudly and explained that kind of truce only happens in the movies, Dad!!! Gee, my son, I smiled, there was no Xmas truce and we were in the movies—so to speak!!!

Like I said, 'twas a major contrast between my earlier thoughts of a kinder, caring world in peaceful flows, and seeing strife and brutal conflicts in real life. A hit over the head via the inconsiderate actions of a few who spoiled the enjoying for so many others. I feel large parts of humankind have grown accustomed to inconsiderate doings—both giving and receiving, in often unthinking mean actions. It seems like they need to do as they do, to be noticed beyond just surviving, primal flash backs of survival and fighting the prowling hungry beasts in prehistoric times, and now fighting with the evolved conditioned beasts that come from within.

Warring modern tribes of differing colored beliefs and territories mixing it up in *moral combat* with other tribes of *colors*, producing shitty hues of drab bloody messes. Their inconsiderate actions spoil everyone's enjoyment. Alas, and indeed most thankfully, some folks have left those negative ways behind, and continue upon their joyful quests chasing playful rainbows, ever so hopefully flowing along discovering an array of beautiful colors—sparkling aurora borealis dancing upon a starry midnight sky awaiting discovery.

Those roaming beasts play upon our fears, greeds, and jealous doings, spreading about as a deadly black plague. The long feared outbreak of a world-wide killing virus is actually of our own doings, done in our continued undoing of a once upon a time more considerate humankind, evolving into being social, where mutual survival found safety in their collective numbers from the harmful beasts. However now, eons later, the stalking beast has our number, and as words of folklore from long ago relate, the number for the eve of destruction is 666. I fear the beast that now comes, comes raging forth from within us all. Like that nuke dude inventor Oppenheimer wisely said about the first gigantic evil blossom from the billowing atom bomb explosion becoming death, destroyer of worlds. Our playing with the once treasured gift fire maintained in a protective pit has evolved into the invention of portable volcanoes that can move mountains away with destructive force. Harmful fire burns with sick cold flames within us.

Cold fires coming from within us, in the sick gripping fears of unaccepted differences making for strife upon strife, in the sickening fright from what horrible unknowns lurk in the darkness, in the sick avoidance of the threatening unknowns and things that go bump in the night—some bumps that don't ding you with marring dinks are fun. In the sickly greedful philosophy of, *fuck them before they fuck you*, grab all you can and control what you can't grab, dump on greedy guilt-games, grind in shattered pieces of all those broken dreams—dreams taken far away with restrictive betelling put-downs from others of, *you can't do that!!!* Those once bright passions deep within flicker out, sucked off by the rage of the evil fire demon, scorching fragile shells into combustion and causing heavy heart burn!!! Fear pisses on passions and the fire pit soon makes yucky smoke!!! Fear discourses so mindlessly onward with outrageous acidic anger burning deeply!!! Fears angrily blows all the joys out of passion!!!

The beast within is found in sick grabbing greed to feed ever expanding fabricated wants, like a craving monster always consuming everything, like a black hole in space sucking everything in and giving nothing out. Gathering stockpiles to stash away in greedy locked up tight places, so driving is the *greedy drive* that we've been conditioned to never, ever, be without, by hoarding everything within—perhaps as protection from the inconsiderate acts of others, perhaps as a way to save a few joys for when strife takes other joys away. All the excessive greedy holding in, smothers the badly smoking fire pit out. Glutton greediness grinds all the pleasure out of passion!!! *Farewell sweet birds of joys, I wish I knew you all better!!!*

The beast within stabs at the innards with every sick jab of jealousy, insecurities lashing scornfully out at others, envy of others and their joyful doings done without anger, feeling imposed frustrations by the guiltless doings of others passing on by enjoying their life—the casting of self bemoaning wishes of wanting all they have. Heavy resentfulness fueled with imposed guilt, playing upon entrenched uncertainties, are so very nasty and judgmental. Jealous frustrations feeding on fleeting ways of grasping upon the fading illusions of security, in a world of ever changing elusive securities. Jealousy dratfully dams off natural intercoursing flows and dampers out the flames of passions in the fire pit!!! Jealousy jinxes joys away!!!

The evolved monstrous beast is reflected in those gangs of different colors mixing it up on Christmas Day. Methinks the Prince of Peace would be way unhappy with all those unpeaceful actions that have been done in the name of peace. All those lives lost in endless conflict throughout the millenniums, because of differing symbols of beliefs, are such a senseless waste of humankind. Generation upon generation have sowed the monster seeds, generating the endless deadly energy for evil weeds to creep all over the land with scents that foul the air. Continuing on with each newly flourishing conflict rooted in frightful anger--minor actions of mindless slipping and snipping interpersonally, to sinking all the way down into the major mess of all out worldwide wasteful warfare.

If I had survived trying to bring my message of *Light & Love & Peace...* to the combatting tribes on Xmas Day, I'd sure have awakened in the locked psycho ward of the nearest hospital—only a nut case would try to stop fighting tribes or else have really big balls!!! My balls are just about average—there's no truth to the rumors that my balls are pure brass, and I'm sure those warring factions would have painfully stomped my balls flat for butting into their rumble!!! Thusly, knowing the limitations of my peacekeeping skills, I decided to forego enjoying the end of the movie. Not too much enjoying to give up to keep my balls out of harm's way. See, I figure that those fighting tribes are way into serious fighting, not the *look nice* fighting on television, where they take turns getting hit and come back to be hit some more. Those real serious fighters go for fast, very harmful take-out blows—quick and painful. Ouch!!!

I did pass on enjoying the end of the movie and not getting mixed up in their fight. I really dislike fights. The USAF trained me to be a very dirty, serious fighter. The kind of fighting that instantly takes the ability to fight out of an aggressor—not very nice looking and very hurtful and most effective and deadly. Passing decades have drained away my fighting strength, and I really don't miss that kind of deadly force. What remains with me from that other time in my life, is now purely for my defensive needs to move from harm's way. Lots of the military training and conditioning was also mental with lots of focus on how to avoid getting pulled into a fight. Pissing contests get so messy!!!

The key to ending the fighting is the *enjoyment factor*. What a difference it might have made *if* the movie audience had told the young combatants to sit down and watch the movie or take their fight outside. Oh, but being a mass media society has conditioned us to be watchers, and only seeing what's happening as long as we aren't involved in the real fighting. Strange, how those watchers have never seen a thing when the police ask about what was happening. The *what if* comes into play *if* the collective audience had stood up to the fighting faction and told them to take their grossly inconsiderate infighting elsewhere, that their actions weren't welcome here. Use the hook to pull those bad actors off the stage!!!

However, messy media has spoon-fed generations of viewing audiences with all kinds of violence and televised warfare. With those talking heads reporting everything with all the possible hype about a crisis about to happen—or what might occur. *The sky is falling, the sky is falling!!!* Sadly, the movie audience would have most likely been into watching the gangs rumbling if they hadn't been so close to what was going down. Add in the high potential for some gun play, and you have major hurts happening, and fired bullets are equal opportunity hitters. Those senseless bullets will also befall the watchers too!!!

Too often, the peacemakers, peacekeepers, and peace brokers, get caught in the middle between warring tribes, and thusly, they get double fucked dead!!! Peacefully, they try with all their *might* to *make* a lasting peace that is so often broken before the ink is dry on the peace treaty, and then the *might* moves onward, homeward bound. There really isn't any peace when the peace is enforced at gun point. That only builds upon the already present anger and resentment that soon erodes away the frail bonds of peace. All too soon, those spreading angers and fearful resentments breaks the peace to pieces!!!

Centuries of endless, mindless wars happening continuously, fighting for the thrill of fighting, these days as money making sports, exciting viewers by showing off honed skills for taking the opposing foes apart on a white lined field of glory. Play nicely within the lines, with judges running along in the flows of battle, to make sure the combatants stay within the lines, and sort of try to follow the rules, or they get fucked-over for having fucked-up national sport TV!!!

Just imagine, two opposing generals are ready to have their forces do down and dirty fighting on a marked battlefield—or at least as dirty as they think they can get away with while the zebras are watching their teams. Of course, some will agree, a threesome of forces going at it on the field of play would sure make for a much more challenging game. Sort of feeling the sensations of going two-on-one has a unique way of conveying the feeling of being ganged up on, getting fucked going and coming, attacking and retreating, amassing their forces with one or the other, joining together to get their licks in on the other, their united strength flowing together against the common foe. Then, as the goal is close at hand, the flows change again, and teams retreat, yielding yardage so bloody in capturing inch by inch in hard fought gains.

The cheers and the cries from the spectators enjoying the melee of triple plays, the balance of flows waxing and waning with all the surges of aroused energies, mixing and merging upon the field of play, as an endless flow of fresh soldiers await their opportunity for taking their honors in active duty on an even playing field, regulated by fair-minded former players of the game and spectators too. Now they are peace making officials and no one dares to fuck with a zebra!!! But those zebras have to apply the rules fairly as blesses and curses as infractions happen in play. Indeed, with instant replay for all the game watchers to see and agree with all the calls of the on-field judiciary system—instant justice with the blow of a loud whistle and all the fans give peer-review via pay-per-view, and they get to vote on questionable foul calls via the all connecting world wide internet web.

Spectators acting like inconsiderate assholes will be transported post-haste to the current field of play, where they take their anal retentive activities out on the battlefield and bang lots of heads available for banging. Ah, drafting outrageous spectators into play brings a realness of the game to all the fans. You got a bad-ass banging dude dinging away being very inconsiderate, and off to the games he/she goes. Presto, with their ego running amuck, off they go to join the game in play. Oh, didn't I mention that these games are mostly unisex, the modern army, so primally brutal to have gender mixes combatting in a clothing optional free-for-all. It brings a whole new level to the ageless battles between the sexes!!!

City site selections for hosting the games is done entirely with bribes. The city bringing the greatest amount of potential for happiness and benefits to their area of spectator-residences from hosting the games, wins. The site approval committee dudes get to party during the games with the host city fans. The construction of the site facility is totally designed for the joyful comfort of spectators. Bringing outside food and drink in is encouraged, and 'tis a joy to freely share with neighboring spectators. Of course, food stuff is available at the coliseum at affordable prices. Drunks run the risk of being put instantly into the game. A selection of play-by-play announcers are available from a basic, *Look at that bad ass running down the field!!!* rambling style, to a blow-by-blow provided by diehard blowfarts, too old to play the game as once was played, back when they last played.

Special event games are held during nights of the full moon for the jubilant venting of moonlight madness. The police and Emergency Rooms get a break too, because most of the crazy going on happen on the playing field. Every player and spectator is a star, and all of the longer lasting, more experienced gaming players/spectators are known by their scars from stretch marks of playing experience. Full medical coverage is extended to all players/spectators, and their rightful dependents, to take care of putting limbs back in place, repairing damaged parts, smoothing out funky dings, etc . . . et al.

Those bad feelings of anger bringing about unsettling disagreements are taken at once to the field of battle, where the rules of the game are enforced to make certain that everyone fights nice and plays within the drawn lines. All the fans get to see all the televised excitement of the games—mostly commercial free, and apart from the games, there's peace in the valley and all throughout the lands. Right!!!???

Alas, that's not how it is in the world today, wars kill while games thrill. The games are big business with so many people sucking off the gaming tits, and the players getting paid so much money for what they enjoy doing, and with all the costs mounting, the fans get royally fucked!!! For way too long, the thrill of turning more bucks is so often the basis for going to wars. Sadly, lots of people have seen the ongoing strife of warfare as a growth business—just as long as they don't have to do any of the actual fighting and dying!!!

So if peace is to come into widespread being, then the doing of peaceful ways needs to come about in the one-by-one ways of all folks interacting. The sparkling of light that happens with good feelings in peaceful harmony aligning. That's the simple path to rediscovering peace. Peace that is longer lasting than any would-be peacemakers can make, by forging foes together in a contrived manner. Peace isn't a manufactured product, rolling off an assembly line, built according to government specifications and assembled by the lowest bidder. Peace is the glow that comes from deep within. Merely speaking the words of peace can't make peace spread throughout the world. Only the daily doing of caring deeds brings peaceful ways into a long time turbulently tumbling world. Peace starts with one person with one person living in peaceful ways.

One person sharing a smile with another can start a reaction that's more powerful than all the toys of war.

One person taking the time to be considerate of others helps to lead folks away from inconsiderate actions.

One person cleaning-up their own messes helps to show others how we need to pick-up after ourselves.

One person not making snap judgments about the different ways of others, grows acceptance of others.

One person unwilling to follow angry ways that have been harmful for so long will help to end the pain.

One person finding more enjoying in the living of life today helps to stop the sad bemoaning of what isn't.

One person caring about their godspark shining, soon shines through the faddy phony appearances of shells.

One person who doesn't need to draw lines in the sand, marking the restrictive limitations for others.

One person accepting others as they are today without their imposing expectations of remaking others over.

One person being respectful of the space and ways of others and not venturing in without an offered invite.

One person letting go of the frayed shroud of cloaking guilt, greed, and jealousy to walk freely into the light.

One person casting off the revenge of generations in hand-me-down anger from long ago wrongs done.

One person reaching another with caring ways, and they reach another, and in turn touch another, and another, and on, and on, and on, slowly making a positive influence to help create a world glowing bright with light & love & peace.

One person following a peaceful path does indeed make a difference.

On the next page is the message that was emailed and spread via the internet around the work . . .

****

Light & Love & Peace...

Alas, methinks these are the three bright blessings that could benefit humankind in the here and now, and in the approaching midnight blue twilight of this closing 20th century. Aha, such joyous hallowed hopes to greet the dawning of an awakening millennium.

Light that sparkles away the darkness that has befallen the strife driven masses in the world. Light that outshines the greed, guilt, and jealousy that has besieged humanity. Light that slips us from those gripes of greedy ways of wanting the newest, the biggest, the *'gotta-get-mine'* and *'fuck-you-over'* attitudes of the human race. Light that casts off imposed guilt shadows that have ensnared humankind for thousands of years. Light that sheds jealous sensations that strip away our self-esteem and dulls the brightness of our godsparks. Light that enlightens our path with learning along the way. Light that bathes the world with the tender touches of twinkling stars, where each and every being has the space to gleam in their own light.

Love that grows freely and basks in the beauty of the light. Love that blooms unimpeded by restrictive *'should's'* and *'shouldn't's'*. Love that willfully whispers in tingling twinkles, and speaks in vibrating volumes as godsparks are aglow. Love that touches with the kindness of consideration for one and all, while keeping self, true and whole. Love that frees you to be yourself to enjoy all of life's energies in continuous flow. Love that accepts the differences of individualities without needing to change anothers way of being. Love that is for giving, as well as forgiving of friends. Love that is mutually accepted, without the need to be defined or confined or contrived. Love that openly embraces, without strangling the life out of love.

Peace that begins deep within yourself, where your inner truths are known and pondered. Peace that conclusively brings to rest haunting hurts from yesteryears. Peace that transcends the eternal quest for illusive perfection in an imperfect world.

Peace that propels us beyond the entrapments of expectations and past the entanglements of tattered traditions. Peace that does no harm to any being. Peace that is truly for real, and not based on begrudgingly made compromises nor dangling deterrents. Peace that glides endlessly with the naturally balanced courses of the universe in harmonious peace.

A dear friend, Nony1, asked me to bring her the gift of *'world peace'* during this holiday season. Ergo, this is my humble effort, and my hopc is that if you find some resounding alignments within these bright blessings, that you'll share them with your friends, and hopefully, they in turn will share likewise with their friends. Thusly, the energy of these thoughts may eventually spread around the world in an enlightening, lovingly, peaceful living array.

Enjoy often!!! EnjoyOften@aol.com

****

Take care and enjoy often . . . John

A CUP OF FIRE

Step into a magical time machine with me
and travel far, way back in time,
back to eons of long ago, when the earth was young,
and the society of humankind was very primitive
of thoughts and in doings,
and being social together was a grave matter of survival.

Thoughts were way less complex then,
mostly about food, water, and safe shelter,
and social doings were gathering together for survival.
Because there was strength in numbers.
The primal law of nature is, only the strong survive,
in a rough, raw, new world, evolving with growing life.

The sun and moon played tag
chasing each other across the sky,
much like they continue to do today.
When the sun was providing daylight,
there was seeing safety from the beasts.
Beasts that would come and try to eat them
if they got caught out in the open all alone.
Hunting and traveling was done in groups
because there was safety in numbers,
safety from all of the hungry animals
that prowled all about wild land,
ready to gobble people up
and spit them out,
same as today.

When the moon was full,
there was also safety of sorts from those nasty beasty things
that came creeping in the night, because humans could see
what was threateningly near.
Then, guided by the moonlight,
they could take quick flight into safe hiding places,
away from those frights
lurking in the night.

Two of the early lessons were:
only go venturing into the dark
when the full moon was shining brightly in the night sky,
and,
don't eat the yellow snow.
Ugh, yucky not good, never eat the yellow snow!!!
They were too busy surviving a rough life,
to spend anytime
pondering about the meaning of life!!!

These prehistoric beings discovered fire.
Perhaps zapping down from the sky
when a thundering lightning strike
brought flames to a struck tree,
or maybe a volcano belched lava flows of fire
from mother earth's open mouth,
in blazing outrages of hellish eruptions.

Then too, fire could have come like a falling star,
glowing brightly with the flare of changes,
like a piece of burning sun plunging to earth aflame,
like an enlightening heaven sent gift,
to keep all humankind warm in the fire light,
safe from prowling beasties.

Fire was both a great blessing of brightness,
and a curse of horrible burning pains.
So fragile the tiny glowing spark
leaping to ignite the waiting tinder,
that the smallest puff of a breeze
could blow the frail flame away,
and a downpour of rain could quickly put out
the most raging fire.
Or the most cursed horror, because the accursed wildfire
could leap with avenging ease beyond the fire pit,
escaping like a raging wildness from the deep hole,
and spread with a destructive roaring rage,
consuming all within the burning path,
scorching the earth bare of life.

Leaving ashes and a pale dust
after the raging whirlwinds
of the licking flames
have passed on by.
Slowly smoldering out, extinguished by self-consumption,
leaving the stench of charred waste
in smoking ugly ruins . . .
ashes to dust.

Primitive humankind learned to become respectful
of the ferocious ways of fire.
Controlling those wild flames, by keeping them trapped
in a round burning pit surrounded by rocks.

A congenial circle
of warmth and light in the night,
and perhaps,
the first circle jerks came to being.
When those primal folks who got too hot
from the blazing flames jerked quickly away,
when their abundant hair caught on fire from the heat,
in those crude early hearths.

Fire could keep savage beasts away,
and the taste of slain animal flesh
was greatly enhanced in favor,
to become yummy good tasting,
after toasting well done in the fire.

When hunting and gathering parties
strayed too far afield questing,
and the darkness of night covered the land,
then the light of beckoning beacon fires
would guide them back to their safe haven
of warmth and fire light.

Then came the first night,
when someone tossed a strange looking leafy bush,
into the fire pit flames.

And from those odd green leaves
a strange smoke did indeed come,
bringing a lifting floating sensation
that was so pleasingly delightfully new!!!
Their primitive minds were blown,
most joyful was their natural high.
Upon those wacky whiffs of smoke,
they did a collective hippie trip,
stoned by the fire pit smoke.

Surprised,
they all were by the gift of joys from the wacky smoke.
Laughing loudly when the little round seeds
from the dried flowers of the bushy plant,
snapped, crackled, and popped-off,
in the heat of the magical smoking fire.

Oh my,
so frolicking and carefree
were their shared primal raptures,
knowing simple joys in their primitive life.

Because life was way simple back then,
now freer of savage beastly fears,
and socially not yet into cultivated cultured fears,
from unknown nasty beasties captured within them.
The complexities of future advancing curses,
were not yet hindering them.

They really didn't worry
about what was *in.*
With them, skins were always *in style,*
and no ties had been invented like nooses to slip necks into.
They weren't fashion smart enough
to start each day slipping their head into a noose!!!
The telling of lies was unheard of,
what was real, was what there was!!!
And there wasn't yet greed and jealousy,
working harmful plays, upon the young society of humankind.

The simple truths were,
they were safe from the beasts
and basking in the delighting warmth of fire,
freely enjoying most willingly,
unfettered to drift upon ancient blissful joys
into a dream filled restful slumber,
enjoying the pure guiltless sleep of untainted innocence.

The early thinking skills of logic and reasoning
were floating around within their shared learnings.
They knew sharing learnings were good for all,
and all did ponder upon the applications of learnings.
Knowing sharing wacky weed fire pit smoke,
was most relaxing and uplifting,
and off they all went floating into a deep sleep.

Freedom from fear they were safe to sleep,
sleeping in the peaceful healing flows
of sweet wellness keeping slumber.

And that fateful night,
when the wacky weed smoke came for the first time,
their sleep was so deep and long
that they all slept very late the next morning,
until the sun was high over head in the sky.

When they awakened,
they were shocked to discover that the fire had gone asleep too!!!
All the ashes were bone cold,
without even a trace of a lingering ember!!!
Dead cold, bummer!!!

Major problem!!!
No fire in the burning pit 'twas sort of,
kinda like,
all the electricity going off,
cable TV service being disrupted,
and not being able to get a dial-tone.
All this happening at the very same time.

They just couldn't start the fire up again
with a simple flick of a 'Bic',
rubbing two sticks together
hadn't been perfected—or even thought of,
and iron couldn't be used
to strike an igniting spark from a piece of flint,
because iron hadn't been discovered yet,
and no free matches were available,
because *7-11 Stores* weren't yet opened.

Now those gatherings of cave folks
usually had at least one dude,
who was a wee bit smarter
than the average cave bear in the clan,
their acorn fell slightly farther from the ancestral tree.

This wiser dude's only job was to be the keeper of the fire,
the tribal tender of the blessing gift of those warming flames.

However, the fire keeper had to make sure and certain
to always keep those home fires burning,
and now those untended fires had burnt out!!!

With the fire out of the pit,
the rocks had long ago gone stone cold,
and that keeper of the fire dude was now in way deep shit,
as he carefully raked the gray ashes to dust,
hoping for a telling ouch upon his spread fingers,
from just one remaining lingering ember.

With just one small glow of an ember seed,
the keeper of the fire could grow the flames anew again,
then he'd become the hero,
leading the clan in chants of thanksgiving
for the rebirthing of fire.
But not a spark could be found,
and even his backup fire pit deep in the cave,
the first form of real fire insurance,
was totally devoid of a single flickering flame.

Now the fire keeping dude,
being in way deep shit
for having failed to keep the fire flame alive,
was sure he'd get all the blame for fucking-up!!!
So being a cave-wise smart dude,
he did some quick ass-covering thinking . . .
and he blamed that wacky weed smoke
they had all inhaled most joyfully last night,
for taking all the fire away.
With all that delicious drifting smoke, the fire got poked out,
and now they were, sad to say, fresh out of fire!!!

Sure, he could have been truthful and said
he fucked-up big time and the fire went out!!!
Because in all of the enjoying of that uplifting weedy smoke,
he failed to take notice
that no one bothered to toss more logs into the fire pit,
just before everyone fell asleep where they lay.
Like everyone in the clan,
he had been exhausted from all that happy inhaling,
and lustful communal playing about,
in the comfortable wonderful warmth,
of the smoking fire.

Yeppers,
'twas a wee bit of a stretch,
blaming the crazy smoke,
but plausible,
because no one wanted to admit
that their collective frolicking
distracted them from feeding the hungry fire.

So they all wanted to believe the story
that the wacky smoke,
had taken the fire away.
Their believing was much to the relief of the fire keeper,
because he had heard perfectly horrible tales
about other fire keepers who had failed
to keep the flame alive.

They were quickly banished from their clan,
and no other clan would welcome them in.
An ousted failed fire keeper dude being exiled out of the group
was a major fall from grace,
and debby and wendy and suzie too!!!

But they believed his story about the wacky weed smoke,
so the fire keeper dusted off the portable fire carrying vessel,
while the clan's three strongest and fastest runners
made ready to run to the neighboring clan,
to borrow a cup of fire.

Fire was very easy to share.
A cupful of fire, is like a cup of water,
there's always plenty for everyone,
except when there's none!!!
Indeed, at times there's way too much of both!!!
However, fire and water sure don't mix,
fire needs a purchase to start and water is always running . . .
babbling away, on the way to the salty sea.

With much cheering and good wishes,
the quest for fire runners took off at a trot.
Over hill and dale, and on across the plain they ran,
dodging hungry animals and big mud puddles,
for the six to nine sun trek to their nearest neighbors.
Who'd surely lend them a cup of fire.

Hopefully, the neighbors won't remember
the little mix-up that had happened,
when their hunting parties exchanged exasperated shouts
over the slain animal in question,
by a far away water-hole, many moons ago,
when times were harder.

Meanwhile,
back at the cave,
the fire keeper was busy demonstrating his fire keeping skills,
by cleaning ashes and bones out of the fire pits.

Then ever so carefully,
he arranged the dry tinder in an especially arranged array,
like he'd been taught by other wise fire keepers before him.
This arrangement would allow the new alighting flame
to grow and roar with life to bring light and warmth,
once again, into the now dank dark cave.

About a day away from the neighboring clan,
one runner got jumped by a hungry lion,
a big mean lion laying in wait,
for a meals-on-heels to come running by.

The other two runners did the lion in with their ready spears,
but the one who was to have been the meal,
had his left arm badly mangled by the speared dead lion.

They continued their fire questing trip,
with the lion carcass slung between their long spears.
They'd share the gift of the freshly slain lion
with their neighboring clan.
For another basic rule of survival is:
waste not—want not!!!
And their shared bounty might help to amend
for the wee bit of trouble back at the waterhole,
so many full moons ago.

With the walking wounded runner
carrying the empty portable fire container,
off they went toward the light of a distant fire
of the clan just next door across the plain.
They were indeed most grateful for the guiding beacons,
glistening from the mouths of multilevel cave dwellings.

When they were within voicefall,
they called out a greeting to the folks by the fire light,
letting the other clan know,
that they were but three weary neighbors
from the cave clan in the hills where the sun goes
into hiding from the night.

They also yelled that they bore the gift of a way heavy lion,
who wounded one runner before dying in ferocious battle,
and they were looking to borrow a cup of fire,
please!!!
And they were seeking shelter from the darkness,
rest, and food for their return trip,
and of course, the swapping of news tales,
for the telling joys in kind sharing ways
was the highlight of visiting.

Well, let me tell you,
those multilevel cave clan folks,
came rushing out of their multilevel caves
with multi-chords of merry greetings and warm welcomings.
The long ago ills done at the waterhole,
were long forgotten,
off-set by the simple joy of helping
these welcomed weary visitors from afar.
Visitors who were bringing a heavy lion for feasting,
a wounded one fallen in battle for tender healing,
and they needed the most vital sharing of fire.
Without sharing the given gift of fire's flame
their neighboring clan could perish in the cold dark.
And best of all, they had news stories waiting to tell!!!

Now the quest for fire runners were soon fed and warmed
by the tribe's large common fire pit,
which the tribe was now gathered all around.

The most important story for telling first,
was how the clan's fire went dead cold.
Sharing learnings about fire was very critical to know.
Lessons learned about fire could mean all the difference
between knowing the joys of creature comforts in safety,
or falling prey to the ravenous beasts
prowling about out there in the dark of night.
Blazing flames kept the monsters at bay,
away from their cavern, with the light and heat of the fire,
the beasts would always run fast away, far away from fire.

And with the beasts gone deep into the darkness,
the clan was safe to play in the cave,
and lay all about by their cozy fire pits.

However,
when the fire went out,
their fate was really in the pits,
until the tended fire sprang back to raging life each morning,
and burned brightly far into the next night.

Each lesson learned about fire
helped to keep the clan and their fire alive.
Lessons like,
pissing into the fire pit
kills the fire and makes stinky yucky smoke,
also,
snow falling from branches above fire,
makes fire go out—but not so stinky,
and,
big thick logs burn longer and brighter
than small thin twigs,
but,
small thin twigs were necessary to start the fire growing.

Thusly,
all information about fire survival lessons
were way important to share with nice neighboring clans,
'twas essential for their very continuation!!!
And indeed, so very neighborly to do so freely!!!

Of personal interest to the multi-level main keeper of the fire,
was to learn the fate of the failed fire keeper.
He sincerely hoped no exclusion from the tribe had happened
to a brother keeper of the fire.

Being shunned away from the safety of the tribe
ain't a good thing,
when being a meal for a roaming hungry beast,
is a sure to happen thing for one-alone!!!

Therefore, the fire keeper listened closely,
about how the smoke from the wacky bushy weed
had gotten everyone marvelously high in fine spirits,
spacing them all so lustfully into wild party enjoying,
until they all fell into slumbering exhaustion,
most joyful sleeping so blissfully.

And then, that wild wacky weed smoke,
which had been so very delightful,
did indeed,
steal all the flames away from the fire pit,
while everyone lay sleeping soundly,
and the fire just went up in smoke,
so to speak.
The clan's fire keeper, was not to blame,
the wacky weed smoke did it!!!

Upon hearing this tall tale,
the main keeper of fire chief for the multi-level clan,
knew what his brother fire keeper had done
in covering his sorry ass by blaming the wacky weed smoke.
But in saving his ass,
he did indeed,
foolishly condemn the helpful herbal weed.

The keeper of fire,
had a keeper of the fire intern bring forth clay pots full of holes,
with wacky weed smoke coming out of the holes.
The head fire keeper dude carefully explained,
that the holy clay containers allowed the wacky weed smoke
to be enjoyed by one and all in moderation.
By setting aflame to but a wee bit of weed,
without getting totally torn and stoned dumb,
from wastefully tossing the whole bush into the fire pit.

Ergo,
with responsible usage of the wild wacky weed,
they naturally enjoy most blissfully,
in freedom from the fear of having fire pit flames stolen away.

Also, the keeper of the fire
had taught everyone in the clan,
how to carefully tend the flaming fire pits,
an ongoing living trust—way better than costly fire insurance.
Throughout all the multi-level caves,
many small fires were always burning,
each with the ability to light anew,
and renew each other's fire,
by sharing the spark of light,
linkings of energy flows,
apart and yet together
in universal flows,
eternal energies
attuning with
alignments,
balancing
insightful
delights,
so basic
in many joys,
enjoying ever more!!!

The hurt runner, wounded battling the vicious lion,
was being tended by the clan healers
doing gentle massages upon his strong body,
enjoying the gladness of primitive touches,
tenderly flowing with natural energies.
Because, universal energy flows helped muchly
with the well being and caring for anyone
badly injured and sick with pain.
Thus were their healthy healing ways
of human kindness back then.
When special herbs and healing touches
were most hospitable sharings,
and always freely given to everyone in need.
In a hostile world,
filled with savage beasts,
those joyful touches felt so marvelous
and so very caring in giving and receiving.

The elder runner of the clan,
from the cave with one big mouth,
told of their fight with the pride of lions,
of being surrounded by the huge cats,
and slaying the bad ass leader of the pride
by the brave wounded one,
in mortal combat.

Of course,
his story got embellished just a wee bit
in those golden olden ways of story retelling.
Because being known for being a doer of admirable exploits,
like surviving savage animal attacks, was way important telling.

Besides,
good story telling was so joyfully vital to humankind,
enduring and winning in struggles for life against the beasts.
Tales about slaying nasty dragons
provided good material for stories too.

With the same joy of telling,
an elder of the multi-level clan
told about a group of women explorers,
who ventured from far beyond the mountains.
From beyond the lofty twin peaks
where the awaking sun slowly rises from,
to chase the night away, bringing the light of day.
These daringly bold women from the clan of high twin peaks,
were searching about the land for a heard-tell-of clan,
who had discovered the secret to make fire on demand.
And it was said, that the unknown clan's fire makers,
would make sparks into fire with anyone who asked
to have the knowledge of lighting their fires any time,
and anywhere they need to create
the gift of fire.
And he went on to tell,
how these visiting big women
laughed loudly at the primitive ways of enjoying mating,
practiced by the multilevel clan!!!

The women had said, rather bluntly,
that the multilevel clan were like wolves,
quickly coupling in an open field
mounting and instantly getting off,
done and gone so quickly in but a few mounted motions!!!
They all agreed, that good mounting enjoyings
were way more joyful when prolonged with variations.
And so the women of high twin peaks did explain . . .
but then, that's another story for another time.

When it was time for the runners to leave, all did agree,
that the healing wounded one would stay
to recover from his wounds.
Maybe the women of high twin peaks would return,
and he could later bring home to his clan
their teachings of prolonging mounting joys,
and the way of making fire sparks anytime and anywhere!!!

The main keeper of the fire dude
had carefully arranged the traveling cup of fire,
to make certain there would be a live flame
when they arrived safely home.
He also made a gift to the neighboring clan
of a few of the clay pots with holes,
for the moderate use of wacky weed smoke.

Six fast runners escorted them
during their long run through the grassy plain.
All those native animals were being very restless,
hungry for sweet meat, running upright on two legs.
One of the escorts did run into a big mud puddle,
and he was up to his neck in quicksand,
before they could pull him free of the hidden sand trap.
Those sand traps seemed to move
just as easy as the moving water traps,
which is just about par for the rough course.
Another one of those safety in number things,
because it took all of their hands working together
to free the runner from the sucking quagmire!!!

At the end of the vast grassy plain they parted on the run,
making haste to get back to the one big mouth cave
before the sun of the next day was done.

They ran late into the night
by the light of the nearly waxed moon,
resting in a familiar thicket when the moon set.
They hid high in the trees, safe from menacing night beasts,
and had time for tending their delicate charge of fire,
which continued burning safe in the portable carrier.

They were on the run again at dawn's first light.
Now racing to outrun an approaching rain storm,
trying to reach the safe shelter of their home cave
before the heavy threatening clouds started weeping,
and risk turning their precious borrowed cup of fire,
into a cold soup of yucky ashes!!!

When they were in voicefall of the one big mouth cave,
they shouted out a greeting yell,
alerting the clan to their safe return.

The entire clan came out to greet them, cheering loudly,
while they handed the portable fire carrier over
to the eagerly waiting keeper of the fire.
He rushed inside to the prepared fire pit,
and used the long carried flame to light the arranged tinder.
In three crows from the cockbird,
the fire pit was brightly ablazing anew.

Grateful thanks were given to the runners,
who had braved the furious wilds,
to run next door to the neighbors
and brought back the cup of fire seeds
to regrow the clan's fire.
Now the whole clan did gather around the fire pit,
to hear all about their great adventure,
questing after a cup of fire.

They told of their bloody battles with lions and tigers,
about visiting with the clan of multilevel caves,
presenting the holy pots gifts to use with the wacky weed
to enjoy the wonderful smoke in moderation,
telling how the multilevel keeper of the fire
had taught everyone in the clan,
how to tend the fire pits throughout the caves,
and about the exploring women of the high twin peaks,
who had visited the clan of multilevels caves
in their search for an unknown clan,
who were said to be teaching friendly tribes
how to make fire any time and anywhere!!!
Also, about those adventuresome women
sharing teachings of knowing more fun joys,
from prolonging mountings with variations of enjoying,
but they explained, that's another story.
And, about the escort runners with them through the plain,
how one was pulled safe from a swallowing mud puddle,
and their triumph in winning the race with the rain storm,
because dark skies were now pouring water.

Thanks to the efforts of the brave runners,
the tribe of the one big mouth cave
sat warm and dry around the beautifully blazing fire pit,
hearing the wonderful tales of the runner's great adventure.

At first,
the keeper of the fire wasn't thrilled with the idea,
about everyone in the clan of the one big mouth cave
knowing everything about the special ways of tending the fire.
Being the sole keeper of the clan's fire,
made the dude feel very important.

However,
when the fire went away,
like during the night of wacky overdoing,
he could have been banished from the clan forever.
For sure,
exclusion was indeed a very deadly bummer!!!

The more he thought about it,
the more he liked the idea,
because it sure would take the heat off him, so to speak!!!

Teaching everyone fire keeping would sure be lots of fun,
were now his thoughts,
and helping hands lighten everyone's load,
more fires could warm every nook and cranny,
in the sprawling cave with one big mouth,
and with lots of drafts.

Also, the hunters taught everyone to make spears,
how to hit the mark with thrown spears,
and where best to jab attacking beasts.
The main hunters had importance in the clan
and the entire clan helped with the major hunts.

And also the gatherers did likewise,
who taught everyone what eatable plants to look for,
and he too, had taught the gatherers
what good burning fuels to collect for feeding the fire,
and the healers had taught what roots and plants to harvest
for flavoring food cooking and healing,
and everyone did indeed benefit from the collective efforts.

Sharing the ways of keeping the fire,
could be a very good thing for him and the clan.

However, he didn't really believe the tale
about an unknown clan somewhere,
who knew the ways of making fire sparks,
anytime and anywhere they needed fire!!!
That was just incomprehensible!!!

Making fire was an interesting concept,
and he sure hoped the women of high twin peaks
would visit the clan of one big mouth soon,
bringing with them their sharing of prolonging joys,
and more learnings about fire too.

Thusly,
the clan of the one big mouth cave,
once again had the gift of fire in their now many fire pits,
to keep all the prowling beasts away,
while they all played in the warmth and light
of the happy fire.

The runners who went on the long quest for fire
were really true heroes in the clan,
their great feat would soon be painted on the cave wall
for all to see,
the marvelous service they had bravely done.

Because the runners brought back their freedom.

Freedom from fear of savage beasts,
sneaking into their cave to eat them in the night.

Freedom to enjoy the light and warmth of fire,
back when fire pit night lights,
were truly security blankets.

Freedom to enjoy the wacky weed smoke in moderation,
that wouldn't take fire away.

Freedom to know a few simple joys,
creature comforts beyond a hard life of just surviving.

Indeed,
the questing for fire runners were true heroes,
enduring a long race across a savage land,
to keep their tribe free from fears that would come in the night,
without the gift of fire.

That was way back in time,
when the survival of humankind
was a more mutual way of being,
and their freedom to pursue happiness
was their collective reward for surviving.

Back in time,
before humankind evolved to become
the very same dangerous beasts
that they feared would consume them.

Back when sharing was natural,
and learning survival skills were basic,
and classes weren't cut,
and enjoyment was in the natural joys of life.

When the sun and moon played tag in unpolluted skies,
when clans had common truths of enlightened learnings,
while holding their own non-threatening beliefs
that did no harm to other beings,
and helping one another
was the way of life,
free of fears,
free of war,
free to share,
free of greed and guilt,
free to be themselves in every way,
free to relish all the wonders and beauties of nature,
doing what comes naturally,
and naturally enjoying,
enjoying nature,
enjoying.

So smart we grew in our ways of evolving,
and becoming as smart as we like to think we've become,
somewhere within all our advancing becomings,
we've lost our natural sharing ways
of mutually being free to enjoy the flows of life.
Others now tend the regulated fire pits,
all built in a similar specified manner,
once vital survival skills have been replaced with button pushing.
Others control the only EPA approved fuels, because of so many
politically made dangers almost everything is now hazardous in
one way or another.

Others decide for humankind what is joyful,
the hype of trite to the masses via easy access media,
and just about everyone is good for 15 minutes of fame.
Others now run not in a quest for fire,
but for only a piece of colored ribbon,
while *we others* only stand and watch.
Others speak about *us* and for *us*,
their words repeatedly ding so hollow as *they* also decide for *us*.

Enjoying
was stolen away
by the cunning beasts
we've evolved into being.

Enjoying
got lost somewhere
when we have to ask the question:
'Are we having fun yet???'

Enjoying
was trashed
with all the stylish
defining done to explain
what was acceptable enjoying,
and what wasn't enjoyable any more.

Enjoying
foolishly fell prey
with those vain vicarious
plastic investing,
in the alluring antics
of self-created celebrities,
entertaining in joys of their reflected enjoying for *us*.

Enjoying
was painted
into the corner with hues
of unrealistic expectations
being saddled upon folks by others.

Thusly,
in many ways
our becoming smartness
has lost sight of the wisdom
found in the more becoming joys,
within the ever glowing playing desires of our godspark.
In short,
in the glitz and glitter and empty dinging dongs,
our collective society has been so very distracted,
and lured into such a zombie state
of controlling conditioned ways of non-being.

Therefore,
the enjoying passions of our godsparks
are flickering and the fire pit smoke is harmfully toxic,
in the chemically charged black smoke from burning plastic,
way different than the natural herbal smoke!!!

Way different too,
are the manufactured joyless sleeps,
rolling off an endless production line as
sweating snoozes and noisy naps at best,
and mind mauling nightmares of the worst kind!!!

Also changed is the tending of the fire,
with lots of bickering and buck passing,
about just who was supposed to toss logs on the fire
and the blame gets passed all around
as the fire dies a fuel starved death.

In our endless quest to make the quality of life better,
the enthusiasm has gone away,
driven-off by every act of mindless interactions
surrounded by careless acts of gross inconsideration,
of leaving lazy slob messes for others to clean-up,
of glutton grabbing to get all that can be gotten
before someone else gets to grab first
and leaves nothing for anyone else.

It has made for a society into wasteful undoings
of telling lies and zapping snaps of coarse anger,
of pursuing rather selfish patterns of behaviors
so frequently totally self-centered,
of doing harmful artificial joys
that are as empty as the smoke and mirrors
repeatedly at the demeaning expense of others,
of leaving the undone work for many hands
to be done by but a few weary hands,
of bemoaning our plight in ways
that are forever blaming others.

Indeed,
we've become the very beast we once so feared
and the beast within is stealing the passions of enjoying life
from our foul smoking fire pit
the beasts have pissed into.

And most sadly,
those neighbors we weren't neighborly with,
aren't about to give us a cup of fire
in our time of dire need.

Trying to sell them yellow snow
made into looking like lemonade snowcones
wasn't at all neighborly!!!

Those hasty and unfounded profound judgments
made to make those neighbors who are different look bad,
with the ill-conceived expectations for improving
our self-inflated statue in the community
was way lacking in every way!!!

Looking at neighbors to only see what they are doing
through jade green eyes that envy only what they have,
are blinded in seeing what they don't have.
'Tis regretful we've tried to be our neighbor's keeper,
only to discover a kept neighbor is no help at all.

We really need to set aside harmful ways of interacting,
that chases enjoying so quickly away.

We need to stop tossing harmful stuff into the fire pit,
that makes yucky poisonous black smoke,
and cokes off the flames of refreshing desires.
We need to spend less time pondering
all those meaningless question
about the meaning of life,
and zestfully invest lots more time
creating and enjoying a more meaningful life.

We need to renew those mutual ways of caring and sharing
by the warmth of our refueled fire.

We need to rediscover the simple ways of enjoying,
and reclaim freedom from ingrown fears.

We need to enjoy life more.

More enjoying prolongs life
and enhances our lives muchly.

Take care and enjoy often . . . John

A Gift of Self in a Nutshell . . .

And then there are those folks
who give as they are able,
as they enable themselves
to give of themselves.

For all we really have to give
is ourselves,
and nothing more.

But first,
we need to empower our inner self,
to shine through shells,
to truly give of ourselves,
and enabling shining from within,
comes from knowing acts of willingness,
to be known as we are.

Most material possessions are merely passing reflections,
reflecting surrounding of appealing trappings . . .
nothing more than smoke and mirrors
that can be gone in a fraction of an instant,
and those decorator appearances
are nothing more than fancy plastic shells,
as pretty as they are painted.

Sadly, there's often no one at home.

Hard shells are turtle-like protective,
others are as clams,
ever nearby armor casings to be retreated into,
or encompassing so completely tight in a troubled moment,
claming up in the puzzlement of silence within.

At times,
silence speaks with volume,
but no one hears the sounds of silence
from inside the shell.

Soft are the feathered ones,
or silky smooth as a cocoon,
as yielding as shell feathers may be,
they are rigid and water does roll off naturally.
Nothing seems to stick or stay very long,
as they quickly flee in feathered flight,
fearful of bumps in the night.

Cocoons are sleepy time changing rooms,
to be shed as part of timely metamorphosis,
discarded shells having served their purpose,
as natural transitions do happen.

Then too there is the natural new shell game,
switching old shells for a seemingly more befitting covering,
ever switching to change into a better fit,
always slipping free of outgrown skins,
always in new skins.

And the only universal constant is change,
ever changing and exchanging one shell
for another and another,
as the changing cycle goes unchanged,
but always exchanging,
changing changes.

Spinning bouts of frenzied energies coalesce
into always busy thorny shells,
so engrossed in bolting to here and being there,
to do this and/or take care of that,
in the gotta do nowness of right now.

Their ever ready active energy is poised to zap
those who venture too near,
warding them off
with their busily buzzing being stinging,
keeping all folks
from disrupting their focus on current priorities,
demanding instant doing.

Sadly, their driven desires to always be doing,
is so often their undoing,
always dinged with waiting undones.

Veils are the concealing shells
of alluring mysteries laced with frustrations,
causing endless pondering about what's hidden
behind those multi-layered shrouds,
so flowing and light they appear to be,
cunning illusions to entice thee.

So quickly they do teasingly entangle,
all who venture into their entrapping web,
so seemingly up-close and yet impersonal,
these untouchable apparitions are.
Look upon them,
but don't you dare touch.

The tease is their mystery, under a shell of veils.

Exposure undoes their tempting mysteries,
but teasing frustrations under their shells,
remain untouched.

Weary be the worn shells eroding away
by the blowing sands of time,
made brittle as life flows go down the drain,
with endless regrets over undone never did joys,
never to be joyfully done,
made weak and so frail,
by uncaring inconsiderate doings
done unto them.

They seem so fragile,
as if a single simple touch
will shatter them to pieces...
while they mournfully bemoan their
oh pity poor me songs from bygone times,
times of *might have been joys* lost along the way.

Overt shells are overbearing,
self-inflating with their hot airs of self-importance,
ever so quick with fixing answers
from their affixed point of all knowing fixations,
sitting on top of a highness of their making,
rendering false judgments
upon those who are different
from their ways of thinking and being.

Thc zcal of their all consuming ego,
won't peel free from the pearls of wisdom,
they believe they hold for everyone,
because there often isn't yet a pearl there,
only the gritty coarseness of an abrasive grain of sand.

Their shells are so preposterously pompous
and so absurdly exaggerated.

Chameleon-like are shells,
in changeable moods of mix and match colors,
ever adapting and changing and molting
to blend into the foreground.
So eager are they to fit in anywhere,
they become part of the background too.

They might be right before your eyes,
but their reality isn't to be seen
as they continue to hide,
appearing to be here
when they aren't really here or there,
as they blend into nothingness,
fading shells of phantom illusions
and nothing more,
nevermore.

The hardest part about freely giving the gift of self,
is reaching out beyond our affixed shells,
to let our godspark that dwells within
shine through protective shields.

To accept others as is,
accepting whatever there is,
that's offered free of conditioning shells,
then lovingly befriending flows,
come brightly aglowing with light.

Methinks,
when we grow from within
to touch others with caring kindness,
the harmony of kindly touching,
transcends beyond the need
for confining protections,
clear of imposed guilt,
free from grabbing greed,
and far above dictated restrictions
that keep way too many people
locked into needless shells.

The cherished giving of self
does align us with similar mindful folks
giving of likewise compassion along the way,
balancing with each other,
as begifting friends bring sharings of self,
delighting godsparks aglow.

Thusly,
I am as I am,
and you are as you are,
then when we are free of these shells,
we come to know the beautiful joys
of truly gifting ourselves.
All that we have to share
are the glows of our godsparks forevermore,
and the more we freely give
of ourselves in kindness,
the more of ourselves there truly is
in the reality of enjoying life
free of hindering shells.

What comes gently into being is
light where there was cloaking darkness,
love where once there was clinging fear,
and peace in our merging merry energies
of giving and receiving
balancing flows,
enjoying life
ever mindful
evermore,
ever joyful.

Light,
love,
and peace
be with us one and all,
my friends.

Enjoy often . . . John

ODE TO A UPS TRUCK

Painted in a unique hue of dark brown,
sparkling clean in the early morning's light,
pushing away from the loading dock,
loaded full with neatly addressed packages,
mostly wrapped in paler shades of tan brown.

Weaving about the rush hour traffic,
the driver knows the best way to go,
taking flight across the jammed byways,
making up time upon flowing highways,
heading for their well known delivery area.

They carry the joys and needs for many,
the belated birthday gift for aunt Suzy,
Fred's brand new desk top computer,
the awaited replacement part for Shirley,
business records for accountant Harry.

Boxes of special ordered inventory,
tubes carefully holding movie posters,
large flats of hard copy documentation,
all kinds of strange shapes and sizes,
each one important to those awaiting.

In the bed of these brown vans,
ride the tireless efforts of so many,
all packaged with care for shipping,
from lots of exotic places far away,
now entrusted to the caring driver.

The last leg of their passage is here,
and soon all the packages will be there,
each one delivered with a friendly smile,
and a *'sign here'* in the magic block,
with that, the daily delivery job is done.

The once heavily loaded dark brown van,
is riding almost empty of outgoing cargo,
gone are all the assorted parcels for today,
save the ones that couldn't be delivered,
and the pickups for delivery tomorrow.

Back to the terminal they now return,
their work for this day is finally done,
parked neatly aligned in marked rows,
silently they recall their joys and woes,
over a long drink of gas and a bit of oil.

So when you see a UPS truck in traffic,
or briefly stopped in a marked loading zone,
give a friendly toot and a wave in passing,
for you never know when in that brown van,
there might be a package addressed to you.

Take care and enjoy often . . . John

This ode was inspired while watching and waiting for a UPS truck to arrive with a delivery I was eager to receive. That was the day I learned that a UPS truck is like the watched pot that never boils while you are watching the pot, and a UPS truck doesn't arrive while you're looking for the truck to pull up. Also, I figured if that other John dude, the Keats one, could write 'Ode on a Grecian Urn' in 1819, then I could surely write one in 1997 honoring a UPS truck.

THANKSGIVING SOUP

On Thanksgiving eve my grandmother would start preparing her very special soup for dinner the next day. She was my father's mother. Her given name was Emma, but everyone called her *'Nanny'*--and that was back in the times before nannies came to be fancy live-in child care providers. She was a very special lady and contributed giving care for just about anyone needing a helping hand, a bite to eat or a listening ear. She always had a pot of coffee on the stove, and time to sit for a spell. She was a wee bit of a short lady of about 5' and thin as a rail, but way big as a person. As small as she was, Nanny was a human dynamo of natural energy.

She taught me how to take care of myself by teaching me the basic skills most guys would rather not know about. Nanny showed me how to do wash, iron out wrinkles, how to sew on a button, and stitch a patch so it wouldn't show too much—*waste not want not* was perhaps her favorite saying. She never got upset when I made a mess because I was sure to clean up after myself—*you made the mess, you clean it up!!!* Sure, you could eat in the living room and watch TV, as long as you carried your dishes to the kitchen when you finished eating—*Now, not later!!!* She truly believed that men needed to know how to do for themselves in real world living ways. She also allowed me to build a small arms range in the basement so I could practice target shooting after I qualified for an NRA small bore team. Nope, she didn't live in a big country house. My grandparents owned a very neatly maintained small row-house in the south east end of Lancaster, Pennsylvania.

She also taught me her method of cooking, not from a cookbook, but in the touch and taste ways of cooking. She believed that most cookbooks had recipes that took far too long to make, for the limited amount of eating enjoyment that came from all the efforts involved in the fixing and the cleaning up afterwards. It was fine if what you were eating looked pretty, but the proof of the pudding was in how your mouth liked it, and more importantly, how the meal felt in your tummy. Nanny believed that the only thing a high priced dinner fed, was the hungry ego in the mind. She'd say, *'tis better to feed the feelings of the heart so you don't get heartburn!!!*

Nanny's special soup of Thanksgiving was always good in all ways—especially fruitful with lots of good feelings. One Thanksgiving, as I was entering my teenage years, when I foolishly believed I knew everything—as young teens are inclined to believe, I was helping Nanny make her soup. Whenever Nanny cooked anyone handy was a possible free agent to be drafted into helping. So there I was chopping onions, as I asked her, *"Nanny, with the turkey and stuffing, and all the side dishes of fresh vegetables, and pies, why do you bother to keep making your vegetable soup every Thanksgiving???"*

"Well it's not a vegetable soup, this is my special Thanksgiving soup that happens to have some vegetables in it," she smiled and continued to explain, *"And, I mostly make it as a reminder of a Thanksgiving during the war, just after you were born, when all we had for that dreary Thanksgiving was a wild turkey from the Quarryville kin. Uncle Amos blew that bird's head off with his smooth bore rifle while he was taking a dump in the outhouse. That turkey would come into the barnyard after the chicken feed, and take off running at the sight of a gun. Amos had put his rifle in the outhouse the night before, thinking he'd get a shot while he did his morning sit-down business. That's when he shot the bird right in the head. His boys shot a flock of cockbirds for their Thanksgiving dinner, so his son Casey brought Tom turkey to share with me."*

"Oh, the soup is to remind you of uncle Amos???" I asked, knowing that wasn't the reason, and knowing she'd love to tell me more of her story.

"I don't need no reminding of him," she said with a laugh, *"I took one look at that old Tom turkey, and figured a bird that tough would need lots of cooking to be fit for eating. There also wasn't much here in the way of food stuff to make much of a festive meal with. Ration coupons and the end of the harvest from*

the small Victory garden made for lean times. While I was plucking that big bird, I figured he'd take a heap of cooking so I thought I'd first roast him, then pick off the meat and make a heaping big pot of turkey vegetable soup for our Thanksgiving meal. Making soup would stretch the vegetables, and with the herbs and slow cooking, that old wild bird's meat might get nice and tender with flavors and be real good eating."

"Your soup is to remind you to cook old birds longer???" I asked, and at that time I might or might not have known that there are various kinds of birds!!!

Nanny laughed, *"That's true, old birds do take longer to prepare, and once they're stuffed, they need more time to cook off too. The important part is in the preparations and what goes into the pot. Some folks don't even have a pot to piss in. The big old soup pot reminds me that I'm grateful to have a pot to cook my Thanksgiving soup in, and a nice clean indoor flush toilet to use when I need to!!!"*

"Oh, yes, I'm thankful for indoor plumbing too. The out-house down on the farm is stinky and full of spiders and bugs and a stack of old Sears & Roebuck catalogs!!!" as I remembered visiting Grammy Moore down country on the Herr farm and having to use the outhouse. Ugh, way stinky!!!

"Those spiders and bugs won't bother you, and during the winter you'll never be sitting there long enough to notice the smell," she said skillfully dicing spuds, *"And that reminds me that no matter how fancy the ingredients are that go in, everything comes out about the same in the end. During that Thanksgiving we didn't know when the war would end. Your daddy was off in the army to fight the Nazi Hun, and some folks had stars in their windows for fallen soldiers and sailors who wouldn't be coming home. That Hitler fellow was a horrible beast--a monster trying to control the world, and he had to come to an end, or freedom as we knew it would surely cease to be. We didn't know when that ending for him would come--but we knew someday the war would end. We did know your daddy was safe, because we*

just got 'V-mail' from him the day before, and at the end of the time when he posted that letter, he was okay. We were thankful to be at the receiving end of his letter. Lots of folks didn't have letters from their loved ones off to fight in the war."

"Well, those kinds of ends, like good letters from people far away and Hitler blowing his brain out with his pistol, are good ends, but . . ." I was saying as Nanny stopped me.

"All kinds of ends are good ends. Look, we've been using all kinds of odds and ends from the vegetable bin to make this soup. Some of the carrots are limp and the celery might be a little wilted and the green string beans have seen better days, but mixed all together and cooked in the soup, those odds and ends will be just fine. When you're watching football and your team is winning by a close score, and time runs out ending the game, that is a good ending. And the same is true, that when your team is losing, and the lost game is over, you're grateful that the losing game is behind you, and you learn from the mistakes made in playing the game, and then you look forward to the end of the waiting for the next game to begin, so you can try out what you've learned and practiced. The end of waiting is a good ending to be thankful for too."

"Now that's silly, Nanny, being thankful for endings!!!"

"Not silly, think about it, without endings there wouldn't be no beginnings, without beginnings there would never be anything new, nothing would be started, nothing would change, so an ending is nothing more than a change. The end of the summer is the beginning of fall, all the end is, is nothing more than changes of time passages in transition."

"That's why you put all your leftover odds and ends in the Thanksgiving soup, to remind you of changes???" I asked, thinking I was sort of following where Nanny was perhaps going with this change tangent she was on.

"Well, my soup also reminds me of how some things stay pretty much the same—even with changes. Each time I make my special soup, the odds and ends are different and always in differing amounts--you know my adding a pinch of this and some of that way of cooking--but the taste and flavor of the soup are just as pleasing and nourishing regardless of the changes in ingredients. Folks are like soup too, the odds and ends of life experiences may shape and change them, but the supporting flavor of the essence of their being is usually pretty much the same. The greater their variety of life experiences, the wider their spread of odds and ends for the soup. Everybody brings different odds and ends to help to make my soup special—that's the magical mix that gets blended all together."

"You make it sound like people soup, like people being cooked in a big iron kettle, like cannibals used to cook people in the Saturday afternoon movies!!!" said I, being less than thrilled with the concept of cannibals cooking people in a big kettle in the spirit of giving thanks. And why I said it then totally escapes my recall—perhaps trying to make a joke out of the big soup pot, and visions of parts of people making up the brew of soup bubbling in the pot. Ugh, people parts!!! This was long before that serial killer Jeffery Dahmer dude did his yucky things with his victims' chopped-up body parts in the Milwaukee area. Ugh!!!

"That's just the right image of my Thanksgiving soup!!!" she said much to my surprise, *"My soup is made in a big kettle, and everyone is welcome in the making of my soup. They're all welcome to toss in their odds and ends of life experiences, and share the flavors of their life with whomever else is into enjoying the soup. And I only have one special soup rule that will cause you to be unwelcome in my soup making if you break the rule. The one rule is: Don't piss in my soup!!! My soup will not be fouled with anyone's harmful ways. You mess up my soup and you're gonna be banished for a long time from my soup pot!!!"*

Now, at this point I was a totally speechless young teen, and this dear wise old lady, who is my grandmother, is slicing up carrots and talking with me very matter of factly about not taking a leak in her soup pot!!! Ugh!!! yucky, bad thing, like not eating the yellow snow!!! It was difficult of me to think of her keeping anyone away from her table. Nanny was a very kind and helpful person to everyone she knew. The only time I remembered her getting really upset and uncomfortable with someone, was when we got on the trolley to go up town to market, and a woman already on the trolley was wearing the same dress she was!!! The other woman made evil eyes at Nanny!!! We got off the trolley at the next stop, and walked back to her home so she could change her summer dress. No way, could I see her banishing anyone or doing harm to someone in anyway.

She went on saying, *"My Thanksgiving soup reminds me to be thankful for all the people who have brought the flavors of their lives to mix and mingle and merge together in my special soup of life. Warmed and always cooking in the glow of my god-spark, all are welcome as long as they follow the do no harm to anyone rule. When someone pees in the soup, their gross inconsiderate action spoils the makings of the soup for everyone. What they're putting into the soup is so tainted with their vile bitterness that it is overpowering, and the unique blend of flavors in my soup is at risk of being ruined, unless they leave until they learn not to mess up my soup pot with their foulness. You know I ain't got no time for inconsiderate people—they won't be allow to bring their spoiling ways into my life—or my soup!!!"*

I'm getting a warm fuzzy feeling, because what Nanny is saying is sounding very coarse and yucky bad to envision. However, she's making good sense about how nasty doing harm is, and that's what messes up the soup of life for everyone else. Those inconsiderate slobs spoil everyone's space with their nasty ways of being. Every year that I had Thanksgiving dinner at Nanny's, her special soup would always be different, but it would also have that same wonderful home cooked flavor that could never be put in a can—not even Campbell's, because Nanny cooked lots of natural love into her Thanksgiving soup.

"The first Thanksgiving I made my soup during the second World War, our neighbors shared with neighbors what little they

had to share. All of our neighbors were always welcome to come and have some soup, especially the neighbors who didn't have anything to contribute to the makings--they were the most grateful ones sharing the joys of our Thanksgiving dinner. You know, you always seem to appreciate something lots more when you don't have something that was taken for granted. What they brought to contribute to the soup was their good cheer and company over a bowl of hot soup--and the warmth of their gratitude for being invited to have hot soup to eat was their very special contribution. That's the special remembrance of my Thanksgiving soup, all the merry goodwill and cheer of enjoying sharing life experiences that folks bring love to make a simple bowl of soup into a festive meal," and then she added with her knowing smile that sparkled with her unique brightness, *"and remembering to give thanks for nice indoor flush toilets too!!!"*

Nanny was a remarkable lady and a most amazing teacher about the flows of living life that makes up the soup. Her book learning was the most basic reading, writing, and arithmetic, but her ways of reading human nature were far beyond the learnings of that time. I never heard her say a mean word about anyone, except Lee Harvey Oswald and Adolph Hitler, she called both of them *worthless scum bags and the world would be a better place if they had never been born!!!* She passed gently away in the late fall of 1968, while she was shopping for a bargain at one of her favorite department stores in downtown Lancaster. One of her fond joys was finding a bargain on sale. I believe she's smiling with my recall and sharing of her loving way for making Thanksgiving soup.

Indeed, she did banish people from her table for doing harmful things. Once in the middle of a Sunday dinner, she told a relative to leave the table, her house, and never to return again because of all his harmful actions. I never did learn what he had done, Nanny just said he ran out of chances with all his sincere promises and blaming everything on others when it was all his foul doings that were wrong and harmful to everyone, and she would have nothing more to do with him. True to her word—from that day on she would never even mention his name or take part in any family gathering where he would be attending. She never said a bad word about him, but I heard tell he was bad mouthing Nanny. I asked her why she didn't do something about the lies he was telling, and she explained that folks who knew her will know what the truth is—those who didn't know her didn't matter, and that he was just digging is grave deeper.

I thought Nanny was being way too harsh and I couldn't think of what he'd done to be shunned by her, until many years later I was in NYC for a business meeting. Walking to the train, I passed a jewelry store window that was displaying a fancy WWII metal that my father had given me. The metal had strangely disappeared years earlier, and I knew it was mine because one of the small stones was missing, the same stone that had been missing on mine. When I got home, I called a friend and asked her to please check out the metal—and to buy it, if the price was reasonable. She worked in an office building near the store, and she said she'd go to the jewelry during her lunch hour the next day. The metal was gone!!! The store manager said he had sold it that morning, he had taken it on consignment from the friend of a friend, and he wasn't at liberty to give out the name. However, my friend had a friend who was a NYPD detective, and he stopped by and got the name. Yeppers, the very same relative Nanny had banished from her table had stolen from me too!!! And I was just a kid!!! Ugh!!! Nanny was right about that relative whose name has never been mentioned in years, he really pissed in the makings of the soup of lots of folks!!!

I'm sorry my son never got to meet Nanny. She was gone before he arrived. Now he only gets to know of her through my sharings about her, and I'm biased by the wisdom of her ways. Methinks this is a good bias to share.

Take care, have some good soup, and enjoy often . . . John

NO SHIT!!!

Listen my friends you shall hear,
about the time that came to be,
around the second Wednesday of the following week,
or kinda thereabouts, in the bizarre month of Bramble.

For it came to pass just about then,
that strange and wondrous magic did happen to take place,
and various body parts were graciously graced
with the ability to be verbally expressive with each other,
that's right—those body parts could really talk!!!

Now being very humankind like,
they naturally got into bantering about
just which of all these boldly talking body parts
played the biggest and most important job
in keeping the body healthy and properly functioning.

"There is no doubt in my mind,"
said the ever thinking Brain,
"that I'm the most important part,
for without me doing all the thinking
you'd all be just a mindless mass of nothing!!!"

"Not so, not so, not so!!!",
the bleeding Heart did beat out,
"for without my endless pumping of blood,
my dear ego draped Brain head,
you'd be nothing more than lumpy gray matter!!!"

"Ohhhh, surrrrrre,"
rumbled the growling ever hungry Stomach,
"and without me digesting and converting
all kinds of yummy food stuff into energy,
you couldn't keep on pumping for long!!!"

They continued to exclaim the many merits of what they did,
and why they were all so very self-important,

as they went about their jobs of keeping the body working,
while sustaining their boastful bickering banter
about their respective vital functions.

Now, not to be too heinous,
but with a blast of foul smelling gas,
the lowly Anus did shout out,
*"I'm more important than all of you,
and what's more, I can prove what I say!!!"*

"You can't be serious!!!" said the Brain with snobby distain.

"You're nothing more than a butt-hole,"
said the beating ever beating Heart, *"and nothing more!!!"*

"You are so beneath all of us," said the Stomach,
"and a dumb-ass asshole can't prove a thing!"

"Oh but I can prove the bluntness of my point to you all,"
said the humble Anus, and with a huff of passing gas,
the anal opening where the sun don't shine added bluntly,
"N O   S H I T ! ! !"

And thusly said,
the cute little round butt-hole did close up most tight,
so tightly in fact, that if one were to look very closely
from a bottoms-up eye view, there was no asshole to be found!!!

The snotty Brain laughed, *"Just a bunch of hot air!!!"*

"Yucky dumb hot air and nothing more," echoed the Heart.

The greedy Stomach said with a cocky grumble,
"I can force that stupid asshole open at anytime I want to!!!"

So time did pass, but not a bit of shit,
moved through the closed bottom portal,
for the asshole did remain securely shut
without as much as a single fart escaping.

The Stomach became very bloated,
the belly button that once was an innie,
all too soon became a grossed-out outie,
and sure enough, a bad tummy ache
was what was really happening!!!

The Heart tried in vain to keep on pumping,
but the swollen Stomach kept on bumping
into the now straining-to-pump Heart,
struggling with heart burn-out, was barely thumping,
because the Heart was now Stomach humping,
upsetting the panging with pain tummy, even more!!!

The Brain was struggling to think this through
in an all too logical brainy way,
and was soon faced with the grim fact that its gray matter
was about to become very brown—as in Shit-for-Brains,
don't you turn those blue eyes brown!!!

Now we're talking a condition of major anal retentiveness,
because no shit did pass,
no passing shit as the hoped for expelling results
from eating those usually purging prunes,
not even the yucky foul tasting castor oil
could allure the striking Anus to allow a shitty movement,
nor did the threat of an enema bring about a gushing flow,
because between those smooth ass cheeks,
was nothing but joining smoothness,
nicely flowing curves, but not working right now,
because within the fanny crack,
there was no hole.

Their collective pleading cries and sorrowful sobs
for much needed relief could be heard,
bemoaning their shared shitty plight,
begging to amend their reconsidered judgments,
but have no doubt about it, my friends,
the Anus most certainly remained tightly closed!!!

Alas,
'twas in the eleventh hour,
in the runny month of Prune,
when they all did at last agree,
that the awesome elusive asshole,
was indeed the most important part of all.

Thusly, it indeed came to pass that the Anus did open
with a mighty venting rush of expelling gas,
permitting a cleansing outpouring of accumulated shit,
holy shit, shit, shit, and even more and more shit!!!

The Anus was heard to tactfully explain,
"We're all important in the part we have to do,
we all depend upon each other in turn,
and I know I have a shitty job,
but the shit work has to be done,
because shit happens!!!"

So when next you bare your buns to grace the eternal throne,
and when all the shit in this sitting has been smoothly passed on,
think a kind thought about your awesome Anus,
and perhaps take pause, when you are about to call someone,
a *"Stupid Asshole!!!"*.

Remember the job ain't finished, until the paperwork is done,
and a neat clean Anus is indeed a happy hiney-hole,
and not at all dumb or stupid!!!

Enjoy often . . . John

CIRCLING PATTERNS

Take a mind trip with me to a scary place,
a very fearful place, unlike any place
your thoughtflows might conjure
into a cognitive form
of non-being.
In this place thoughts don't flow in usual ways,
your thoughts are all scrambled about,
at times overloaded with mixes
of sensory input so boggling
that the brain doesn't
have the ability to
process all of it,
as brainwaves
fail to connect
in usual ways
of connecting
all together,
not at all.
Where what's up might appear to be down,
and down sort of seems to be sideways,
and sideways isn't a place to be,
because what seems to be,
isn't what really is,
as it seems to be,
and you don't,
know what is,
or what isn't,
real or not.
Here is where everything that goes bump
in the deep dark of night is dwelling,
where most of what we know
as reality is always unreal,
always threatening,
always there,
frightening,
awaiting,
you.

Here in this place where fright is constant,
where even the most tender touches
bring screams of painful hurts,
but you don't feel it as pain,
and bangings in the head,
that become a harmful
knowing of self-made
compulsion based
relational reality,
of pain you do
relate within,
but not as,
really pain,
so unreal,
harmful
to you,
hurts,
ouch.

A brutal reality pounded into your basic being,
to experience just a brief fleeting touchstone
of being a total stranger in a strange land,
devoid of all the usual reality links,
so empty of the common means
to grasp upon any realness,
so totally out of touch,
except for the pain,
pain rains down,
rains in your,
hard to stop,
mind hurts,
rain pain,
painful,
endless
harms
ouch
pain.

This is no cute trick and not a Halloween treat,
and the sad costume is always the same,
because here you only know a sense
of safety in repeated sameness,
following around the circles,
made safe only because
they are way familiar,
and nothing more,
than mindfully
safe circles,
circling,
circles.
Nothing more than just a pattern of worn circles,
like a top spinning endlessly around spinning,
to go around time and time again and again,
so very small and self-encompassing,
those endless all protective circles
define the confines you know
as your entirely safe world,
never changing patterns,
in a never expanding
world, so enclosed,
in safe circles,
closing out,
closing in,
enclosed
circles.
Patterns are woven as your safety net,
you feel safe in your patterned web,
safe from the threatening world
where minute changes in,
happenings cause you
acute discomfort,
and cries of
distress,
stress,
circle,
spin,
in.

You don't know how to feel loving caring,
your feelings are polarized in between
what you know as only safe circles,
and you the fear of the unknown
that is even now lurking just,
beyond those safe circles,
circles going nowhere,
in your most limited
peephole of reality,
that is seemly so,
unreal to others,
but is so very
comforting,
soothing,
to your,
being
safe,
in.

There is no freedom allowing playing in the sunshine,
no swinging upon swings in the beautiful parks,
your rigid patterns become your entire world,
only patterns build upon more patterns,
so empty of understanding of how
those fixed patterns come to be,
there's not grasp of the cause,
for reasoning is not a part
of your set mind flows,
no logic is present
in this cloudy,
ill-logical,
gloomy,
dismal,
place
pain.

The banging in your head rattles headaches,
the physical stresses from the throbbings
of your head against the cold hard wall,
you sadly know only as solid reality,
with no thought of self doing harm,
nor the stressful fright to others,
as you drum your head to beat
all those missing alignments,
in discords of disharmony,
in your lacking rhyming,
striking brain back into
some comfort pattern,
smacking your head
with hurtful whacks,
repeatedly a trying
to find the safety,
a haven of being,
where patterns
align to bring
momentarily
the security
blanket of
comforts,
no ache,
finding
safety,
again,
there
sit
in.

This is your world, where absolutely everything beyond
the edge of your comfort patterns is totally horrifying,
where caring touches are pushed away as painful,
where loving care equates to a comfort pattern,
and sadly the care provider has little meaning,
where there is no appreciation of beauty in
evolving creation growing free into light,
because no light makes it past the wall
of your encircling protective patterns,
and the only growth is in the ever
increasing complexities of your
locked tight comfort patterns
stacking one upon another,
in the limited orbit of your
circle of endless patterns,
your envelope of safety,
restricted comfy zone,
where you are safe,
to sometimes even
sparkle some in,
a brilliance all,
your own so,
ever briefly,
then gone,
back into,
patterns,
of more
endless
circles
round
orbits
cycle
spin.

You have no concept of the feelings of others,
because your own feelings are all so jumbled
in an unreal mixture of comfort or fright,
and the sad creeping darkness of night
brings all the terrors of unknowings,
always lurking there in darkness,
and in pushing away the dark,
you push away those trying
to bring you the comfort of
their always caring love,
a real love you have no
concept of knowing,
your world is only
safety or threats,
and in-between,
is nothing but
your maze of
all patterns,
so primal,
tracking,
patterns,
of circles
going on
around
circles
round
circle
to be
safe
in.

You can't pop a pill to fix the alignments of brain waves,
no doc frankengates can rewrite your operating system,
and you won't find a shrink to help solve the puzzle,
and there is no remote hope of divine intervention,
because all hope is a concept that escapes you,
but you don't feel a sense of hopelessness,
because 'hope' is an unknown concept,
and you have no way of knowing that,
all of the marvels of modern healing
can't frcc you from ever locking
patterns entrapping you in ever,
never working mind-settings,
of always circling patterns,
spinning an endless web,
that keeps you trapped
under guises of safety,
never to venture out
beyond the patterns,
of your closed mind,
closed to the world,
beyond the painful
spinning patterns,
encircling about
your full mind
of encircling,
comforting
sameness
patterns,
circling,
around,
circles
cycle
spin
sit
in

Now some might say in jest, *'wow, what a trip!!!'*
Alas, but this isn't a mere trip of your making,
this is a life's journey of being ever plagued,
to circle endless upon the same old paths,
'tis as if all of the bad karma ever done,
is now coming back to hit you again,
and again and again and again and,
again and again and so on ever,
this is no bad hangover in the
morning with a headache,
the headache hangs on,
ever with you dinging
endlessly away with,
dinky dinging dings,
of the patterns that,
never do work out
beyond all those,
ever encircling,
same patterns,
of sameness,
always into
the same
patterns
circling
around
circles
cycle
again
safe.

Now right about now you are thinking as you're read this,
Gee, John is really rambling on and you with this pattern
thingy and wondering if there are any points to all this,
but there's no wondering here in this ugly starkness,
to wonder about, beyond the circles is too scary,
and this place doesn't know joyful wonderings,
there's no enjoyment here to bring a smile,
no echoing sounds of playful laughter,
expressive looks are sharp contrasts
between the almost ever present
appearance of the blank stare,
and screams of total terror,
where everything has the
potential to reproduce
fearful tantrum cries,
and there's no way,
to think about any
point in all this,
because often,
those patterns
do seem to be
so pointless,
as patterns,
sameness
no point,
patterns,
circling
circles,
safety
there
spin
in.

Others will define what kind of day you are having,
you lack the ability to do any kind of defining,
one day continues on into the same patterns
of tomorrow and the dry endless sameness,
living in the same patterns of non-being,
and birthdays happen with no meaning,
and there are no more holidays here,
only the dull sameness of patterns,
all the numbers on the calendars,
are only patterns of numbers,
and never anything more,
the bleakness of all your
being is the safety of
your ever so present,
patternings, day,
after day after,
pattern after,
day pattern,
of patterns,
endlessly
circling
endless
circles
around
orbits
safe
spin
in.

Now you are here in a room full of people about you,
you overcome your terror of being surrounded by
so many odd strangers, and there you sit among
those who talk with words you don't know,
and no frame of reference to understand,
they're so unable to interact with you,
and your safe patterns aren't such to
allow you to communicate with
those who are all about you,
there you sit as an object
of inattentiveness and,
nothing more than a
physical being of
an empty person
in attendance at
this very bizarre
social gathering,
you are lost in,
the mind traps
of your circles,
of patterns all,
safe patterns,
so protective,
safely inside
your circles
of patterns
encircling
all around
the circle
of cycles
circling
cycles
round
orbits
again
safe
spin
in.

Sadly, folks avoid you fearing your affliction is contagious,
thinking that by being around you will cause them to be
as strange and as impaired as you seem to be to them,
they talk about you and ignore you because you are
the way you are with your circle patterns around,
you and about to keep them out and you safe in,
safe behind arrays of complex patterns you've
built as the only world of reality you know of,
and of all your patterns you know them well,
those safe patterns are the very keystone
of you inner most being that holds you,
kind of, sort of, almost oddly together,
or at least as together as is possible
in a world of such fixed patterns,
strangest formless unrealities as
your all encircling patterns do,
always so undefined as your
unreal threatening world,
all marked safe in harsh
patterns of unknown
makings of circles,
spins of no reason
so out of rhyme,
in a timeless
no place in
continuing
patterns
circling
around
circles
space
safe
spin
sit
in.

This isn't a seasonal place that comes and goes away,
changes of seasons or a place you outgrow in the
usual sense of growing beyond with maturity,
you are stuck here forever and ever more,
always the frightened stranger in a world
filled with fearful ugly strangenesses,
the strangest of nasty strangenesses,
hearing all languages as an alien,
trying to link together all those
odd patterns of sounds into
a pattern of expressions,
to fit into your patterns
of safe comfort needs,
as defined in your,
endless patterns
of patterned,
all patterns,
in circles,
so spins,
around
cycles
even,
odd,
and
out
or
in.

You've just had a very brief visit into the jumbled world,
of an autistic person,
and the challenges of what they *live*
with every moment,
day after day in their ongoing
insistence on patterned sameness,
as self-preservation behavior.
So unable they are to cope with
any kind of change,
insensitive to pain,
non-goal directed,

life so barren of meaning,
except for their patterns of non-being,
their only way of being is in patterns of circles,
spinning circles spinning,
in endless cycles circling,
continuously cycling,
endlessly,
in constant unchanging patterns,
locked into their fixed narrow world,
without a key to unlock changes,
jailed in a jumbled mind-cell,
fit in a restrictive place,
in a surrounding universe that's always changing,
where the only true constant, is change.

And here are we,
in a world that is ever expanding,
where we have the ability to change and grow,
building beneficial patterns that we learn from,
as we learn not to do harm to ourselves and others.
Where the circle is the wheel following life's path,
and your path is ever changing,
always with motion,
changing.

Where there are those in distress,
about the developing flows of changes in life,
bemoaning the creeping changes of aging,
or gaining a few pounds here or there,
as if it is so horrible to change so,
yet we manage to cope moving onward,
with the changes that are always happening.

And then too, we often shun away those who are different,
doesn't matter what physical impairment they have,
their challenging disadvantage sets them apart,
or maybe they have a way differing mindset
from the way your mind is set into your ways of thinking,
or flows in a discourse that are different than others,

their differences puts us off,
pushing away those who are different than we.

Often we get swayed by the allure of appearances,
locked into the falsehood of security,
securities so subject to change in the eroding sands of time.
The flows of the universe are ever changing for all,
except for those locked into patterns,
where no change is coped with,
bccausc their patterned universe never changes.

Those who are unable to change,
unable to adapt with the ever changing energies in flow,
risk being devoid of having any meaningful feelings,
clinging to their artificial appearances,
appearances certain to change with time passages,
in passing.

Be understanding of those locked into changeless ways,
some folks just lack the ability to flow with life changes,
others are just way too weary to change much at all,
and some folks just need to believe more in themselves,
believing enough to make those transitions,
of being more joyful with the flows of life,
and stop wailing about what they don't have,
and appreciate what they've got,
while enjoying a wide variety
of life experiences and,
enjoying more often.

For more information about autism logon to:
http://www.brainnet.org/autism.htm
thusly at last another ramble ends,
another request by a friend done,
in the kindness of sharing.

Thank you for reading through all the patterns.
Take care, my friends, and enjoy often . . . John

FORGIVE ME...

The other day upon a bus,
I saw a girl with golden hair,
and I thought, gee, it must be grand to be
as young and as beautiful as she,
and when she rose to leave,
I saw she had one knee,
and walked with a crutch.

A short time later,
I stopped to buy some pipe tobacco,
and the young lad who waited on me
was just as cheerful and as friendly as he could be.
I lingered and chatted with him awhile,
trading jokes and laughs,
as I was about to leave,
he thanked me for sharing the time
to bring a few smiles.
He told me he enjoyed talking with folks like me,
and knowing the music of laughter,
because he explained,
'You see, I'm blind.'

Later that afternoon,
I stopped to watch a group of children at play,
Ah, their merry laughter filled my ears with joy,
but one young lad stood apart from all the rest,
and I asked,
'Why don't you run and play with the other girls and boys???',
but he just looked on with a distant stare,
and then I knew he couldn't hear.

Late that same night,
a telephone call summoned me to the city morgue
where I was asked to identify a man I hardly knew.
Oh sure, I'd worked with him a few years ago,
but I never really knew him.

And as I looked upon that shell that once held his life,
I saw that even in death he wore a frown,
because he never laughed
nor shared a smile.

And here am I
with more life ahead of me,
with two legs to carry me wherever I want to go,
with ears to hear whatever I need to know,
with eyes to watch my world grow.

Forgive me...
when I whine,
I have so much,
and the world
is mine.

Enjoy often . . . John

Parts of the above poem were a gift shared with me from my friend Grover from my Jaycee years. We sort of traded back and forth different ways of including this at the conclusion of each of our various speaking engagements. I've indeed taken liberties embellishing and expanding upon the original poem.

THE BULLFROG

A recently divorced woman was very horny, and she decided she needed a pet, to help take her mind off her cravings for the joyful delights from carnal knowledge that she had been missing since she split from her husband. The attractive woman thought a smallish dog she could teach a few cute tricks to might be nice, or perhaps a cuddly little kitten might just help to alleviate her rather disturbed and compelling condition. While thinking about her plight, she recalled seeing a new pet shop that had just opened for business in a nearby shopping mall, and so, off she went to get herself a pet. Shopping always did wonders to lift her out of a depressed mood.

She found a parking space close to *'Exotic Pets'*. Upon entering the shop, she was amazed that the shop didn't have the usual cages of adorable dogs and cats seeking customer's attention by doing charming tricks, nor colorful fish swimming about in bubbling tanks. There was only one large aquarium filled with exotic fish occupying one entire wall. In fact, the store was very neat and clean, although sparsely furnished, sort of like the waiting room in a high priced doctor's office. The well groomed clerk explained that the store didn't stock any commonplace pets, but instead, each exotic pet was especially selected to fulfill the erotic needs of their many happy customers.

He tactfully asked what her need was. She blushed and said, that since her divorce, she had been very horny and had hoped a pet might help to take her mind off her lustful yearnings. The attentive clerk smiled a knowing smile, and explained that he had something very special that he thought would be ideal for the woman. He excused himself and went into the back room for a few minutes.

He soon returned with a fully enclosed twenty gallon terrarium. *"I believe this will suit your needs very nicely,"* he said smiling broadly, as he proudly pointed to a very large dark green bullfrog sitting in the center of the terrarium. The lady looked with disbelieving surprise at the big ugly frog and said very mockingly that she didn't think an amphibian would be of much *exotic* comfort to her.

"Aha", the smiling salesman replied, *"but this awesome amphibian is very special. He has been carefully trained to perform satisfying oral sexual gratification upon women!!!"*

Overcoming her initial reaction to laugh off what he had said, the lady's eyes lit up as visions of the bullfrog's long tongue lashing out to capture flies danced through her head. If the bullfrog could catch a fly with his talented long tongue, then his talented long tongue could also . . . mmm, and so went the lustful logic of her relishing reasoning. She eagerly agreed to the purchase price of $369 for this potential prince of a big bullfrog. She quickly paid for her purchase, while the clerk was explaining that the bullfrog was completely guaranteed—exotic erotic oral satisfaction as promised, or her money would be cheerfully refunded. As she left the store with her bullfrog, she thought that even her friendly handy vibrators didn't come with a money back guarantee—and with a bullfrog *batteries weren't required!!! Oh my, the many possibilities!!!*

As soon as she arrived home, she drew a hot bubble bath, poured a glass of chilled champagne to celebrate her good fortune at making such a fine purchase, enjoyed a wee bit of the magical herbal natural smoke, and relaxed in the soothing soft bath water. Her thoughts of joyful erotic anticipation now playing out in her fantasy mind. Thinking about what a switch it would be that when the frog kissed her she'd be the one who would feel like a *princess!!!* Her joyful thoughts drifted about like the Calgon bubbles surrounding her, as she enjoyed her building blissfully mellow buzz. She arose from the bath refreshed and ready to enjoy her new *trained to bring exotic erotic oral delight* pet bullfrog. She carefully dried and lightly powdered her body . . . mmm . . . she was clearly looking forward to having a really brand new erogenous experience this very night.

She turned off the bedroom lights, after she lit several scented in-the-mood candles around her bed, to help get her new froggy friend in the mood, and she comfortably arranged her nude body upon her queen-size bed. Spreading her legs wide open, she placed her prized bullfrog between her upper thighs, closed her eyes and waited and waited . . . and waited . . . and waited . . . and waited.

The bullfrog said, "*Ribbittt!!!*" and nothing more . . . the frog just sort of sat there in front of her inviting pussy and deeply croaked, "*Ribbittt!!!*" once more, without moving toward her most glorious offering. Well, the lady wasn't sure if the bullfrog was trained to respond to a spoken command. She didn't recall the clerk saying anything about any kind of special instructions to follow. So, looking right at the bullfrog she said, "*Please eat my pussy now, froggy.*"

And all the big bullfrog did, was once again reply with a deep resounding, "*Ribbittt!!!*"

With a wee bit of frustration starting to come upon her, she thought maybe the bullfrog needed a visual aid, so she reached down to her pleasure place to show the frog where to apply his long tongue, playing her fingers all along her neatly trimmed and shaved pussy, and she shortened the command to, "*Eat me, froggy, eat me!!!*" And all the green frog did say was, "*Rib-bittt!!!*" once more.

Maybe the frog needed a very clear and present target for that marvelous prolonged tongue to find. So she started to play with her pussy more, in such a way as to slip her clit free of the fleshy hood. While she gently held her aroused clitoris between her fingers, she said, "*Here froggy, lick my clit!!!*"

Again the sitting bullfrog only uttered in the same very deep toneful, "*Ribbittt, ribbittt!!!*"

The frog hadn't moved as much as a half-a-leap-frog hop closer to her, so she moved her glorious pussy right up close and personal like to the trained frog. And the only reaction that came from that big old frog was a repeating reverberating, "*Ribbittt, ribbittttt, ribbitttttt!!!"*

Now her increasing frustrations started getting to her, because of her expectations about what the frog had been promised to do, and this dumb frog hadn't yet gotten into wrapping his supposedly talented tongue around her clearly offered clitoris to bring an end to her horny feelings. She was hoping she didn't need to exchange him for an especially trained *horny toad* or a sleazy *lounge lizard.* Out of pure exasperation, she threatened the bullfrog with him becoming a fried frog-legs dinner, telling him that this night someone was sure to be eaten—either he could start eating her, or she'd have his nice big frog legs sizzling in a hot frying pan. And again came nothing from the old bullfrog but another, *"Ribbittt, Ribbitttttt!!!"*

She changed her approach, and tenderly kissed the frog on the top of his cute little froggy green head, thinking maybe the frog needed a bit of foreplay before he'd start performing his princely joys of oral delight on her waiting wetness. However, all that came from her tender kisses was merely another more prolonged, *"Ribbbbitttttttttt!!!"*. . . and nothing more!!!

She was getting very angry. Feeling that she'd been fucked over by the swindling salesman of exotic pets, and not in a fun fucking way for her. In a mad huff she was off the bed, pulled the sales slip from her purse, and phoned the store, not really expecting anyone to answer at this late hour.

Indeed, she was surprised when the gentleman answered on the third ring. She told him bluntly that the damn frog wasn't eating her wet pussy, she was all hot and bothered, and she was about to make a meal of frog legs—if the damn bullfrog didn't start performing on his guaranteed promise of satisfying erotic oral joys upon her!!! She was very pissed, complained loudly that he had cheated her, and she was feeling left rather high—in more than one way . . . and in some ways not at all dry!!! The clerk apologized profusely, begged her not to cook the poor old bullfrog, wrote down the lady's address, and said he'd be right over to make everything right with her. Assuring her again, that he would stand by the complete satisfaction guarantee.

Ten minutes later, he knocked on her apartment door, and the woman, who had calmed down some with another glass of champagne, answered the door wearing a sheer midnight blue nightgown from Victoria Secrets—and nothing more. He said he was very sorry that the frog had failed to perform as the frog had been so carefully trained to do, and he was at a complete loss to explain why the bullfrog hadn't brought her the promised joys of many orgasmic oral delights.

He asked her to please help him to solve the predicament of the non-performing bullfrog, by demonstrating the very same position she had assumed when the bullfrog failed to do as he was most certain the frog could do so skillfully. She was so hot and horny and ready for almost anything at all to happen, that she gladly obliged to show him just how she had positioned herself. Thusly, she did slip off her sexy negligee and assumed her former invitingly accessible position, with her legs spread wide open and her hands reaching down to bring attention to her waiting pussy with the big old green bullfrog in place between her open thighs—just like before. The frog made no movement, and indeed the bullfrog only declared, once again, another deeply uttered, *"Ribbitttt!!!"*

"You see, sir, I've positioned my pussy in a most inviting manner," she said rather pointedly and most proudly, *"But your specially trained bullfrog won't have a thing to do with what I'm offering so openly."*

"Oh yes, I do see, my dear lady," said the salesman while looking directly at her delightfully offered pussy from the lucky bullfrog's point of view.

Then, as he moved the frog out of the way so he could move his mouth closer to her delicious pussy, and he now addressed the frog saying sternly, *"Now listen to me carefully, Mr. Bullfrog, I'm only going to show you how to do this ONE more time, now pay attention . . ."*

Alas, the lucky lady was smiling because she was enjoying in a more conventional way than what she had been expecting. The rough shell of the above story was by an unknown author from somewhere in cyberspace. I took great liberties with the humorous short story in doing some creative enhancing and changing things about in rewriting. There was no especially trained exotic bullfrog, but the horny lady wanted to believe that there was. Her wants and needs created her bizarre expectations that the bullfrog would indeed most becomingly become her princc charming, and she'd be coming too.

That's how life is with many of the expectations we all tend to create. We want to believe that people, products, and services will be just as presented and promised to be. We want to know and have that special magic of what's being offered to us for purchase. We've been conditioned into a place of wanting to believe!!! Believing that the frog will turn into a real life prince or princess. Believing that there is a way to turn lead into gold.

I do know of an old toy maker from long ago, who did indeed discover the secret of turning lead into gold. He bought a bunch of lead ingots, melted them in a smelting crock, and poured the molten metal into his carefully crafted die-casting molds to produce an army of toy lead soldiers. Then he polished and filed off the excess metal flanges, and painted cute little faces and colorful uniforms on each of the toy soldiers. He put a price tag on them, and presto, he had certainly turned lead into gold and silver!!! Of course, in reality, it was his creative efforts and skilled craftsmanship that had actually increased the value of the transformed lead. Underneath the pretty painted colors on the figures of the little soldiers, there was still pure lead. The old toy maker had taken the raw lead material and improved upon it. Those creative improvements made all the difference in the value. Improving upon the raw material is really what does away with expectations and increases the value of life.

Folks buy all kinds of self-improvement books expecting to improve themselves just by reading the book. They are hoping to find all the secrets, to bring them whatever kind of miracles they are seeking from the woven words within. They expect the author's words will some how help to magically transform them into whatever they hope to become. Some folks even become self-improvement book junkies. Jumping from one popular improvement fad book to another, with their expected hopes that leaping into the flashy buzz words, will bring about the improvements they surely expect to find—and perhaps find an improved better self between the pages, maybe even a become a better person between the sheets too!!! Alas, the truth of the matter is that those words might point you in the right direction, but those skillful words don't hold instant miracles. What rings true for some, might ding hollow for others. The only way I've found that really works for doing my style of self-improvement, is what aligns true with my own individuality. The viewpoints of others might be sort of helpful and informative, but the most effective course to self betterment comes from within the being, where the values of your unique godspark dwells.

Sorry if you bought this book with expectations of finding all kinds of magical answers for yourself within my wordsmithing efforts. Gee folks, I'm still working on trying to figure out lots of the questions for myself!!! So I'm sure not going to profess to having the answers for you!!! I certainly wouldn't be presumptuous to believe that the few answers I've found along the way for me, are the same answers that will work for you. That's the problem that I see with lots of those well meaning folks with their self-improvement books, they've convinced themselves that what works for them, will work the same way with all their readers. Too often what works for those authors, just doesn't fit the needs of all the others reading their books.

Alas, this book is only my hopefully continuing collection of life's reflections expressed from my introspective point of view, along with my most sincere hopes that parts are enjoyable enough to bring you a few smiles. Perhaps, some of the shared parts you smiled about, will plant the seeds of mind blossoms that might grow within your thoughts. Also, parts might cause you to reflect upon some of the harms you've experienced along your path and hopefully, see then a wee bit more positive than they felt to you at the time. Right about now, I know a few editor friends who are dratting me for addressing the readers directly—traditionally, that's just not done in the body of the book!!! Hehehee, so much for writing traditions!!!

Meanwhile, back to the nice lady with erotic expectations who bought the exotic bullfrog. I'm sure you figured out by now, that the salesman had an expectation game plan too. Indeed, the bullfrog had been trained to do nothing at all—except to sit between her legs and do nothing more. He had been waiting patiently for her very distressed telephone call. And you know he was extremely eager to fill in for the bullfrog, so to speak. However, these days, way too often guarantees just aren't stood behind, or in this case laid so delightfully on the line, to rightfully provide complete customer satisfaction as promised.

Purchases made with the buyer having great expectations that aren't fulfilled, will all too frequently hear, *"Read the fine print!!!"* or *"Sue me!!!"* Ugh, that nasty *sue stuff* is a no win legal game!!! Sue is a real bad ass and best to be avoided—and the best laid plans, with even the fewest expectations, and a really smart lawyer, are sure to get all fucked-up when you go and do the courting sue thing!!!

Now, that lady also forgot the common sense part that *if something sounds too good to be true, it most likely isn't true at all.* Ah, but she wanted so badly to believe it was all true. Just like most of us want to believe the best. Also, the cunning salesman had priced the *trained* bullfrog at a high enough price, to create the seed of belief, that many hours of training and conditioning had gone into teaching that exotic bullfrog. However, the nature of the training was only to teach the bullfrog not to try to play leap-frog with pussy!!! Also, with a $369 purchase price, the lady was certain to call for a refund—way different than buying a $19.95 vibrator, batteries extra, that doesn't work. Thusly, cometh the salesman, and eventually the lady too!!!

We all have expectations. Having hopeful expectations are what turns dreams into reality. However, we also have the ability to decide which expectations are pure bullshit, and which have a possibility of becoming reality. There's lots of truth in the belief, that when you have few expectations, you have lots more appreciation for whatever positive stuff exists, that goes beyond what you expected. Those folks with great expectations never seem to be happy with what there is, and I guess in some ways that's a plus when their hopes and dreams are composed of healthy realistic expectations.

I guess that Columbus dude could have sailed most of the way to where he expected to find the *New World*, and then said there was nothing there and sailed back home without finding a thing. However, he sailed onward with his great expectations based on his belief that he'd find something. And we all know he did find something, even if he didn't discover what he thought he'd discovered. Much earlier, by several hundred years, the Vikings had discovered a beautiful green island with hot bubbling springs on the edge of the cold North Atlantic, and they had the foresight to call this marvelous place Iceland. Those Vikings were a silly crazy bunch of joking dudes, because they also discovered a much bigger island, more to the north and sort of in the center of the very cold North Atlantic and out of the flows of gulf stream. That island was all rocky barren and covered with ice and snow. They named that island Greenland!!!

You see, those tricky Vikings were doing a big reverse on the expectation game. They figured no one would mess around exploring and settling Iceland because of the unwelcome image created by such a chilly name. That was way good thinking on their part!!! Also, the suckered ancient mariner explorers would quickly sail off to find Greenland, and the joke would be on those fools expecting to find a lush green land. Not!!! Hehehee, those Vikings were smart ass dudes, and they sure kept old Randall Cunningham playing at Quarterback too!!! Way to go Vikings!!! Okay, I know that's football stuff . . . but I get to have some fun too!!!

Thomas Edison, who mostly did the electrical wiring in this old house as pick-up work way back when, he really had positive charged expectations too. That was during the time when Edison had his little workshop laboratory in New Jersey, and he was very busy playing around inventing a better light bulb. A light bulb that would burn brighter, safer, and longer. He had the expectation of finding just the right kind of element that would be the best compound material to use for the filament in his improved light bulb. Now, he not only had the expectation that he'd eventually find it, but he also had the driving determination to try thousands of potential materials for the fragile light bulb filaments looking for those elements that worked the very best of all. Indeed with all of his tireless research, he did find the correct combination of elements that worked best, and the rest is light bulb illumination history.

Seems like these days, lots of people have way too many expectations and not very much driving determination to stay with working through, to find the good stuff that does burn much brighter, safer, and lasts longer. Folks seem to have a very long shopping list of what they expect from their relationships, but they often lack the abilities to think for themselves and act in ways that are true to themselves. Frequently that shopping list of expectations has been put together for them. Others have imposingly shaped your relating concepts, and they are telling you just what you can expect in *your relationship*, and how things *should* be for you. And when those expectations aren't all there as expected, just as you were lead to believe they'd be, then big time frustration happens. Unfortunately, there's really no determination to look at what works and what doesn't work--except of course to give lip service about trying to get beyond the expectations. Therefore, for many long centuries, humankind has spawned multitudinous societies filled with a whole host of hand-me-down expectations, with each new generation growing more frustrated with imposed gotta-have-it-this-way expectations. Sadly, with all those frustrating expectations being dumped upon us for so long, the unique individuality of self has gotten lost somewhere.

Some folks set out on quests expecting to find themselves and their individuality that they surrendered along the way.

Naturally, there are those who will mistakenly call their quest a *mid-life crisis.* I've wondered why they want to wait until *mid-life* to find themselves??? I sort of thought of it as an ongoing process. And how do they know when *mid-life* has been reached anyhow??? Call me an optimist, but I like to believe I'm still decades away from *mid-life,* especially with the way life-lines keep getting extended with all the medical research being done to prolong a healthy life. I've also wondered what it is that they hope to find during their announced discovery quest to find themselves??? I personally hope to discover those nude hot springs in Iceland—heard tell they are bubbling warm and lots of fun, but you know, I gotta find out for myself—and that's very different than finding myself!!! I *hope* the nude hot springs are not another Viking joke. Oh, and I want to check out those spectacular Northern Lights too!!!

I do believe lots of what's happening with this *mid-life crisis* stuff is some kind of a cop-out, when *40 something* folks start acting like airhead teeny-boppers, and they're trying to get in on some of that mindless *bopping* they believed they missed out on a few decades earlier. Now they seem to be trying to turn back the hands of time, and get into some of that young teeny-bopper stuff. Okay, not *bopping* jail-bait, which is major bad trouble at anytime, but they go chasing after someone much younger than they are—and still an airhead. Maybe those questing folks are thinking that perhaps some of their youthfulness will rub off and linger with them, sort of like drinking from the lost fountain of youth. I could be wrong, I often am, but I don't believe the youth transference thing works that way. Besides, mature folks of many varied life experiences are much more worldly, often unhindered by expectations, and so knowledgeable about joyful doings and much more interesting to talk with.

Questing for individuality often creates a crisis—*mid-life* or at any other time. The crisis of reclaiming individuality might tilt relationships out of whack, when some folks who are into relating, mistakenly start to feel that another's desire to regain their individuality, is a threat to them. All that nasty stuff of greed and jealousy, dings into being and zap the potential for sharing joys about. The negative kinds of expectations come into play. Instead of feeling the joys of knowing a fuller person, comfortable with who they are as a whole being, they see the loss of someone who they once upon a time had control over. I believe the deepest regrets I have are the ways in which I knowingly and unknowingly controlled folks I had and have relationships with—and also the ways in which I allowed myself to be controlled. The whole controlling thing is a bummer, and people who think that control is some kind of expression of love, really have some perverted expectations about what love is all about!!! This control thing and what's expected are everywhere, and each of those yieldings to, *it doesn't matter,* takes parts of their unique individuality away.

The individuality of enjoying is lost to the strings of control too. A real simple example would be movie reviewers, they pass on their judgments about what movies they deem worthy of seeing. Your selection of a movie is based on their expectations for what they were looking for in a movie. Ah, 'tis wonderful when those movies they have criticized for not measuring up to their esteem educated expectations, are a big hit at the box office. And in some ways there is just no accounting of the changing tastes, or tastelessness, of the public. You might also know the feeling of seeing a movie that got *rave reviews* from most of the critics, but when the movie is finally over, you walk out of the theater feeling that moving picture show sure wasn't worth the price of the ticket or the investment of time!!!

We've grown accustomed to having the expectation of being told what's good and what's funny, dumped on us. Television sitcoms come complete with canned laughter, to let the viewers know what the show's producers expect you to laugh about—even if you don't find those parts of the sitcoms to be laughable. This is a carry-over from early live television, when TV shows were broadcast live with real live studio audiences. The studio had a sign that would light up to tell the audience when to *applaud* and when to *laugh.* Ah, those timeless chains of conditioned expectations are taking away the individual joys of laughing with what you feel as being funny to you. Not to worry if you are at a loss about what is funny, those TV sitcom producers will gladly peg the laugh meter for you!!!

Sadly, vast segments of society have grown lazy in doing enjoying. Our controlled enjoying conditioning, now needs to be prompted by others telling us what *they* have judged to be humorous, so we all know just when to laugh. Oh my, the whole thing with being told when to laugh is just so very laughable—and so very sad indeed to feel we lost the ability for knowing spontaneous laughter. Especially when you think about how our ability to find our own ways of enjoying humorous situations, has silently slipped away within their contrived controlling expectations. Okay, Laugh Out Loud now!!! Not!!!

Also, we've gotten into doing conflicting expectation, like when you go to see your doctor and you expect sound knowledgeable medical treatment. However, the doctor has the expectation of covering his or her ass and orders all kinds of additional tests—just in case he or she gets sued later for malpractice. There's that bad ass sue again!!! Then there's the insurance company, the insurance carrier that has to pay for all those extra ass-covering tests, and of course, those insurance dudes have the expectation of making a profit too. So, to fulfill their assured profit expectation, they up the cost of insurance coverage to cover all the ass-covering and still make a profit—most likely reducing insurance benefits as part of the never ending process. Yes indeed, conflicting expectations and differing values really do cost everybody, and lots more than just the artificial values of money!!! Ah, but money often figures into expectations.

High costs come when expectations are accompanied by ultimatums. Those warning strings attached, to have you do something as expected. You are expected to study for a test, because if you don't pass the test you'll get a failing grade. Simple cause and effect situation that has long been linked with measuring learning. The teacher needs to know that the course work is being studied by you, and at the time of the testing, you've retained at least enough of the studied information to pass the test. The expectation is that you'll apply yourself to doing the necessary studying to earn a passing grade. The over-riding ultimatum is that if you don't apply yourself to learn what is being taught in the class you'll fail.

However, in doing your course work of life and interactive relating, those ultimatums can become downright deadly. Like the lady with the non-performing bullfrog was about to have the *ultimate* meal of costly fresh frog legs!!! The same thing often happens when people have a relationship that isn't happening as *they* expect their relating would be. The ultimatum gets swung like a cutting sword and parts of the relating get cut off. Major bummer when the one being threatened with the ultimatum doesn't yield to the tossed intimidations—when they don't concede to the demands of the expectations being forced upon them. There comes a point when the expected efforts necessary to continue on in a high maintenance relationship, are just too overbearing, and parting happens. The flows of mutual benefits have gone into being one sided, and those cutting ultimatums sadly bring ongoing relating to an abrupt end, with no hopes for a workable compromise being achieved.

Ultimatums are deadly weapons. Way back when I was an airman going through the USAF Air Police Academy, the instructors teaching the small arms phase of the training, stressed over and over again that you must never pull your weapon unless you are fully prepared and mentally able to use it. Bluff with a gun that you don't have the gumption to use, and you could find yourself very dead. Lots of those people who pull a gun to bluff with, are found dead—shot with their own gun!!! People often seem to toss about ultimatums so lightly, never believing that their threatening weapons would be anything more than a ploy to bluster the other into doing what they expect them to do as they are told to do. However, there comes a point when folks wake up and find that the ultimatums of expectations have cut off too many pieces of themselves, and the relating ends in the rotting ruins of the shattered parts that once was a mutual union—before the nasty undoings, were so deadly. Alas, 'tis time to be done and gone from the overwhelming shadows coming from expectation fulfillment, via imposed ultimatums. And you might even hear them exclaim, as you go out of sight, that they're sorry and they really didn't mean it!!! And of course that's said with the departing stopping expectation that you'll give them *one more chance!!!* I don't think so!!! Not when you feel your very life being threatened by their deadly actions.

And then of course, there are those who will say that the fulfillment of expectations is a way of proving love. Ugh, that stressful, strifeful proof factor!!! They explain that if there is love, then you must yield to doing just what is expected of you—expected by them, their family, and their friends. Assumptions get made about that doing of stuff as expected, as if those controlled doings are some kind of magical measurement of love—wouldn't it be marvelous if the joyful non-measurement of living love could be via the sharing of countless orgasms. This measuring thing is what ties love on a string, that pulls you along by measuring just how *your doing* as expected is being measured!!! The truth is that living love is impossible to measure—and enjoying many orgasms is way more joyful than counting orgasms. The *doing as controllingly expected* does nothing more than take the life out of being once loving joyful folks, and turns them into nothing more than a lifeless plastic marionette, with the ever demanding *lover* pulling all the strings.

Eventually, the tangled mess of controlling strings gets cut—when you love them more when you are apart, and back in touch with your missing parts. Sadly, lots of those string pullers, have no concept of the harm they are doing, with all the expectations they are so into doing. Values get shifted about in the spinning of valueless expectations, and 'tis wisely joyful to get into the flows of acknowledging and accepting differing values. Too many folks try to push and press into place their values that don't fit with the other, and this gets them into a very fixed anal retentive mess!!! Now I do believe the eternal flows of the universe are arranged as fateful tricksters, because just when you think you have values aligned, along comes shifts in the sands of time, and time brings about changes in values. Bingo, changes in expectations too!!! I'm not sure if those hippies had this kind of flow in mind when they were talking about going with the flows of what's happening, or more likely the head flows of going with the natural herbal flows . . . flowings . . . enjoying flows.

Hippies I've known along the way have been unique in their individuality and respectful in accepting and mutually giving. Against the harsh background of an increasingly unpopular war, they had the guts to urge folks to *make love, not war!!!* During those early birthing years of the hippie era, I was in the USAF in SAC, whose motto was *peace is our profession!!!* The other unofficial part of the motto was *war is just a hobby!!!* We had enough nukes to glow the planet with the deadest, brightest, and longest light ever, and along come these laid back hippie folks!!! Those hippies had some interesting concepts about truth, joys, and *make love, not war!!!* The open ways they were into enjoying openly, so free of expectations. Most of the hippie homes I visited were joyfully filled with thoughtful consideration of others, neat and clean reflecting the self-discipline to clean-up after themselves, and mutually sharing naturally with upkeep and collective maintenance. Your welcome there came by invitation, and with your being respectful of their ways, and not being a snob or a slob.

Snobs are aloof as they float on air farts because they falsely believe their shit smells like the aroma of the sweetest fresh clover. They are aloof and wrapped in snarling appearances of being in disagreement with life, and are upon an ill-fated course that's so uncaring of others about them, expect to use them and try to control their undoings. Snobs smartly render unasked for answers for others—others who might still be trying to figure out hard questions. Sort of feeling like Jeopardy, double Jeopardy, all three daily doubles, and final Jeopardy all at the same time!!! With the snobbish expectation to do when and as they say, because they have all the perfectly right answers for everyone!!! Becoming a snob is a hand-me-up thing, or for a snob wannabe, *ass-pealing* to measure-up. Lots of comparing and measuring-up happen with snobs, always doing mindless banter with their self-inflated snobby ego overwhelmingly engaged. Snobs are sadly so anally into themselves and full of their own shit!!! Perhaps they would be happier if they'd send their bloated ego out to a distant star for a tune-up.

Sad too, are the shitty slobs of the world. These grossly inconsiderate people who go through life leaving their messes for others to clean-up for them. The slobs have been created by their holding expectations that others will always come along and pick up after them. They are created mostly by well meaning mothering hands, who have been so accustomed to cleaning up the messes of their offspring, that those young ones never learn to take care of their own shit. Slobs lack the basic motivation to do it themselves, because they've come to expect others to do the cleaning up for them!!! Now, some mothering types feel, that by continuing to do the cleaning and picking up, they are fulfilling a loving need by providing for their offspring, while bemoaning what a huge mess they always have to clean-up. And then they wonder why their lazy ungrateful offspring has become such an uncaring slob??? Slobs carry into life woeful expectations that others will always be there to take care of their messes. What a bite in the ass it is, when the slobs might eventually ponder why they don't have the motivation to do for themselves. The parents of the slobs often wonder also, why their offspring lack the motivation to move out into making a worthwhile life for themselves. Gee, I wonder why???

Another kind of expectation is the kind that has someone assuming you'd know something. Almost as if they expect you to be a mindreader and you're expected to know what they are thinking. You get saddled with their judgment about what they expect, *assumed* works too, you *should* know, and then they get all bent out of shape with the discovery that you don't know what they assumed you should know!!! Perhaps they said something to you at some point in time, and now you're expected to do an instant recall, and factor those said once upon a time bits of information into the here and now of what's happening. Seems way unfair to have to carry such an expectation, in having to have rapid perfect recall about everything that was said way back when. Failure to accomplish the instant recall feat could bring about a curt, *"Nevermind!!!"*

Expecting perfection is the breeding ground for mental breakdowns. This whole perfection compulsion is a myth that people seem to be obsessed with, in questing after flawlessness as some perverted form of self-flagellation. Expecting everything to always be just so perfect in every way, when that's not how life is in an imperfect world. Shit happens!!! Real world things happen that no one has the ability to control, and those *unexpected* variations of occurrences have the means to mess-up the sought after perfection of the most perfectly made plans. The lady with the bullfrog had planned a perfectly blissful evening that didn't go as she had planned. However, I'm sure she quickly amended her erotic plans with the help of the sly, eager salesman, who had done some delightful plotting of his own. You could say she went along with the flows that were joyfully happening, and most likely came out ahead of the game. Also, the exotic bullfrog made out okay, when he didn't become the threatened meal of frog legs!!!

You know of course, that there are no magical exotic bullfrogs that can do all kinds of wondrous things as promised. However, I could tell you about the magic of the golden unicorns . . . but that's another story for another time. And of course you know that those talking bullfrogs in the beer commercials are all computer generated. Sure they are funny and cute, but they aren't real live bullfrogs, and besides, real bullfrogs don't drink beer!!! Frogs have natural hops!!! Also, real bullfrogs hop for Dr. Pepper . . . the friendly pepper upper!!!

Take care and enjoy often . . . John

George Birthington's Wash Day!!!

Yuppers folks, the George Washington's Birthday Holiday has been changed and merged into Presidents' Day by an act of Congress. They took away our first Presidents' birthday celebration, by acting in congress in an open chamber to spread the celebrating around, in a way that's supposed to honor all US Presidents, with one federal holiday during a three day weekend. 'An act of Congress' is not to be confused with 'an act of God', which is no cause at all to celebrate, because insurance companies get to blame God for loss of property and such!!! Therefore, enabling insurance companies to get out of paying claims off by sticking poor old God with all the blame!!! God gets blamed for everything!!! What's been paid in premiums for insurance coverage, well, those profit-heavy insurance companies get to keep all the money they can get out of paying out.

This insurance stuff really has nothing to do with observing Presidents' Day, just my way of explaining the basic difference between 'an act of God' and 'an act of Congress'. However, at times, Congress does indeed play at doing acts of god too—or at least they like to think they do!!! So much for the original separation of the church and state concept!!!

Back when George Birthington's Wash Day holiday—my father sent me his mangling of George Washington's Day in 1962 on the back of a letter. Anyhow, the holiday could float into being any day of the week that February 22nd happened upon, and likewise Abe's B-day on February 12th, and lest we not forget the potentially costly February 14th, Saint Valentine's Extortion Day!!! It dawned on those Congress folks, who decide to change things *for the better, for the good of the people, for special interest groups with money, for special favors,* that the shortest month of the year had more holidays than all the other eleven months—especially when you include Ground Hog Day, observed for decades by the Slumbering Ground Hog Lodge of Quarryville, Pennsylvania, every February 2nd!!! Quarryville also has a Slumbering Ground Hog Lodge too, but the other one gets all the national media play!!!

Part of what this Congress of wise persons did when they wrote and passed the national holiday's act, was to create *Presidents' Day* on the third Monday in February. That way, all those folks who do foolish things on Valentine's Day can take full advantage of Presidents' Day Sales during the three-day *federal* holiday!!! Those special Prez sales are going on everywhere, as if directed by President Bill in-between his ongoing Presidential directing—*"more to the right, Monica, oh my!!!"* So you now have the capability to frolic more on Valentine's Day, via viagra!!! The celebrating of V-Day still floats to whatever day of the week February the 14th falls upon each year. Then those frolickers get to pay more taxes for their merriment by buying more token gifts at Presidents' Day Sales. Seems as if the feds have figured out how to tax certain aspects of loving too!!! But of course, some merry folks will avoid the taxing sales and paying Excise tax by frolicking joyfully on Presidents' Day as well. Free love lives forever, down with panties and Excise taxes!!!

Happy Presidents' Day is like an oxymoron wish—rare are happy U.S. Presidents, at least in recent times. Seems like 'tis a warm wish that's extended for the elected leader of our nation to be happy. However, as soon as a President is getting into being happy enjoying whatever, however, and wherever the Prez is enjoying, the press comes along and bites him in the Presidential ass!!! You could say they want all the details on the tail the Prez has been detailing, so to speak!!! Now, it really doesn't matter how discreet or indiscreet the President is being with his personal enjoying, snooping *news* snoops stick their noses into the Presidential doings, and soon everything the Prez has done or is doing becomes a sordid matter of public record, available for nightly viewing, thanks to ensuing starring investigations that leak all over the news shows.

Instead of delighting in living in the White House, the Prez sadly discovers that life in the glass house isn't all that joyous. There's no joy when whatever takes place between consenting adults in the privacy of their doing, is subject to recall at anytime—that sure isn't happy and can be so undoing!!! What a bummer it is to discover that what was thought to be mutually joyful, is later reshaped with selected recall to support charges of sexual harassment. It matters not if the charges are true or false, the charger has the instant advantage with the media edge, because when those fuck-and-tellers do their slanted cackling of once private parts in their twisted retelling, they have the starring spotlight. Then not so entertaining news shows do their show-and-tells to tease the public into tuning in to learn all the dirt that's being dug up!!! However, the fuckee has the shovel, and the once-upon-a-time fucker is getting buried!!! The fuckee uses *breaking news* as a first strike move, to tell just enough to tease the news-buzzards with juicy crumbs.

Forgive me if I say I could care less about who's doing what with whom, and it matters not how or where or why it was done, as long as only consenting adults are involved in the doings and no barnyard animals were used in their activities. The intimate details of those doings tales, matter not to me, but I do hope they both enjoyed their doings. One sided doings are such a bummer!!! If indeed Bill enjoyed some doings of oral gratification in the oval office, so what??? Was Monica having fun too??? What saddens me was his need to lie about the fact of his actions to the nation on television. Foolishly he sought false protection behind his lies. Methinks that rather than trying to cover his own ass, Bill was trying to maintain the illusion of white wash that surrounds the White House. Or maybe his lies were done with rightful concern for saving his ass and trying to stay out of even deeper shit. Alas, he'd have been ahead of the phony political contest, if he'd just explained that, yes, he and Monica had indeed enjoyed a bit of *fun and games* at the office—so what???

Ever since young George Washington copped to chopping down a mythical cherry tree, it seems that all the other Presidents have had this burden of having to do a major piece of work at the head of government and never tell a lie!!! At least not a lie that wasn't covered by plausible deniability. So the Prez has to do a heavy job, playing high stakes poker without tipping his hand when he's bluffing, and he has to be prepared to back-up his bluff, while he's telling the people just what public opinion polls say the public wants to hear without telling a lie. Then you mix in playing politics, you know the *'I'll scratch your back if you scratch mine'* stuff. Those political doings being done, as they say, for the general well being and good of *we the people.* Good for you, if you like eating out of a pork barrel!!! Way too salty for my tastes. All things considered, I can almost understand why Billy played the game out the way he did—all except his lies on national television. Someone should have told Bill that 'tis hard to fill an inside straight when the deck is stacked!!!

We have become a populace of prodded sheep!!! Our wool has been shaped and groomed by the teasing of mass media—*it* must be true, because *it* was on television, radio, newspapers, magazines, online, and in the chat rooms!!! Pestered people are polled for collective opinions, with their differing points of views sheered off when their viewpoints didn't fit the shimmering jells of the norm—which really wasn't a true and meaningful average, because spin had been added and data looped off!!! *We the people* are ever eager to foolishly buy into wanting to know the bullshit from the rich and famous that abounds all around—depending on the style of package the bullshit is in. Of course all political bullshit will be marked down *blue-light specials* for the Presidents' Day sales. I do believe that people who buy into gossip will eventually choke on the bare splintered bones of those tattled tales being boldly told.

I'd have a wee bit more respect for Prez Bill if he'd have said way back when, *"Yes, I tried grass while I was in college, so what???"* Instead of showing off his dumbness by saying he didn't inhale!!! Duh!!! Seems like so many people get into a place of rewriting their life history when they become some kind of famous person, or at least they think, in their own shining ego-painted persona that they are sort of famous. Ugh, those things of discovery and exploring we all did once upon a time, that later in life we wish we hadn't done, or perhaps we wish we had done them sooner!!! Those kind of things we no longer want to claim as ever having done, like getting high and/or drunk in the heat of the moment, or otherwise!!! The real pissers are the sheep herders who are in a place of *do as I say and not as I do*—and then they vigorously lie about what they do, did, didn't do, are doing, or haven't done!!! Can they spell, *double-standards???*

I say, yes, I confess!!! I did it!!! When I was a sophomore in high school I copped a feel of Rabbit's big tits. I did it because I just had to know if those beautiful bouncing mounds under her hot pink fuzzy sweater were really real!!! Yeppers, I boldly reached from behind her and cupped her breasts at the end of the second period while she was picking up her books!!! In the middle of the third period class, I was called to *the office* where the assistant principal asked if I'd fondled my classmate Rabbit??? Yes I did, said I. Why did you do that, he asked. To find out if they were real or only a bra stuffed with Kleenex. Don't you know it is wrong to fondle a girl's breasts in school, he asked. No, I didn't know that and I did it between classes, and she did seem to like it, answered I. Well, a teacher saw you, and when the teacher asked her about it she said she didn't like it so don't do that any more. Okay, said I. Then as I was leaving his office, he asked, were her breasts real??? Oh, gee, sir, said I, a gentleman never tells.

From cupping Rabbit's breasts, I learned that just because something is right in front of you and so teasingly enticing, doesn't mean what's there is really there for your enjoyment, enjoying it could be a fatal attraction. Even when what was done was perceived as having been enjoyed then, everything changes when confronted by a questioning authority figure, and then there is a clear and present danger that all of their enjoying that once was enjoyed, will now be disavowed by *the enjoyee.* What seemed like a good idea at the time, suddenly is under the probing spotlight, and the joy that once was experienced quickly vanishes in the harshness of the burning probe—witch hunt.

Those 'probing' questions aren't the, *"was 'it' good for you too???"* type of pillow talk, but rather the hard cross of an inquisition with fire in hand, and looking for someone to burn!!! The moralistic, those always righteous people of right minded pious judgments, are there with a hammer in hand to nail accused asses to the wall, *"we're running short on nails, could you cross your legs???"* The public display of the crucified is a warning of what happens to offenders when their offending doings are uncovered, or the moral mindless, contrive, convincing cunnings that in their eyes foul offenses *might have* been done.

However, in their holy quest for righteousness, those so morally masterful ones become rather immoral, butting their noses into private places that are really none of their business. So much for the defunked, *"not my brother's keeper"* concept or coveting thy neighbor's ass—cute ass that it may be. They wildly wail out, *"'tis the public's right to know,"* or so these outspoken, self-proclaimed keepers of the public's moral rightness want everybody to believe the *facts* as they believe!!! Methinks, I don't need to know all that!!!

Ugh!!! Give me a break from this *'public's right to know'* bullshit. I really don't need to know if Bill got blown away in the oval office by Monica or by whomever. Bill getting a blow job pales next to the years of wasted worry about a perhaps sexually frustrated, power crazed, Presidential finger on the red launch-the-nukes button, when a single push of that button would have given the entire world a glow job from an atomic blow-up job!!! But of course, those were the years of the 'cold war', the iron and bamboo curtains, the red tide, the evil empire, and massive weapons poised for assured mutual destruction, big time boomers ever ready to strike and blow the world away in a matter of minutes. Now that is a possible Presidential blown job I want to know about, and the truthful potential for some nuclear wad blowing about to happen—before someone says, *"Oooops, I didn't mean to push . . ."*

I'm certain, that *'for the public good',* we have never been told how many times things got down to the bare bone, and at the very last minute the big time boomer of a blow job didn't happen—and thankfully, life, liberty, and the pursuit of happiness continued on. While respective and respectful heads of state once again slip safe guard shields over red buttons, saving an unknowing world from another close call. I fail to equate Billy boy getting off from some oral joys with the same importance as the entire world being offed. To elevate a common *'blow job'*--ugh, I really dislike that term *'blow job',* 'tis sucking that's happening, not blowing!!!—to a Presidential act of high treason against the people of the United States of America really offends me. That is what really blows!!!

I do indeed endorse honoring all Presidents who didn't push the red button, after Harry *'the buck stops here'* Truman sort of pushed the button, made ready for him by FDR, to stop a nasty big war on the other side of the Pacific Ocean. I really don't care about those other buttons on a blue dress that never made it to the cleaners . . . 'tis just those red buttons that give me major concerns. Of course, you might recall that John Dillinger had a major problem with a woman friend wearing a red dress!!! Blue dresses generally don't have red buttons—right???

Those nailers with hammers develop corruptness too, because they lament about *'the state'* staying out of *'church matters',* and then try to impose the supposed morals of their churches upon the state of affairs. Now that just doesn't seem fair, sort of like they want to have their holy religious cake and eat it too!!! Maybe that's one of those holier miracles of eating and still having. However, it could be your cake they're eating. They don't want their religious freedoms abridged by the state, but they want to stick their religious noses into the business of the state of the nation. Our *'we the people'* country enjoys the freedom to worship according to the various religious beliefs—as long as they are acknowledged as being tax exempt, approved, God-fearing, religions. Witches, pagans, druids, native American Indians, and others with differing ways of honoring the natural powers that are flowing in the universe, are exempt from enjoying those freedoms, and they're required to pay taxes too.

However, churches are exempt from financially supporting the state, because approved churches don't pay taxes—so much for rendering unto Caesar jazz. At the same time, churches take their needful *'God-given'* right to impose their contrived religious beliefs upon others, and continue their ways of butting into and overseeing the doing of state affairs. Those approved religious dudes have effectively set aside the basic, all those bothersome *'separation of church and state'* statutes, except when the churches find such separation not to be in the best interest of the churches—like not paying taxes. And when it is in their best interest, to grab the news spotlight to moralize and admonish the immoral who got caught with their pants down or their hand in the till. Not fair at all!!! If you don't play the game you don't get to make up the rules!!!

And which is the singular holy voice that speaks for all the various religious denominations in the United States of America??? Even within the various religious sects there is discord. Martin Luther did some fancy nailing of his own, when he nailed a hit list of religious wrongdoings onto the church door. His way of saying, *"This same old shit from the unholy roaming church just doesn't cut the mustard with the common folks anymore, go away unholy dudes, and peddle your self-indulgence papers elsewhere."* Several religious groups, like the Amish sects, have almost nothing to do with the government or with other religious groups. Those Amish folks are still into doing life in way old fashioned ways of living and worship. The native American Indians also tried to have nothing to do with the government and to follow their natural ways of believing. They got screwed out of their land and their way of life in just of couple of centuries. The *'white man's greed'* for *'fool's gold'* and to control all the land, as far as the eye can see, did the Indians in, and put them out on the reservations. Out of sight, out of mind!!! The vanishing Americans are vanishing.

Methinks that government truly needs to be of laws, rather than of men/women. The laws are supposed to be for and applied equally to all the people, and the people elected to govern are only suppose to administer those laws in ways that benefit the people—*all* of the *'We the people'*. Ah, if only the ways of doing government affairs these days were that simple like it might have been thought of way back when our nation was born. The problem is, all those laws that made up the making of our big government, have gotten to be so very complex and abridged with exceptions and additions, that lots of wrongness creeps into governments and makes a royal bureaucratic mess of the law.

The ministering ministers seem to be more into playing god than administering, and the 'ad' that's missing is the added value by the direct involvement of *'we the people'*. The fewer number of those who govern, are usurpingly sucking off the dwindling values of the masses composed of the greater number of *we the people!!!* Thusly, the masses' values are being sucked dry, while being force-fed bullshit about what's being done for *'their well being'*, and being *'such good people'*, they don't need to worry about being picked clean to the bone. Then you have all kinds of special interest groups interested in ensuring their special interest values, swooping in for their piece of the pie—the cake has already been religiously eaten, and the whole mess gets to be a media blitz, because those special interest values relate to bucks, and bucks beget fucking business, and the fucking business bucks is good for their fucking business interests—too bad if the sucked dry folks are getting fucked over again!!!

Oh my, what a fucking mess!!! And all those political foresighters are amazed that many of us aren't all bent out of shape over those *'the alleged'* oral gratifications in the oval office. What's funny is when politicians get into fucking other politicians, but what's not so funny is when we all get fucked in their political fucking too!!! Who is the next politician in the pork barrel??? *We the people,* the taxpayers, we are the ones who get to foot the bill—yes indeed, pun intended!!!

No shit, those guys investigating this who-did-who stuff really paid tax dollars to have the President's cock checked out to see if his cock was the same cock described by an *'alleged'* Presidential cocksucker!!! Did they get a second opinion??? And they spent more tax bucks to see if *'alleged'* cum stains on a blue dress were a DNA match with the Prez!!! And I gotta say, this whole grand jury thing with doing the secure closed cable TV bit, that must have been the most costly private television production ever!!! No commercial messages to pay the freight—only lots of tax dollars, way boring viewing, and they didn't even have the foresight to cut a deal on the video distribution rights—so all the gutter rakers could order their own personal copy of the Presidential deep shit!!!

You know, I can see the value in getting my nose bloodied defending personal freedoms—life, liberty, and the pursuit of happiness, but I have no desire to get my nose dirty poking it into the personal business of other people. Thank you, I've got my own business to stick my nose into and to stay busy with. Their yucky political business is different than my business, but unless their business is doing me harm, 'tis not my business until my liberties get linked into their shitty mess.

Tell me that Bill fucked up something or other in trying to reduce the federal budget, but I really don't need to know about his supposed fucking around!!! Tell me that tricky Dick did some major string pulling to rig his re-election, and then did a major cover up and cutting off heads during his bloody Saturday night in August massacre—that kind of head stuff and fucking business matters to me. Yes, because that upsets the very process of government, those actions impede the functioning of *my government* and that was high treason. JFK was a heavy thinking dude, he might have had some good ideas taking shape before he got zapped with a hit job in Dallas, and as for Jack enjoying the sexy shape of beautiful Marilyn, well that really didn't involve me, except I'd have liked to have enjoyed her too!!! Her tits were for real, not Kleenex!!! Much ado was made about Ike and his prolonged relationship for seeking joyful comforts with his aide, a cute British bird assigned to him while he was generally doing WWII. Bottom line is we won the war and *'I like Ike'* was later elected to be our President, *so what???*

In the early 70's, I had lunch with Mamie on her famous *Gettysburg farm.* An inconsiderate member of the luncheon group asked her about the *real truth* of Ike's *wartime romance* with the chippie. She smiled a killer smile at him, and said that what Ike did was of no concern to her, that was Ike's business, and his business really doesn't concern the young man asking the question either!!! Ugh, I'm always astonished at the crassness of inconsiderate people asking questions that are none of their business. I do believe she was rather nice with her curt reply. She was a classy lady. On the fireplace mantle in her living room was a beautiful sculpture of a graceful school of swimming dolphins. The work of art was most impressive with fluid motions, and I got the personal impression that Mamie was real good at going with the flow.

Many of our forefathers fought a hard bloody fight to free us from the harsh rule of a far away king and courtly royal dudes in no so merry England, and yet we have made our elected President into some kind of a sitting king and our elected representatives into courting dudes. Our own homegrown American brand of elected royalty consummated every four years with a thorny crown of popular votes!!! Bullshit!!! Royalty my ass!!! The President works for me, and for you, and you—or at least that's who the President is suppose to be working for!!! Yeppers, he lives and works in the White House—that's only a rental property with a four year lease that comes with the job!!! It isn't a royal palace, and the oval office isn't some hallowed hall—it really is just a rounded kind of a room with a neat view of DC. Believe me, I was in the oval office on a school field trip back in the 50's. I remember Bert Long even cut a loud fart in the oval office!!! Beans for lunch was a very bad idea!!!

I wonder what Thomas Paine would have written about the ways of government and statesmanship if he was around to reflect on the goings on in Washington these days. Back when our country was birthing, he had some forward thinking ideas about human rights and the limited role of government. Then too, I'd like to hear about Ben Franklin's take on the whole sorry mess. Methinks Ben would have been amused with the *alleged* antics in the oval office, and way upset about them making much ado about nothing!!! Most likely he'd be way pissed over the vast amount of overspending and all the do nothing people sucking off the big government tits!!!

Anyhow, the idea of Presidents' Day is to celebrate and honor all of the Presidents who have served our melting pot of a country, and those who mostly served themselves from the pot. Are we really expected to eat this slop??? The Presidents who led us into war . . . and those who finally brought us out of wars, conflicts, police actions, peace keeping forces, black ops, etc et al, and those few Presidents who wisely avoided wars for as long as war could be dodged. Those special Presidents who pursued peace, courted peace, and sincerely believed that they had indeed helped to forge the tools to secure a lasting peace in an ever changing world where peace is such a myth.

Presidents' Day, a time for reflecting upon the Presidents who spent way too much money—grossly overspent lots of money—running up the national debt and increasing an already high federal budget into big time bad numbers . . . and those few Presidents who quietly reduced federal spending and tried to decrease the national debt. The Presidents who had visions far into the future . . . and those who sadly only looked with narrow tunnel vision, and couldn't see beyond the dome and the craziness trapped within the *beltway.* The Presidents who figured out how to balance payments to Peter and Paul while keeping Mary happy . . . and the Presidents who dumbly asked, *"A musical group from the sixties, right???"*

The Presidents who hunted quail and eagles—before they became endangered species . . . and those Presidents who hunted tail and found out they'd become endangered too!!! The Presidents who wisely redefined the land mass of our country creating national parks, gifts from the past we give to future generations as we enjoy the natural beauty today . . . and those who messed around and up masses of land masses—*but of course, you will fill the holes in, right???*

Those Presidents from humble backgrounds who rose to the grandness of the demanding office . . . and those who were humbled by the overwhelming demands of the office and overcome by ever changing tides of the general accounting office red ink. Those Presidents who were leaders beyond the taunting pulls of the beltway . . . and those who were led by the different pulls of so called public opinion polls, so helpfully provided by all those *in the loop* special interest groups with selfish hidden agendas.

Those Presidents who tried to *do the right thing* for the sake of the country . . . and those who believed that whatever they did was *the right thing* . . . and those few Presidents who did very little or nothing at all. Those who honestly tried to keep all the promises they made while getting elected and re-elected . . . and those to whom promises made to the voters had no meaning at all—tell them whatever they want to hear to get the buttons undone, oh, I meant to say, to get the votes!!! Those Presidents who left the comforts of a private life to serve the nation . . . and those who sadly discovered the President has no private life to enjoy because the all seeing eye of the gotta know everything media is everywhere. A time to honor those Presidents who were a real *peach* in the high pressure *elected* office . . . and those who really did lots of *impeachable* acts while serving in office—no way is getting a bit of joyful gratification in the oval office an impeachable offense!!!

While you're enjoying Presidents' Day, pause in your pondering of all those offered sale items, and reflect on how happy you are knowing you ain't the one in the White House!!! Perhaps Presidents' Day is best a time for honoring the memories of those Presidents who did the least harm to the country. Those who did their utmost to fulfill and keep promises made to the voters who voted to elect them to serve *on their behalf* in the high office of President. Those who dealt fairly with one and all, and not just the voters with the deep pockets. Those who employed the powers of the office for the benefit our country, and not just to look good in a thirty second sound bite on the network nightly news. Those who had the vision to see beyond the trappings of Presidential power and disregarded the false belief that might makes right, the might isn't right that costs a life to be right—that's just wrong and harmful. Those who overcame the tossing about of anticipation and got into bringing ideas off the table and built constructive concepts into fruitful reality, beyond the fucked up unreality of politics, as usual, where it takes forever to get anything *out of committee* to get anything positive done. Those who had the balls and the brains to try to make a positive difference in the working of *our government*—or at least tried their very best to make changes away from all the usual political bullshit. Those very few Presidents who tried to work at unfucking the fucked-up mess of government, and didn't contribute more shit to the continuing fucking mess!!! Those human Presidents who continued to laugh joyfully and cry in sorrows shared with we regular average folks-- *'We the people . . .'*

Be it what it may be, unless you work in retail sales and support, you most likely have Presidents' Day off to go to all those sales where folks are working hard to sell you stuff you don't really need—sort of like a real world civic lesson in politics, all in the spirit of the celebration of a national holiday that you need as a holiday to get a day off work!!! And many of us will have to put in extra hours at work to make-up for the holiday time taken off to shoppingly celebrate Presidents' Day.

Take care, my friends, and enjoy often . . . John

NEVERMIND!!!

Did you ever notice
how a conversation can be flowing along,
and then all of a sudden you hear
those thought stopping words,
"OH, NEVERMIND!!!"

Now, maybe you were just pausing
to reflect on what you'd been asked,
or perhaps you were trying to focus
on what had been said to you,
but before you could reply comes,
"NEVERMIND!!!"

Possibly you were distracted,
your attention pulled ever so briefly
into another direction,
but before you could say a word,
you get zapped so quickly with,
"NEVERMIND!!!"

Oh my, you're perplexed,
unfruitfully you try to recall
just what had been said that you missed,
what was it you didn't hear quite right,
trying to grasp what had been said
before you got mind-slammed by the,
"OH, NEVERMIND!!!"

Admitting the question slipped right by you,
and asking them to please repeat
what they had just said to you
so you could respond to them,
begets nothing but curtly said,
"WASN'T IMPORTANT...
NEVERMIND!!!"

However,
what was said matters
and is important to you,
but you're left in such a lurch
feeling like a bit of a jerk,
because you've been left hanging
with that ever dangling,
"NEVERMIND!!!"

Now,
trying to be mindful
of this discourse
that has gone off course,
you plead for a chance to amend,
once more asking them to please repeat
whatever they had just said,
and all you hear
is the dull dinging echo of,
"OH, NEVER MIND!!!"

Perhaps . . .
the off the cuff remark or inquiry
was only said in passing,
or maybe the sayer had second thoughts,
and now decides not to pursue
the possible path
their query could have taken,
thusly their abortive,
"NEVERMIND!!!"

Could be
their asked question
might have opened a can of worms,
then the asker takes a hasty pause
and doesn't want to get into
such wiggling matters just now,
and so they keep the lid on with,
"OH, NEVER YOU MIND!!!"

Methinks,
a common reason
for such an ugly utterance
often appears out of impatience,
and when your instant reply
isn't immediately forthcoming,
then comes their scornful,
"NEVERMIND!!!"

Also,
could be
'tis an old habit
that some folks
just keep on saying,
because they're somewhat lacking
in the good social grace of having
a meaningful conversation with another
who is truly trying to be attentive
to whatever they are saying,
until they show you
their lacking consideration
with their thoughtless slapping,
"NEVERMIND!!!"

Now,
some folks
really get all upset
by words considered
by them to be profanity,
but when you think about this,
this is truly a very nasty word
that is most vulgar,
because of the crudeness
of what the word does
when rudely injected
into a flowing conversation
'tis indeed most foul and very disgusting,
and dripping with lots of negativity is,
"NEVERMIND!!!"

Please . . .
be very mindful
of the negative power
this inconsiderate
and coarse word has
to disrupt your course
of doing verbal intercourse,
to tarnish the beauty of sharing enjoying,
to snidely snip off opening mind blossoms,
and cut the fabric weaving friendships.

'Tis way nicer and more joyful to be,
"EVER MINDFUL!!!"

And
please,
do indeed,
be ever mindful to
take care
and
enjoy often . . . John

HATE...
where does it come from???

Well, we've discovered how to love,
and sadly, we've also learned how to hate!!!

We discovered love feels good, delighting in good lovings
'tis such a joy, fluffing up with marvelous warm fuzzies,
sharing loving flows in positive ways of relating together,
aligning balances and harmony uniquely into unity,
evolving naturally with unconditional accepting,
those precious shining loving giftings of ourselves.

We are taught how to hate, for some hating comes all too
naturally, for other's 'tis a self-destructive learning process,
learning to be fearful of all who are different,
made afraid of mysterious unknowns said to be lurking near,
making for the vicious venting of vile anxiety angers,
ever so quick to lash out with hatred at any perceived threat,
clinging to a false sense of security in hateful courses as hatred
both consumes and defines all those who follow hateful routes.
Eventually, they erode away by their endless strife.

My ancestor, Ben Franklin, once wrote of life in colonial times,
"Only two things in this world are certain: death and taxes!!!"
Methinks Ben missed the certainty of babies being born
as long as folks continue doing what comes naturally,
and he did his share of spreading about natural seedings,
as he surely enjoyed being natural very often!!!

Death is the greatest unknown, the final secret told only in
passing, the fatal finish always somewhere out there.
Death—ever waiting nearby to grimly come reaping,
when the midnight hour tolls the bell for the newly dead.

Left-behinds defined mortality, regretfully undertaking to
explain and cope with the *untimely* loss of the beloved deceased
for those survivors grieving out sorrows from their losses.
Because only the living feel the relentless pain of death.

In death, the recently departed have left all pain far behind them.

Gentle are the beliefs of resolving missing ones by celebrating their departure—with a going away party, as if they've embarked on a long journey of no return, honoring and biding loving farewells for their timely trek across the great waters to happier hunting grounds, traveling beyond clear deep azure blue skies, moving endlessly with the sun and moon and stars.

Some believe death fulfills the religious promise of expiring into the power and glory of heavenly peace, the *reward or punishment phase* of eternity, to an awaiting eternal heaven or hell, depending on all of life's deeds and misdeeds done.

Harsh are life-to-death transitions, where rendered spiritual judgments determine between assured rewards of everlasting life, for those judged to be without sin the opening of the pearly gates await, or perpetual torments in the hellfires of damnation, their souls burning for all eternity in sinful cleansing fires.

There's also an old belief of some faiths, that atonement is made for offered joys, foolishly passed upon as being unenjoyable, sort of like a, *did you enjoy life to the fullest* answering.

However, regardless of the judgmental ruling, there's the imposed fear of being judged on life's qualities, and when the time of passing arrives, wondering if those granted absolutions and forgiveness really took away all the wrongs one had done.

Others believe cycling reincarnation recycles spent lives into renewed life forms, with each new cycle presenting fateful opportunities to improve upon the qualities of previous lives.
As a good friend would say, *clean cup move down!!!*
What goes around comes around, now pay attention this time!!!

Hopefully knowing each passing with less harm done,
as rebounding hurts previously inflicted unto others,
now return upon those once hurtful doers.

Also returning are all the joys and kindnesses shared refreshingly flowing anew, ever balancing from lifetime-to-lifetime, growing life lessons as pathmarks, becoming merrily older with soulful-stretch marks, earned from your doings along this traveled path.
Did you do love,
or did you do harm???
The answers are in self-truths of deeds done, forming awaiting awarenesses to experience life lessons to be learned from.

And some other people think of death as abruptly befalling in a mere instant, all done and gone into nothingness,
'roger, go at throttle up,',
'top of the world, mom,',
'over and out',
finished,
the end,
enda,
bye.

Abrupt as, *here one moment—gone the next*,
as the last grain of sand falls through the timeless-glass,
that's all she wrote folks, Elvis has left the building!!!,
fading away into an endless void that's unavoidable
and unexplainable too.

At times, the abruptness is so lightning fast
that the lifeflow departs the body.
However, the energy gets trapped in this world's reality,
as a lingering spirit--a mere ghost of who they'd been.

Some sham slammers try to claim to be communicating with earth-bound hauntings by cryptic messages from the great beyond, cunningly conveyed by profit minded intermediaries. So very eager they are, when the price is right, to decipher and explain hidden meanings, making good ill-fortunes from others grief and foolishness, a marked-up price tag for their *clairvoyant services,* playing upon the grief-stricken fears of not knowing, messages alleged to be from beyond the fearful unknown.

Death and dying beliefs are fertile breeding grounds for hatred
from people believing in differing devout creeds,
each believing their faith is the most faithfully true one.
Some religions implant early seeds that their doctrine is the only
righteous one, and all others are doomed.
Such omnipotent egotistical propriety causes destructive distress
and hatefulness towards *unfaithful* folks not worshipping
as the truly faithful always do.

Then, in the continuing strife soiled saga of humanity
comes the *save them* or *slay them* phase.
When *saving souls* is an option, the non-believers are raped of
body and spirit, ageless beliefs are plundered away never again
to be honored or celebrated, superseded by the new and
improved updated religion.
Of course, idolizing gods with human sacrifices,
being killed as offerings, was way brutal and dumb too,
and such a horrible waste of perfectly good virgins!!!

The slaying part is twisted hate, unlashing vile viciousness,
surging out at folks because they hold differing beliefs, and at
those living unacceptable lifestyles, and those loathed, for simply
looking different, judged unworthy of being accepted as they are,
shunned for thinking thoughts deemed to be sacrilegious, and all
of these would be transgressions are determined by those said to
be self-righteously so ordained, and yet, from their hateful ways
they won't abstain—while staining others.

The religious Big 10 carved in stone clearly include the one that
says *don't kill,* but humankind seems dead-set on killing others.
The killers always seek exceptions to the rules, absolution from
the sins of their own creation proclaiming that what is done is
done in the name of all that is holy—done for the good of all.
I believe the common person who has just fallen by warring
ways would take exception with the *good of all* part in dying
in the political ways of resolving *holy* belief differences.
Let those who do harm to others experience the same harmful
ways being done unto them—and then some.

Meaning that if you come to take a life with a knife, the life of the person you come to take is rightfully empowered with the survival rights to turn the blade back upon you in the defensive protection of saving their being—safe from harm.
The would be doer of the harmful knifing, learns an instant karma recycling lesson in *do no harm—thy will be done.*

Thusly, it comes too often to pass, that humankind foolishly plays at being godly by boldly taking countless lives and salvageable captives, in the holy name of their righteous god almighty, so scripted in pious words that might makes right, and thusly it is written that *might prevails* to make right to smite the sullied scoffers, hatefully hound the heretics, implode the inane idealists, impede the imperialist infidels, and fool the fleeceable foolish, etc . . . et al.

The lead keepers of the one-and-only all powerful faiths, judge who among you are the scoffers at beliefs, who are the heretics of the true words, which ones are idealists who dare to dream changes, who are the unclean infidels to be purged from life, and which are the foolish faithfuls ready to kill for them!!!

I've often wondered, with all these different zestful zealots divided by all their almighty unholy indifference's each so affirming in their true perspective on righteousness, if holy wars are really a congress of unholy gods staging a huge cosmic free-for-all-cock-fight complete with pecking and clawing!!!

They wager on their differing *faithful followers'* abilities to uphold and defend their so *godly* projections of the god and goddess, as they appear to mortals to be visions of perfect beauty and boundless strength, all seeing and all knowingly god-like, as their ungodly fickle-fated-fingers do stir things up in harmfully, horrible fights, fatefully moving about humankind into conflicts.

Methinks something got lost in retellings of olden times, and the part about god creating humans in god's image sort of came out butt backwards, because it does appear that humanity has gone about creating a variety of Big Gee's in the images of human

concepts of gods and goddesses, and those impressions of the Big Gee's are ever changing, according to needful illusions.
Those eastern religions had some very interesting images of god and goddesses they thought up long ago, with several arms and a couple of heads on some of them.
Methinks these gods and goddess grew beyond conflicting, and into enjoying having so many hands to play with.
Bet they were lots of fun to play poker with too!!!

Meanwhile, humankind's hateful debts continue to increase.
Now overdrawn at the universal karma bank to such a colossal amount that the world is in an unhealthy tilt from all the heavy bad karma debts that humankind still hasn't learned from.
New generations are indentured by previous generations, with centuries of amassed dues and indebtedness mounting.
The bloodthirsty commerce in vengeful strife continues inflecting more prolonged hateful killing, pay-backs begetting pay-backs upon pay-backs from long ago fought bloody battles, as fresh hatred always bleeds anew, taking an eye-for-an-eye, thusly, rendering seeing beyond ancient hates an impossibility.

Hate comes from taxing ways, the rendering unto those who take their due regardless if equitable or not, 'tis an imposed tariff, no questions, no discussion, no debate, no rebate, about the fairness of what amount is reasonable—squeeze every drop out.
The choices have been made by others, the taxed are stuck with supporting all those impositions, the only consideration is how much can be gotten, the hateful greed of gluttony is so taxing.

When there's no say in what's happening in their lives, humankind boils over with angry pissed-off frustrations, becoming embittered by those trashing individual liberties, encumbering freedom of expression—*for your own good,* and imposing mindless hypocritical restrictions, done under the guise of being for our protection—*our good,* doubled over with dinging *double standards,* those *do as I say, not as I do* kind.
And our *well being*...the *well being* of *us folks,* gets lost in the angry fast shuffles of holy card dealers, gets royally fucked again by the *fickle-finger-of-fate.*

But all too often the befalling *ill-fate* is the self-fulfilling anger of people's increasing hatred.

Once upon a time we discovered how to truly love, in a time of innocence before hateful harms bled the mingled bloods of generations in battles with kin, staining the earth with spills of animosity done, a fall from the comforting graces of primal love.

Do loving life with me.
Let godsparks shine brightly banishing angers and scorn,
judge not the beings of others, leave harmful ways alone,
and hate will die dead away, and killing conflicts will no longer
play havoc upon the lives of humankind.

Turn away from vengeful doings, revenge is a very cold dish, best garnished with understanding of the others' anger, painful lessons learned from the *harms* done, offset their hurts with the living of life to the fullest, filled with shared joys as life goes on.

Know that I honor you where your godspark dwells as the uniqueness of your being, thusly aglowing when godsparks do indeed align freely with individualities, accepting the joys of differences, discovering the vibrating harmony found in the array of differ harmonizing notes.

All beliefs are different even when folks believe, they believe the same beliefs, those believed beliefs are differently believed, by those who believe, they believe in those very same beliefs.

That's the remarkable uniqueness of humankind, the differences in saneness makes the difference, all the difference between doing love or harm.

I respect your differing beliefs as I trust you to respect mine.
There is a bond of trust that may be a long time growing,
sadly, the trust may be snipped off into the wilts of distrust
when differing beliefs and values conflict—*shit happens!!!*

I may choose to share my individual beliefs with you, but I won't tax your being you by forcing my beliefs upon you, nor take away from you the essences that makes you uniquely you.

I have no time to fear the afterlife, way too many harms in the reality of this life to contend with to worry needlessly about the hereafter, and when this passage nears concluding, I'll surely rage out vainly at the coming of the final night.
Raging not with hatred at what does eventually come to be,
but raging with passions to know more joy—more merry,
to play with one more idea—birthing a mind-seed into a bud,
to create another pondering concept—thought stretching,
to conjure another rambling for sharing—prolonging flows,
to meet a new unknown friend—strangers are unmet friends,
to relish joyous laughter with true friends—laughing freely,
to bathe in the free flows of good fellowship—hate free,
to hopefully see the dawning of many more tomorrow's,
where there is no greed, no guilt, no jealousy,
no angry lines drawn in the sand,
and no hate to stain anyone's fate.

When there are to be no tomorrows
as twilight's heavenly final curtain falls,
then I'll just go with the departing flows
that eventually await us one and all,
smiling as I come to know
the greatest secret of all.

Take care and enjoy often . . . John

MOTHER'S PARTING GIFTS

My mother's life was being consumed by cancer. The slow dying that comes creeping from deep within the body, feeding like an ugly hungry beast upon her innards. From all outward appearances she looked just as fine as ever. Oh, perhaps a bit more weary, maybe her eyes sparkled slightly less brightly, but her warm loving smile was ever present. Nothing about her looks betold the horrible battle raging inside her, taxing her straining system to fight the deadly cancer. Sadly, the cancer was gaining as my mother continued her silent struggle to prolong life, holding on to her unspoken dream.

During the early part of her war I was in hiding. I'd been told that as a parting shot my second ex-wife had given a contract to a 'hit man' to take my life. She was crazy. The 'hit man' even crazier. What was even more bizarre was that I knew the guy!!! Indeed, he once was a professional for hire doing *wet work*—and he was also a professor of political studies. Thusly, I took the advice of the police and got out of harm's way, left town quickly and disappeared, leaving the experienced police to handle the nasty matter of arresting this very bad ass dude.

From deep in hiding, I kept in daily touch with my dad by phone. My mother would have been way more stressed if she had known why I'd gone out of town so suddenly. She would have lovingly been worried about my safety as only mother's can do. All she had been told was I had to go out of town on business to help a friend, which was indeed true. I was visiting with a friend who lived in a *cave* in the middle of nowhere, and I was doing the business of staying alive. I longed to be at my mother's side, bringing her a smile to help to ease her mind away from her pain. The doctor said her treatments were working as much as could be expected, but more tests were needed.

Finally, my father had gotten the *unofficial* word, that the *hit man* had dropped from sight too. The police and feds believed he was hiding because another *contracted matter* had gotten rather messy for him, and now he was on the run as the one being hunted. *What goes around, comes around.* There was a small chance that he was still in the area, but now he had also gone-to-ground, and it was unlikely that he would be looking for me.

Cautiously I returned to the area, and I was able to visit my hospitalized mother. With each trip to the hospital, I carefully took a different route, varied my attire, and used a variety of entrances. Later, I found out that the police had increased their patrols in the area. They had several plainclothes officers hanging around in case the 'hit man' tried to stake out the hospital waiting for me to show up. Seems the *hitter* had made a few *hit lists* of his own—with a bullet!!!

However, all that was important to me, was to have time with my mother. That precious time of knowing death's door would soon be opening for her. A time to share a few cherished joys in smiling recall together. To make amends for trespasses into her space—"Yes, mother, I was the one who took your new bottle of dark red finger-nail polish when I was nine to paint a model airplane I was building." She smiled and said she had recognized the dark red color painted on the wing of the model airplane I'd just finished building. Hours upon hours for us to talk about anything and everything except the ending time creeping closer at hand. Avoiding talking about dying, as death lingers near, coming closer and closer with each passing day.

During visiting hours, relatives and friends were often there in her room, and I'd come and go from her bedside with the flows of her need for privacy. Some of the family and friends I wanted no part of—the show and tell crowd. They weren't visiting to bring her comfort, their only reason for visiting was to be able to say they had been there to see her and remarked about what a sin that she look so sick. Much of what they seemed to do in life was done simply to be able to say they'd been there and done that, without experiencing really having been there in spirit. Nothing more than their painted plastic shells were there, and thankfully only briefly.

"Yes, mother, I found those old pictures daddy had taken of you, those magnificent photographs he had hidden way in the back of his night-stand." She nodded and smiled her special smile, that spoke in volume of her joys in knowing that I had seen her in all her beauty, once upon a time when she was young and carefree. Odd that I could now talk with my mother about seeing her altogether expressive photos as she talked about that time in her life before I was born, but I could never tell my father about my appreciation for his creativity and professional camera work capturing my mother's beautiful *au naturel* splendor. Seems like he always had way too many shells to try to get through, and at the time, so did I.

My mother's health was holding status quo—neither getting any better nor getting any worse. I developed an appreciation for the positive nature of status quo—so far so good. All the time, the dark shadow continued to stretch nearer—not good. As she grew weaker, the time spans between drawing blood for tests and treatments started to be varied. I was with her when she told her doctor that she wanted to leave the hospital to celebrate Christmas at home with her family, promising that she would be back in the hospital right after Christmas. The doctor smiled saying he'd see what he could do to make that happen.

"Yes, mother, Doris and I were playing *I'll show you mine if you show me yours* when you came looking for me out behind the shed that sunny summer afternoon, and I lied when I said we weren't doing nothing but watching those big old bumble bees buzzing all around the sweet smelling honeysuckle."

Again she laughed and smiled and said, "I knew that, Johnny, you were always interested in learning more about the birds-and-the-bees. And how you got an early copy of Peyton Place and rented the book out to the neighbors for a quarter a day really surprised me!!!" Extraordinary how mothers always seem to know far more than we smart-ass kids believe they know. What remarkable parting gifts to be able to share with her joys in these smiling knowings, held so long in silence. Strange how it happens, that there's so much that's natural about life that just seems so impossible to talk about at the time.

Days passed too quickly, and nothing more was heard from the doctor. My mother asked me to please remind the doctor about her request to be home for Christmas. Friends were visiting her when I went off to find her doctor. He was a special-head-doctor-type dude. I found him on the phone and waited out of earshot until he finished his call. Then I approached him and respectfully asked about my mother's request for a temporary release to spend this Christmas at home. Seems only reasonable to be able to spend what little time you have remaining, being as you need to be and doing what you're able to enjoy.

The doctor did a song and dance about still waiting for more test results, and his not being sure about her insurance coverage involving a holiday release. I felt like I was being talked *down to* and being fed bullshit. The doctor said he'd be back to me as soon as he heard back about the tests and got an answer about the insurance. I thanked him and went off to tell my mother what I had found out—which wasn't anything new. She was still visiting with friends, but she wanted to know what I'd learned from the doctor, and for her friends to know too. I watched her mask her sad disappointment from her friends with a smile.

"Yes, mother," I said to her later in private, "I'm sorry I embarrassed you in front of your card club, when they were teasing me about Jane and me being married for seven long years and no grandchildren had been produced. And smart-mouthed aunt Edith asking how do I explain being married for seven years and no grandchildren. And the hush and collective gasp of your card playing friends when I replied, *'Easy, Edith, we frequently fuck for just the joyful fun of fucking!!!'* and you really blushed with the shame of what I had said in front of your friends."

"Don't be silly, Johnny, I wasn't blushing," she said smiling, "I was beaming with pride that you left your aunt Edith totally speechless, and you know how she always has to get the last word in, and she didn't have a thing to say. After *youes* left, all

Edith kept on saying over and over again was, 'Well I never . . . well, I never . . .' and all the rest of us could do was laugh and laugh. I laughed so hard I almost wet my panties!!!"

Treasures of parting gifts from the universe, sharings from a priceless time when you know life *as* a short timer. Opportunities to share things you wish you had shared but never did. Wishes that could have been shared long before but never were, too many shells, or not the right time, or the fear of perceived shame—that cutting guilt. You know, all the imposed holding back and pushing away from talking about *stuff* that everyone seems to be conditioned into not talking about all the aspects of life—generation after generation, as folks continue to shy away from really talking about and living a more joyfully open life. Sad, isn't it???

Time was fleeting, fewer shopping days until Christmas when I called my mother's insurance company. Doing a wee bit of an end run to check on the coverage provisions for my own information. Indeed, the voice of a helpful lady explained, the coverage would continue if my mother were able to be furloughed for her Christmas at home. On the hunch of my gut feelings, I asked if the doctor had been called back with that information. No, she said, he had never called to inquire about the coverage. Nothing had been noted on my mother's record since she had been admitted this time, and any question from one of her doctors would have been absolutely noted. I made a note of that, regretting that it appeared the doctor was lying about having called her company regarding the coverage.

I told my father what I'd found out. He was upset that I had called the insurance company. Jumping on me for butting my nose into what the doctor was doing, that he was *the doctor* and I didn't know anything. I said, "I know when I'm being lied to!!!" Now those words were usually fighting words between us—my father never believed I knew much of anything of importance to him. But my mother quickly cut off the verbal fight that was brewing, telling my father that she had asked me to follow-up on what the doctor was doing. She went on to say that I was only trying to help fulfill her wish to come home for Christmas. Just then, some of their friends arrived, and the three of us put on *company-is-a-coming* smiles, and while everyone was making nice passing phony air-kisses to one another, I left for the nurse's station to find the doctor.

I was at the nurses station asking about the doctor's next expected visit to the unit just when the doctor arrived. I said I would appreciate having a few words with him in private. He said he was looking for me—as we stepped away from the nurses station counter. Before I could say anything, her doctor started to explain, ". . . your mother's test results were the same as the last set of results, she isn't getting any worse, but she isn't getting any better. We're trying to build up her strength, so we can do more tests, then we will schedule her for more treatments, but for right now we just have to wait for her to regain some more of her strength. However, her overall prognosis doesn't look good, because her condition is staying about the same."

"Sounds like my mother is caught in some bizarre sort of a medical *'Catch-22'*, she needs to be stronger to have more tests, and the tests are necessary for more of the treatments, which hopefully will make her stronger, but she isn't strong enough to have the treatments, and in the meantime, her condition remains mostly unchanged. Since her condition is currently stable will you please arrange her furloughed release for Christmas???"

"No, I will not agree to release her on a furlough," he said, and curtly added, "She'd also lose her insurance coverage if she left the hospital to go home."

"Is your unwillingness not to grant her a furlough so she might celebrate Christmas out of the hospital because you're concerned her going home for a couple of days would cause her condition to deteriorate???" I asked.

"Her condition could deteriorate at anytime, regardless of where she is, I want to keep her here to keep an eye on her," he retorted belligerently, "I *won't* sign her furlough release."

"It would mean alot to her, and being home for Christmas would sure lift her spirits. That could help her to recover some of her strength. I'm not trying to play doctor, but I think it would be in her best interest to enjoy having one last Christmas at home with her family . . ."

At this point I got cut-off by the *good doctor* who leaped at me with a verbal onslaught about how he would be the only one to make a judgment call about my mother's medical condition and what would be best for her. He went on and on berating me for butting into things I knew nothing about. Ending with that loaded acknowledging question full of confirming expectations about if he had made himself perfectly clear???

"NO, doctor!!!" I demanded, "I'm not at all clear about why you lied to me about her insurance coverage being null and void if she went home on a Christmas furlough???"

Nuclear blow-up, big time blast, booming into a huge mushroom cloud happened. I backed out of the way of his poking finger zapping into my chest. I backed up all the way to the nurses station, where I picked up the phone on the desk to make an urgent call. Madly the doctor frothed at me, "No outside calls allowed—hospital rules!!!"

"Inside house call and my dime." I replied bluntly, hitting the extension numbers of a phone that was picked up almost instantly, "I have a problem, I need your help right away, I'm at the nurses station for the unit my mother's room is on . . . thank you very much."

Now the doctor was quick to inform me, that calling in my mother's family physician wasn't going to do any good. He was the only one who could release her for a furlough, he and he alone had the final say. I think I said something about an oath doctors take that includes the words *"and do no harm to my patients"*, and that I felt his actions weren't in my mother's best interest and I wanted a second opinion. He said I'd never find a doctor to say differently than he was saying because he was in charge. I said I thought he was wrong in not considering my mother's expressed desire to go home for Christmas. He was just saying very loudly that he didn't give a damn what I thought!!! Now he was interrupted by a loud commanding voice from a person walking quickly up behind him saying, "*I* care what my good friend John thinks."

And there stood the President/Chief Executive Office/Chief Medical Officer of the hospital—the main man. He glared at the doctor as he shook my hand in a friendly greeting, asking, "What's the problem, John???"

The ranting doctor instantly went very quiet, and turned a sickly shade of green, looking at me in total disbelief that I actually knew Paul. No one fucked with Paul—if they did, they were soon history regardless if they were a doctor, nurse, tech, orderly, or whatever. He was the head honcho of the entire hospital. No one involved in my mother's hospital care had known that I was friends with Paul. We had worked together on several community service committees, we'd *do lunch* a couple of times a month. That was an earlier time in my life, when I was able to do volunteer work with 'the United Way', 'the Jaycees', 'the Chamber of Commerce' and the local chapters of 'the American Heart Association', and 'Planned Parenthood', helping them out with some creative ideas.

Paul reviewed her chart, as I explained to him my mother's most sincere request to go home for Christmas, and that this doctor wouldn't sign her furlough. He whispered something to the unit charge nurse who instantly made a phone call, as the doctor was explaining his judgment call, and doing it in a softer, more respectful manner than when he'd been yelling at me. Soon another doctor appeared, and then another, and Paul passed them my mother's chart and asked if they could see any reason why she couldn't be granted a Christmas furlough. Both doctors agreed that going home for the holiday might just lift her spirits, and help her to recover some of her lost strength. Paul signed her furlough paper, reassigned my mother's care plan to one of the other doctors, and relieved the other doctor as the department head—and bluntly told him if he ever heard of him talking like that to a patient's family member he'd be off staff and lose his hospital privileges.

When Paul finished with the doctor, he stopped in to see my mother, and meet my father. A young nurse was giving her meds, as Paul told her the good news that she was going to be able to spend this Christmas at home. She smiled the brightest smile I'd seen from her in a very long time. The same kind of smile as from an excited child knowing that Christmas Eve and Santa Claus visiting were near—a bittersweet coming. My mother beamed with pure delight. She had to promise Paul that she'd be back in her hospital bed by noon on Wednesday, the 26th of December. I know she was so very happy to be going home that she would have promised him anything!!! My father asked him about what had happened to the other doctor, and Paul explained that the other doctor worked for him, and he was being reassigned to other duties elsewhere in the hospital, and now he had taken a personal interest in my mother's treatment plan and making her as comfortable as possible.

After we left my mother's room, I was out in the hallway thanking Paul for his dropping everything to respond to my call. Paul said in the three years we had known each other, I'd helped him with all kinds of projects and never once asked for anything—except perhaps for more Pepsi and a smoke break. He said he'd been told by a mutual friend that I rarely ask anything for myself. Which is true, I have a problem asking for help, I just don't like to impose on folks asking for myself. However, there was no way I was going to allow that jerk to run a *Catch-22* and play god with my mother's remaining time—and ruin her Christmas too.

"Yes, mother." I smiled, precious and few are these times for amending closings in open honesty. "When I had to sit at the kitchen table until I finished eating everything on my dinner plate. I waited until you went into the living room to watch television, and then I'd open the back door and scrape whatever food was left on my plate, into the crack of space between the wooden backsteps and the house on Pine Street. I know you told me about all those little kids in China who were starving, and I'm sorry I wasted food, but I *still* don't like yucky liver, slimy egg-plants, and bushy broccoli."

"I knew you did that, Johnny, that's why I went into the living room." she said laughing. "I still have the remains of the stale bread you stuffed into an envelope you neatly addressed, *'TO: THE STRAVING LITTLE KIDS IN CHINA'* and you secretly mailed it with my *S&H Green Stamps*!!! Tom the mailman brought it back for the right postage. He laughed handing the envelope to me and said, 'It feels like dough!' and I told him it was dough, a piece of Wonder bread!!!"

Mother got very upset about wasted food. She was careful about cooking enough for everyone, but if you put the food on your plate you were expected to eat all that you had taken. Likewise, if you poured yourself a glass of milk, juice, or soda, you'd better drink the entire glass. She'd switch you to water for the next few days to remind you not to waste milk or leave the milk bottle out on the kitchen counter—yes, once milk came in real glass bottles. Water on corn flakes isn't nearly as good as milk, in fact it is downright yucky!!! *Waste not, want not,* was her wise saying which I know she learned from Nanny.

One last Christmas at home, a gift from the universe, the gift of knowing what's what in the nearing passing on of life. Feeling the warm sensations from the ghosts of Christmas' past visiting her again as the smiling haunts of happy holiday joys. Celebrating a symbolic birth of old on the approaching eve of closing her birthing. With all of the joyful focus now on celebrating one last time . . . once more with feeling, truthful feelings. Feeling a congregation of spirits gathering to eventually carry my mother away. But not today, not on her last earthly Christmas . . . this was her perfect day of merry Christmas joy.

A joyous Christmas Day of lingering present opportunities to share parting gifts of life reflections. Gifts with real meaning, gifts that counted far greater than the plastic value of all the dust catching gifts of glitz and glitter given and received over the many years. The gift of the last Christmas was a very costly gift for my mother. Once again she gave the gift of life. Prolonging her life with more pain, pain like she endured birthing me and my sister—I was first and bigger and gave her more pain. However, now her pain came from the anguishing distress of continuing her raging battle against creeping cancer. She was courageously fighting a delaying rearguard action, keeping death off her ass for one last Christmas—abating cancer, buying time, time to give as gifts in parting.

I have no idea about how my father and sister did parting giftings with my mother. My father was mostly into competing with me, until I discovered the freedom of being a non-competitor, making that freeing self-discovery that I have nothing to prove to him or anyone. Having to prove love by cutting off parts of yourself competing is not loving. During my formative childhood years his mental games challenged and stretched my young mind in ways of self-learning, and for those early mind-stretches I'm most grateful. However, 'twas the endless interacting in competing with me that was always present with him. His ongoing nasty mind whacks were abusive in hidden ways—hidden away giving my gray matter stretch marks . . . no time out . . . no half-time . . . no umpire to call foul plays.

My sister is very different than me, and methinks her farewelling wasn't filled with the wellness of closings, but most likely weary from weepings of 'don't go' with perhaps, hopes for a healing Christmas miracle . . . to chase mother's cancer away. Oh, my dear sister, those kinds of miracles mostly only happen in the motion picture shows. Where we differ is my hope would be for a cure for cancer for everyone—miracles are most miraculous when they are miracles for everyone. Sad it is, but I really didn't feel I could ask how they enjoyed their parting gifts—or if they were even aware of the great gift mother gave us on that last Christmas together. Sadly, I fear they only saw the lurking presence of the pruning grim reaper stalking nearer and nearer to mother.

Methinks the grim reaper is a pretty cool dude. With a quick pass of his sharp blade all the grim and gloomy parts of leaving life are gone in a compassionate instant. The shell and unfinished messy remainders are left behind for the living to contend with, and the glowing godspark of life is the harvesting yield the reaper carefully gathers at the parting instant of passing, tenderly transcending that heavenly glow into the eternal energy flows of the endless universe.

Looking back on that time, I can see my mother's memories of spirits from a lifetime of Christmas' past, spinning around her a beautiful saving white light to hold the reaper at bay. Her gathering of angels pointing to her new Christmas star sparkling brightly on the top of her energy tree. Merry spirits singing glorious carols of *'Heaven Can Wait'* and dancing the night of the 'Grim Reaper' away in a twisting shouting whirl of light . . . *rain, rain, go away, come again another day.*

Falsely, I believed that my mother's parting gifts from our last Christmas together were the most meaningful gifts she could ever have given. Later, I'd discover just how wrong I was about these being her greatest gifts. Her gifts in parting were indeed far more valuable than all the gifts with costly price tags and fancy wrappings that are so soon gone and forgotten. In her own simple ways of loving she gave us the sparkling gift of herself. Mother never once let on that she was in acute pain, not a single mention that her time for passing was now even nearer. Not a single word came from her that would have left a hint of guilt attached to what she was saying and doing. No nagging questions from her to solicit from us tacky measures of how much we were appreciating her 'staying alive' efforts. I'm not sure when she came to know that guilt was very much a big bad bummer, but I'm sure Nanny helped my mother to learn about all the harm that lingers from guilt games. Slowly my mother had grown into a place of mildly taking others to task for laying on guilt trips.

My parents were alone at home on Christmas Eve. They also shared one last Christmas Night in bed together. Hopefully they enjoyed together one more time that night. My father phoned me early the next morning saying my mother's condition was worse!!! She was less than stable now, but she didn't want him calling the ambulance to take her back to the hospital before they were expecting her late in the morning. I said I'd be right there, dressing quickly for warmth, and rushed out to my car. I uttered a bright blessing for energy in the car battery, I hoped there'd be enough battery juice to start the car. The starter-motor slowly turned over in the morning cold, turned again and again, and then thankfully the engine sputtered and started. I made good time, driving in the light early morning traffic the day after Christmas, carefully running lights and stop signs, wishing I could find a patrolling cop in a cruiser to ask for a safe escort.

I parked in front of their house. As I got out of the car, I saw four big crows looking at me from their perch on the peak of the roof. They mockingly cackled at me, and I sharply cackled back a 'be gone' at them. I understood the unwanted quote these black winged messagers were bringing . . . nevermore . . . never more . . . never more time!!! For now, the crows took flight into the dawning light as I entered my parent's house.

In an instant, I could feel my mother's energy levels had dropped severely. A welcoming smile was on her lips, but she looked washed out—drained of her natural color, fading to the plight of her loosing battle. Clearly I saw her inner fortitude was very low. I know she must have pulled heavily on her remaining energy reserves to be home for Christmas, and now she was paying dearly. I had the feeling that she was most grateful to pay whatever the cost was, for her one last time of gathering with us around the cheery fireplace on her special Christmas Day.

My father had called for an ambulance, and I called the unit nurses station to let them know my mother would be returning soon, her condition was deteriorating. The ambulance crew arrived, they quickly prepared her for transport, and gently eased my mother into the back of the ambulance. She waved weakly to us and said she felt silly, and was asking why she couldn't just go back to the hospital by car, the way she had come home, with my father or me driving. The medics were on the radio with the hospital ER and they had started an IV drip and were giving her oxygen. I knew she was in the good hands of skilled 911 medical emergency professionals.

A flock of doctors and nurses were attending my mother when I arrived at her room. Paul said something about increasing her meds, that her condition had slipped to a critical point, but she was stable for the time being, just very weak. I said I believed she fought with all her reserves to make Christmas possible. He said he felt cautiously optimistic about her ability to regain her strength to the point of being able to resume treatments again. For now all they could do was make her comfortable and try to ease her pain with hopes for her recovering some of her depleted vigor.

Once again, there were a flood of visitors into her room that afternoon. Bringing her romance novels I feared she'd never read, boxes of candy she'd never eat, and flowers that would wilt away with her. I'd slip down to the snack bar or cafeteria when she had visitors. Paul joined me over a cup a coffee and for one of those off-the-record kind of chats later that day. He said he reviewed her recent test results and there was no chance she'd recover, and she could go at anytime. He also said that often folks will hold onto life until a special day has passed, and then ease themselves into dying with those lasting happy memories in mind. I told him I was certain that's what my mother had done. She fought death on her terms, and won the one battle that was most important to her—while all the time knowing the long war for life had been lost. I thanked him for making it possible for her to win that meaningful last battle her way.

I didn't want to see her like this—this frail, colorless shell she was now—so thin and weak. I didn't want to feel her suffering—seeing her eyes dulled with pain. I didn't want to be cheerful and smiling and lie to her that everything will be just fine—believing somehow she'd get better, that wasn't a hope anymore, because now I knew believing she'd get better was a lie I was telling myself. I knew all of the enlightened rational kind of thought stuff would not make what was happening be any different. I guess I too, had clung to the small lingering hope that being home for Christmas would renew her spirits and refresh her energy to continue her status quo fight. I wanted to believe that even with acknowledging the wonders of her one last Christmas, that this really wasn't her last Christmas, that she'd get better and everything would be just fine—but that's not how things were happening. The cold hard fact was, my mother was at death's door, and maybe she was even knocking to come in from the pain.

Shit!!! All that stuff about it not hurting was blowing me away. That one small sparkle of hope was gone and I knew it was only a matter of time before she'd be gone too. I wanted to be gone too!!! I didn't want to see her die. All those visions I'd conjured up about those happy Christmas spirits coming to keep her safe so the grim reaper wouldn't carry her off was just more mind-shit of my making. Fuck it all . . . seeing her lingering into dying isn't for me. I did my part, I had helped make her Christmas at home possible, I didn't want to believe this Christmas really would be her last one. I guess I was like Nancy, thinking that one of those Christmas miracle healings would happen and she'd recover and her cancer would go into remission, and next Christmas we'd all be together again and laugh about how she beat death's hand with a royal flush!!! And away goes cancer down the drain!!!

Fuck death!!! I knew death . . . been there and done that. Slipping away from Mr. Death several times, each time he thought he had me, I'd slip out of his deadly death-grip. I also looked into the face of a man as I strangled his life away in defense of my own life. He tried to gut me with a knife that got caught on my belt buckle. I stared into his eyes as life left his body. Decades later I can still see his death mask haunting me as a visiting nightmare. Horrible to be up close and personal that way—to bring death to another. How many times had I played at war games in my youth??? Blasting away at pretend foes with cap pistols 'killing them dead' with make believe bullets finding the mark on pretend enemies. But 'tis way different to snuff out the life of another with your bare hands, feeling his last act of pissing soaking through my pants to run down my leg, his last exhalation of foul breath in my face!!! Oh, all those unknowing folks who talk in such a flip manner about killing someone. They have no idea what killing leaves behind as ghastly disturbing nightmares in the mind of the survivor.

Oh, I don't want to be there when my mother dies away. I don't want to take away her dignity when she voids away her shit and pees in passing. I don't want to see her sparkling eyes go dull with the mask of death upon her face. I'd done my part, helped as I could, time for me to avoid being there for the death bell to toll grimly. I could just beg off from being there, make up an excuse of just not wanting to be part of her deathbed gathering. Ugh!!! Now I was in an anguish of my own making, because I knew that no matter what was happening with me, my mother was always there for me—and I knew deep inside I had to be there for her now. If I cut and run, would her spirit haunt me forever??? Tauntingly asking me why I had forsaken her in her time of greatest need??? With no forgiveness, for I'd know leaving her now was wrong—so very wrong to steal away and leave her alone at the steps to death's door.

Thus, I returned to my mother's hospital bedside. Bringing my smiles of love for her. Hopeful she wouldn't notice me crying deep inside and the burden my heavy heart carried. "Yes, mother," I softly whispered to her as I lovingly kissed her pale cheek, "I'm here with you. Right here beside you."

"I'm glad you are here, Johnny," she said in a very weak voice, "I was afraid you'd have to go somewhere and now I need your strength to help me get through this, and to help your father and sister after I . . . ah . . . after I go away. Oh, Johnny, please hold my hand."

I took her hand in mine. I felt the frailness of her touch, I felt the struggle of her energy still fighting a winless war, I knew the pain she was feeling. Then I felt my energy flowing with her, joining with her energy, easing away some of her pain. I felt the harsh coldness of the creeping cancer, felt the icy stings slipping right through my energy flow, there was no stopping this army of marching death from killing off the life spark of each healthy cell the spreading plague touched from within.

The following days collapsed into a visiting hour vigil by her bedside. As friends and relatives came and lied about how good she was looking, how she'd soon be better, and asking about the next cruise she'd be going on—perhaps to Bermuda. Saying all those trite things other folks think you want to hear when you are sick in a hospital bed. The minister from her church came to make a bedside clerical visit. I suppose ministers grow accustomed to seeing people about to die. He asked if she was ready to make her peace with the Lord. She told him that she had made her peace and thanked him for the kindness of his prayers. After he left she said she had made peace when she asked for her gift to be able to be home for Christmas. She said that usually the good Lord has a deaf-ear to her prayers, but thankfully, this time her prayer was answered. Indeed it was, because 'twas fate that had Paul in his office when I called him. Paul had told me a minute later, and he'd have been gone from his office and out of the hospital to attend a meeting at another hospital across town.

My mother's lifeflows became weaker. When I held her hands I could feel less and less of her energy in flow. Her life support systems were closing down. She'd drift in and out of being awake, and at times she seemed to be in a coma with shallow breathing. Her visitors were now limited to immediate family. She seemed to be more into a comatose place than restfully sleeping. I could reach inside her when I held her hands, and feel her lingering life spark slowly waning away.

In the middle of the afternoon of the Saturday after Christmas in 1984, I relieved my father from his bedside vigil so he and my sister could go out away from the hospital and have an early dinner. Mother had been in a coma since late Friday morning. Again I felt her low energy, sitting there holding her passive hands. They felt so cool in my hands. Her remaining energy was tangled with rages of cold prickling pain. I knew I was reaching her, I knew she sensed my presence, my warm energies trying to pull her free from the pain one last time. "Hear me, my mother, know I'm here with you, here for you, lean on me, flow free of your pain . . . " were my thought flows.

Suddenly I felt her life flows of energy increasing, stronger and stronger. Her energy was building, breaking free of the grip of the cancerous pain. I felt uplifting joy, believing she was coming out of her coma, that she'd be awake when my father and sister returned from dinner. I was happy they'd have a chance to talk with her again. Her energy was stronger than when I first held her hands in energy flows days ago. From somewhere deep inside her being, she was massing her energy anew. I could feel all of her energy regrouping free of all the pain she had been battling with. My energy mingled with hers so naturally, in the easy natural bonding of mother and son. Now I again felt joyful hope in believing her special Christmas miracle was truly coming to be. Somehow, she was tossing off the choking cancer, flowing free of the pain.

Now in a surging instant, I felt her energy leaving her body, leaving her body completely, shedding her now pain ridden shell. And then I knew, at that very moment, she was passing over into the afterlife of being, and I was with her, with her as the twinkling miracle of death cut her free of all the pain. She was making her trip to merge with the light, as I followed along in astral flight with the very essence of her godspark moving onward to the light . . .

"Mother, mother, can you hear me???" I called lovingly.

"Oh, Johnny, let me go, I'm free, I'm finally free of all the pain, and I'm in a beautiful place, please, don't make me come back . . . " she pleaded.

"I'm with you mother . . . right here with you . . . "

"Oh no, Johnny, no, you didn't die too???"

"No, I'm alive, mother, I'm in astral flight with you."

"Oh, I know about those out of body experiences."

"Yes, mother, astral flight. I was doing a healing with your energy when it was your time to return to the light, I'm just flowing along with you for part of the way, mother, and I've been here before, and soon I must go back to my body."

"I remembered that night when you were 6 or 7, and so sick in the hospital and the doctors said you wouldn't live until morning. Were you here then???"

"Yes, mother, I was, and came back."

"And you got well, when we thought you were dying."

"Something happened. I think the illness just ran its course. I was able to come back into my body after my flight and my high fever had dropped to normal."

"You're able to go back now and give your father and sister messages from me???"

"Yes, mother, I can do that."

She gave me parting special words of farewell and private messages for them both, as we flowed closer to the light. Then came the time for me to turn back. I'd been given the extraordinary gift of seeing her safely on her way, free from the pain, free of the fearful unknown of what awaits, and now seeing her flowing ever onward to the eternal light.

"Oh, Johnny, I never thought it would be like this . . . "

"Mother, there's lots more to enjoy and see, and now I must go back to my earthly bonds . . . "

We shared our special magnificent moments of closure, a moment of reflecting that it was only she and I when she birthed me into the world—my father was off fighting WWII, and now at the ending of her birthline we are together again—just she and I, like it was at the beginning of my birthline so many long decades ago. My mother and I having a glorious prolonged moment of knowing pure love—free of all those tainting conditions humankind needs to define and bind love with. And a magical moment when we parted and we both looked at each other for one last time in the light, love, and peace of being as one in the universal beauty of the light. This was the true marvelous greatness of her parting gift to me.

I returned from my flight, to the here and now place of her parting. I looked at her shell, empty of her being, her eyes dulled by death passing, her hands cooling like the earth cools when the sun has set. I fondly folded her arms across her chest, gently closed her eyelids, tenderly kissed her on the forehead, and pushed the call button for the nurse. I looked out the window and saw the last golden rays of the setting sun in the western sky. The nurse and an attending physician came in, they examined her, and I told them her time of death was at sunset. I asked to stay here in the room with her until my father and sister arrived back from dinner. I didn't want them to return to an empty room and find a freshly made bed.

As I sat there with her remains in the quiet of the empty room, I thought of all the remainders she left with me. Like her always reminding me to put the toilet lid down and flush, be considerate of others. Clean your messes up as you go along, and don't leave the mess for someone else to clean up, be considerate of others—but mother, I didn't leave that dish in the living room!!! If you can't say something nice about someone keep your mouth shut, be considerate of others. Always give the right answer to the correct question, be considerate of others. Don't ask a question if you don't want a truthful answer, be considerate of others—but mother, you always look beautiful in every new dress. Be kind to dumb animals, they are usually smarter than we believe they are, be considerate of others. Don't lay down with dogs, you'll get up with fleas, be considerate of others. Don't put the dog out just because company is coming, be considerate of others. Don't put on the airs to impress others, that's inconsiderate of you and to them, always be yourself and be considerate of others. Yack-it-tee-yack, don't talk back, be considerate of others. Do a good deed to help another and a good deed comes back to you, do them a good deed without your needing to let anyone know you helped them and those good deeds smile with you from within, be considerate of others. Do a wrong to another, and worse wrongs will befall you, be considerate of others. Be your own best friend, if you don't like yourself it is difficult for others to like you too, be considerate of others. When you find joy in your work there is more enjoyment working, be considerate of others. A kind word costs nothing, but 'tis worth its weight in gold, be considerate of others. A penny saved is a penny earned, and pennies add up to dollars, be considerate of others. Sugar catches more flies than vinegar, sometimes eating crow is a very sweet dish that has to be eaten when you make a mistaken judgment of others, be considerate of others. Don't mistake lust for love, or confuse romance with love, with love there is just love and nothing more, be considerate of others. Be considerate of others, avoiding the messes of inconsiderate people when possible, and when you can't avoid the messes, then be considerate of yourself and avoid those harmful inconsiderate people.

Alone with lingering remains. The remainders of thoughts dancing through my head. Lingering remains of the afterdeath. The afterbirth is tossed after birthing, however, the afterdeath remains are the sparkles from their being that stay to brighten your godspark. The afterdeath is felt in the lasting light of godsparks glowing from the kindness of their touches that now remain. That's the fulfillment of the true promise of an ever lasting life of light, love, and peace for humankind . . .

My father and sister arrived from having dinner, and I hugged them both and told them she had passed on gently. Then I stepped out of the room to be considerate of their alone time with her. Soon my father came out and wanted to know if she had come out of her coma at the end. I told him what she had told me to tell him, and did the same with my tearful sister as they switched places in the room.

When my father was alone with me, he told me I *should have* come and gotten him. Always with the *should* thing!!! My father *could have* known that was impossible to do!!! I tried to tell him about her ease in parting, but his anger and pride kept him from hearing anything. 'Tis the twists and turns of the ego that gets in the way, the pride of keeping up appearances that turns life so fake and phony, and then the only realness that's left is the *faking it* for others. Who knows what is real, and the fall that happens when you are unable to reach out for help—when reaching out wouldn't be keeping up appearances, when help has strings attached, and the fear of hidden agendas, and the gifts still have price tags on them even if those prices can't be seen. That's how non-relating is in competing inter-actions. When relating is an endless quest for always topping the other in abusive competitiveness . . . a few of the remains from my father so woefully left with me. I'm grateful for non-competitive ways of relating my mother taught me.

We parted to grieve in our own separate ways. I called a friend and asked if she felt like celebrating enjoying life with me that night. My personal way of balancing the losses from death, with the primal joys of reaffirming the enjoying of life. Shedding the what isn't any more, and embracing the here and now of what is joyous and so very lustfully alive.

I met my father and sister the next morning at the undertaker's parlor. 'Arrangements' had to be made. Selecting the casket to hold mother's earthly remains. The softness of the pillow for eternal slumber, matching the lining, as if it all that material fluff mattered. Sadly, materialistic trappings do matter so much to the living, the survivors, their way of believing that a comfortable resting container and a plot with a view are essential for honoring the departed. Sad how some folks are honored far more in death than they were when they were alive.

I believe the tradition of having a viewing is a carry over from the days when viewing the deceased was proof positive that they were indeed dead—when premature burials were a bit of a problem. The viewing afforded an opportunity to pay last respects, and unload the burdens of all that couldn't be said face-to-face when they were alive—their shells got in the way, and now all that remains is an empty shell.

The viewing for my mother was very well attended with all the expected relatives, her lifetime of many friends and coworkers from the Dairy Queen where she worked for many years as a cashier. Especially noticeable, were about half a dozen single men who had arrived early and lingered until the last of the mourners were leaving. My father told me they were most likely customers my mother knew from the Dairy Queen. Nope, I knew my father was wrong in the conclusion he jumped to. They were plainclothes police officers, thinking that the elusive 'hit man' might make an appearance after he read about my mother's obituary in the local newspaper. I was the dangling bait. Thankfully, he was a no-show and the funeral services weren't disrupted.

The next morning, many of the same mourners gathered again for the funeral procession and graveside service. The minister had asked if anyone from the family would like to say a few words as part of the service. I said that I would like to speak. I instantly got a glaring look from my father. That kind of look that spoke in volumes, the look that said he wasn't happy that I wanted to speak, but he wasn't going to say anything and make a scene—not now. But if I knew what was good for me, I'd withdraw my request to speak, and I'd definitely hear more from him about it later—that ever present *when I get you home* threat. One of his beliefs was to leave the speaking parts to the professional speakers, and that's what my father was surely thinking. The unspoken contest of competing wills continued on unabated even in front of my mother's open coffin. For me it wasn't a contest, I was determined to speak for my mother.

The minister address was long-winded with well meaning words tailored to eulogize a lady he scarcely knew with big words not at all befitting of my mother. He scattered about a few over used Bible verses about parting souls in concluding. I spoke briefly with simple words, betelling of her mothering love in caring for us all . . . I spoke of her teaching us to do for ourselves and to make do with what there is and not whining about what isn't . . . I spoke of her joys in sewing, knitting, and making and painting all her ceramic *dust-catchers* . . . I spoke of her inventiveness in making delicious meals out of leftovers that never seemed to taste like leftovers . . . I spoke of her mild mannered consideration for one and all and never speaking ill of anyone, and how she wouldn't want her friends mourning her passing in the weeping ways of sorrow, because she had left all the pain behind her and was enjoying the ever lasting promise of light, love, and peace . . .

The funeral procession wove through the city's busy byways, one last slow passing along the streets she knew so well. Finally arriving at the cemetery where a freshly dug grave awaited as the final resting place for the casket and the remaining shell, cold and empty of her life—ashes to ashes, dust to dust . . . and life goes on . . .

Thus, with my saga of sharing with you my dear mother's parting gifts, her treasured gifts increase in value, because a gift freely shared increases the value of giftings. Perhaps I've been able to bring you a few smiles, maybe some tearful thoughts to reflect upon as loving memories from another time, and maybe a slightly different way of thinking about this holiday season called Christmas—beyond the commercialized glitz and glitter of empty gifts in pretty wrappings. Maybe you'll take a pause for recalling the simple joys of the season, the natural warmth of human kindness in the symbol of the brightly burning Yule log, and the good cheer with a gathering of merry spirits lifting high our hopes in what appears to be the darkest hour of winter, for now the days are getting longer as the sun returns to warm mother earth. Precious is the gift of self—precious and few are times shared free from our fears. Bright blessings upon you one and all, my friends. Light, love, and peace be with you.

Take care and enjoy often . . . John

ROMANCE VS LOVE

If Romance be the burning emotions
blistering the heart into a heated ember;
then Love be the motions of shining energies,
tenderly flowing merging godsparks aglow.

Romance is a fire that's hot and raging,
and all consuming and demanding of personal fuel;
while Love is the enlightening light of the flames,
the natural warmth and comfort from the bright fire.

Romancing hearkens awake with clanging clinging bells,
bursts of fireworks exploding in loud booms and bangs
announcing emerging mutations in unification,
fixated fabrications of fragile fantasies prodded together.

Loving fondly plays a medley of harmonizing tunes,
zestfully strumming a merry melee in rapturous jubilation,
of resounding reverberations from a bottomless cornucopia
flowing forth with delighting symphonies of sweet loving.

Romance blows into being like a whirlwind,
huffing and puffing all around *beloved* objects,
fearing rejection, wooing woeful worries,
inflaming excruciating insecurities
with the ominous ultimate ugly threat of leaving
when everything isn't just as expected to be,
romancing comes into blaring being in an instant,
and often goes far away just as quickly in a whimper.

Love is a shining beacon in the dark of night,
steadfast and true through all kinds of weather
helping to guide the ways into safe harbors,
adapting with the adjustments for time passages,
free of fears and worries about delusions
and no hanging about lurking ultimatums.

Romance is often a sequence of *put-on, put-out, put-up,*
with *put-ons* come best seductive courtship appearances
causing *put-outs* and *hooking-up* together to transpire,
and then the *put-upping* with all that follows thereafter,
coping with, status quo-ed, endured ensuingly evermore,
so dingingly different than once done in idyllic courting.

Love is openly aligning, accepting, and attuning,
discovering alignments in sincere beliefs and values,
experiencing unconditional acceptance and accepting,
evolving through life changes with learning attunements,
flourishing to enjoy harmonies in the freedom of the light,
doing love, free of the expectations of undoing themselves.

Romancing brings the risk of souring life into bitterness with
perceptions of somebody's done somebody wrong
when differing values clash in crashes of thundering rumbles
turning blue skies gloomy black with raging irate storms.

Loving is letting the realness of being different shine,
for within those differences dwells the uniqueness of us all,
doing love sparkles your unique goodness more brightly.

Romance frequently has a *Hollywoody* scripted plot
that's full of anticipations to follow threadbare story lines,
filled with expressed expectations to be met on cue,
and when words and doings aren't done just so in accord,
then comes disappointment and crushing critical discord,
when what had been once written to entertain on screen
fails to make the transition from make-believe fantasy
into the ever changing tides of living real life.

Love is like sparkling fireflies in free flight,
venturing out with the heavenly shade of coming twilight,
willfully winging about upon gentle night breezes,
dancing lights twinkling as minute star fragments,
points of speckled light upon a midnight blue sky . . .

. . . but once captured and contained in a glass jar,
the magic of their inner glows soon fades away,
entrapped into dying a slow suffering death
until pulled free in their passing to rejoin universal flows.

Romance is a distorted image on a silver screen
where more often than not, nothing is as it seems to be,
appearances are but painted faces upon a painted stage,
so quickly their plastic smiles come off once off-stage,
projecting fleeting appearances to peering peers,
phony living organisms faking orgasms,
cloaked in heavy costumes of darkness
covering completely the silver-lining within,
entangled in mixes of ever changing story lines
mirroring imaginary illusions,
merely tainted delusions diluted of life.

Love is letting the realness of being true grow,
extending naturally beyond pretentious appearances
into the naked reality realm of being truthfully real,
free of trappings styled in conforming molded plastic,
unhampered by restrictive shrouds that bring frowns,
enjoying life as a continuous intimate experience,
always unfolding with new wonders to behold,
free to joyfully share openly with others,
and equally free to cherish close to self.

Romancing compels measuring, questioning,
How much do you really 'love' me???,
producing declarations of unrealistic proving spans,
like, *as deep as the ocean!!!*, some will foolishly say,
as if love's actual depth might be possible to measure!!!

Loving is impossible to measure
when love is freely growing,
and the answer to the magnitude of flows
is clearly reflected in the brightness
of the godsparks, glowing naturally,
free of imposed comparing measurements.

Romancing is getting a small piece of a diamond rock
all set and mounted on a finger ring,
a dinging thingy to show off fake sparkles,
to gather up the envious awes of others,
and to glitter in fashionable flashes of false security.

Loving avoids threatening rocks,
steering clear of greedy harrowing hazards,
navigating past jagged jealous jeopardies,
rolling upon the free flowing waves of life
as silky smooth as faultless pearls roll about.

Romancing teases bogus warm fuzzies into being
that get kind of kinky with tangled jealous snarls,
all clingy with the dull dings of snapping static,
nasty noises in prelude to going off in a dingful funk,
dinging away once pleasing fuzzies into wasn't's.

Loving eases along with the easy joys of warm fuzzies,
enjoying the happening of exchanges in playing,
singing off key with jolly merry laughter,
free to let your hair down and be as silly as you please,
nice and easy does the wonderful warming doings,
so pleasingly endearing and long lasting.

Romance tends to get all fixed into set ways of not doing,
ways that become so rutted and taken for granted,
that leads into believing that nothing will ever change,
that all things are going to be as they are right now,
now in the same endless cycle of being tied together,
never changing with the flows of life now frozen in time,
where changes are seen as threats to the myth of security.

Love is always changing with renewable flows
that are as endless as refreshing gentle breezes,
shifting the eternal changes in the sands of time,
changes that flutter with benefits on the wings of love,
benefits that enrich life experiences in countless ways
that are always growing in all ways and open for sharing.

Romance restricts with crude lines drawn in the sand,
locks and heavy chains get clicked into place,
and high forbidding walls get built all around,
securing all in, while keeping everything out
in wasted efforts to abate the perpetual passing of time,
time slowly rusts away locked chains and crumbles walls.

Love is flowingly fluid,
waxing and waning and waxing again,
constantly feeling the unspoken certain knowing
of undefined ongoing caring with open sharing,
sometimes the flows are those of gratefully giving,
at other times so appreciative in accepting receiving,
with no tiresomely totaled tallies needed for keeping
of who did what, or when, or why in the tides of love.

Romancing brings crushed and broken hearts,
and shattered dreams as illusions come to light,
weepy tears of anguish from memories of bygone days,
from promises and pledges made in the heat of passion,
tossed away like used tissues stained with sorrows.

Loving tenderly opens up hearts,
and builds upon shared dreams in the daylight,
tears of joys and happy times fill each new day
with lots of new enlightening experiences,
and in kindred spirits of lingering merry memories.

Romance twists *love* all about,
and tangles *love* up in provoked perverted greed,
feverishly wanting this and expecting that in just the very same
fiction fashion as others appear to be doing so *romantically*
upon the formulated pages of *romance novels*,
where cunning novelists craft *romantic love* so perfectly.

Love flows over inevitable imperfections
and fades dinging funks away with understanding,
accepting that the future has not been written,
and whatever will come to be will be.

Romance abruptly concludes at the end of the last chapter
when the final page is turned to blankness.

Love is the never ending story of enjoying life
shared in growing love together ever mindful.

Romance carries the ambiguous allure of forever and ever,
and the dreaded end of forever is for ever a day away.

Love is the here and nowness brightening each new day,
and the ongoing caring and sharing along life's pathways.

Loving is the finest enjoying in life.

Take care and enjoy often . . . John

Love-cycles . . . waxing and waning

In the beginning there is new awareness…
when traveled paths do merge together…
fortuitous findings along their ways…
fateful contacts made in passing…
perhaps as a chance encounter…
or an arranged introduction…
merry they are having met…
cheerful they are upon…
this joyful first day…
of their friending…
to know more…
about each…
other!!!

Connecting with another so appealing…
sparks explorations of commonalties…
sorties soaring into formation flight…
delighting in discovered likeness…
of mirroring shining simulations…
dancing ageless mating steps…
enchanted by the illusions…
becomingly so charming…
awesome allurements…
probing possibilities…
cunningly courting…
conniving cheers…
come catch me…
if you dare…
you can!!!

Fateful acting occurs when waxing together is happening…
all kinds of interactions come about with waxing flows…
with surging passions heating up and melting waxes…
as hot fluids delightfully mingle and merge together…
sealing together their current fated engagement…

Courting time--when the best parts are shown…
only desirable aspects seem to be seen now…
confusing floating upon new blissful airs...
with stretching to walk upon tippy toes…
being careful not to step on anything…
or break eggshells or ruffle feathers…

They're into playing scoring cards…
seemingly so charming and witty…
staying clear of touchy topics...
that would blemish touches…
or conclude the beginning...

Tender touches reaching...
to touch another anew...
new to sharing touch...
and new to sharing...
sharing touches...
way touching...
as touches...
knowing...
all again...
brand...
new!!!

Their illusions are making new enchantments…
weaving silky smooth webs so enticingly…
woefully telling all those little white lies…
which is what are longed to be heard…
hollow words ding in empty minds…
casting about half-truths so easily…
avoiding touchy rejection topics…
by doing way fancy tap dancing…
dazzlingly avoidance footwork…
falsehoods begetting falseness…
believing in: *all is fair in love…*
and in war!!! all is fair game…
'tis only a game now in play...

The battle between the sexes…
wagged by doing deception…
so very cunningly contrived…
continues on taking victims…
pieces of shattered hearts…
tossed so carelessly upon…
the blazing funeral pyre…
ashes of absent truths…
blown upon the wind…
from raging flames…
waxing long melted…
burns so painfully…
as fullness wanes…
into the darkness…
of bumping into…
ill-fated finds…
passing ships…
ill courtships...
floundering...
in tears of...
sorrows...
unsaid!!!

The Hunters

Hunters play at courtship to only partake of the game…
ever questing to capture more fascinating trophies…
each more challenging than the last one taken…
crafting skillful plans for another conquest…

With a whiff of those new alluring scents…
their conquering chase does begin again…

Sadly, hunters only catch and skin…
leaving the fallen meat to spoil…
where it was savagely taken…
and so quickly, so forgotten…

Except for those trophies…
mounted wall-hangings…
tagged 'n neatly nailed…
to the show-off wall…
captured in time...
forever empty...
of meaning...
for one...
and all…
to see...
gotten...
prizes...
never...
more!!!

The Teasers

Teasers are indeed a most tormenting bunch of players…
enticingly flirting in tempting ways to gain attentions…
provoking prodding returns to expand fascinations…

Doing their dance of the moth drawn to the candle…
bolder flirtations fanning burning passions high…
bantering about building up blazing encounters…
reaching in closer to elusive alluring delights…
almost touching flickering fantasy flames…
coming ever nearer, and yet so very far…
until just about first touching happens…
quickly they so teasingly pull away…
their ongoing jesting continues on…
engrossing tauntingly consuming…
passions pull the orbiting moth…
fanning daring flames brighter…
licking ever nearer the moth…
catching frail wings ablaze…
crashing dive into the wick…
extinguishing all passions…
into cold empty darkness…
with no touches known…
of feelings left undone…
only as passing teases…
never anything more…
all gone, nevermore...
it was nothing but a...
now passing teasing...
a fancy displeasing...
and nothing more...
now gone away...
parting teases...
lingering in...
a darkness...
so empty!!!

The Gods & Goddesses

Gods and goddesses are those beings who seem perfect…
floating into empty loveless lives as being godsends…
in all appearances they are ravishingly so dazzling…
expressing themselves with enchanting charms…
all shined up with their seductive perfections…
a faultless manifestation of a dream-lover…
as if stepping from romantic novel pages…
awesome on down to the minutc dctails…
in creating the perfectly ideal illusion…

All to soon a fleeting fantasy persona…
fading as their human imperfections…
soon show through fronted facades…
as the perceived perfection myths…
do pale with reality's awareness…

When the once illustrious beings…
are now seen as merely humans…
not at all perfect as once seen…
by seers who saw reflected…
illusions as those fantasies…
of only make-believings…
made dreamful perfect…
so they could never…
be perfect in reality…
because they are…
impossibilities…
as impossible…
as reveries in…
perfections…
not to be…
known...
in real...
life!!!

The Whiners

Whiners are into bemoaning all their ill-fated experiences…
blowing into lives of others with tales of so woeful plight…
playing pitiful pouting pulls so often deeply depressing…
ensnaring are the ways of their sorrowful expressions…
quick to cast blame and guilt about what befalls them…
telling of self-imposing insecurities besieging them…
wearing scornful tally marks of bad sorrows done…
deadly recounting of retained messy negativities…
insecure with themselves they quest to discover…
erroneous measures of security within others…
latching on, to try to amass some wholeness…
dependently locking upon others valuation…
to appease their ever lurking insecurities…
whining all about anything they believe…
to be different than how they wanted…
perceiving changes to be threatening…
to their fragile way of non-relating…

They constantly seek reassuring…
attentions via manipulations…
craving contrived controls…
with unhappy bewailings…
of finding dubious faults…
pointed fingers blaming…
'tis their negative ways…
crying over spilt milk…
making more messes…
with negative vibes…
pushing joys away…
with the self anger…
about whatever…
they're certain...
ain't right, but...
in their world...
nothing is...
ever right!!!

The Pretenders

Pretenders are into pretending to be what they aren't you see…
shape shifting into forms they want you to see is their game…
saying all those words longed to be heard at proper times…
playing beguiling mind games to steal lonesome hearts…
'tis only mind-messing playing-at-love for pretenders…
acting as the world is but a stage as we all play parts…
actors with scripts in hand—some autobiographical…
reflections of self in the truthfulness of playing self…

When playing self projects to be overwhelming joy…
acting transcends into expressing reality essences…
self-image reflections are shining esteems aglow…
pretense pales as pure tenderness babbles about…
the star has won a life-time staring role playing…
themselves upon the many life-learning stages…

Reading for many parts in life's trying parts…
feeling aches from push-away rejections…
knowing joys of welcomed acceptance…
becoming truthfully so self expressive…
wherein their newly found roundness…
honest open awareness does bubble…
now flowing freely--make-up free…
and letting unlimited outflows…
to become possible to again…
ringing out freedom joys…
in jubilant harmonies…
betelling alignments…
with truthfulness…
of your being…
being you…
truly you...

Pretending...
nevermore!!!

The Gifters

Gifters are into waxing up shines with glittery giftings…
endowments invested in material reality trappings…
far beyond consumable airs of creature comforts…
away from needfully nurturing nursing caring…
surpassing playful gifts of simple surprises…
entangling by snagging gifted expectations…
with those bestowed being ever beholding…
to the gift-giving strings that do bind ties…
disguised as givings linking heartbeats…
but chaining hearts together materially…
imposed gift-controls and rent is due…
time comes to pay ado to the piper…
tap dance to the tune being played…
inter-actions with price tags fixed…
three smiles for one mere dollar…

Sadly, the kindness becomes overwhelming…
each new doing unmeasured in non-values…
of gifting debits and credits are all tallied…
as insincere expressions of the giftings…
do expire upon old spreadsheet pages…
devoid of enjoying upon bedsheets...
gifts with affixed expectations…
yielding diminishing returns…
unappreciated gifting efforts…
once freely given/accepted…
now are withdrawn away…
open offers are declined…
once controlling strings…
are no longer governing...
leaving timeline marks…
of unmet expectations…
unappreciated efforts...
as empty gift boxes...
was the heart in gift…
or was gift in mind...
as expectations???

Alas...
godspark...
giftings indeed...
glow ever onward…
ever brightly delighting…
the smiling giver enjoying…
joyous receiver in blissfulness...
karma gifts coming around again…
flowing gifts of the universe arriving...
in timely fashions just when needed to be...
totally string free of conditioning restrictions...
'tis impossible to restrict the glows of starlight...
always twinkling with the brightness of energies...
beacons of eternal light upon the vastness of space...
and the energies of all those infinite star bright points...
to span those far away distances to eventually touch us all.
Oh.
star
light,
star bright,
shinning so brightly for all in the darkness of the night.

The Seekers

Seekers are always searching for their right one-and-only…
as if someone somewhere out there is needed to bring…
them saving deliverance from their empty lonely life…
existing in a continuous searching and seek mode…
always looking for their *right* next-one-and-only…
to come into their fateful watchful tunnel vision…
their one totally perfect person who does it all…
or at least they seem to do it all at the time…
because seekers do continue on seeking…
believing their own perfect wholeness…
is in discovering parts of themselves…
in a mythical perfect completeness…
in linking with their one soul-mate…
saving salvation in another's soul…
two half-beings becoming whole...
two halves locking one-n-only...
soulfully all together forever...

Until the *Twelfth of Never...*
a completeness evermore...
in a state of being graced...
with their fated mating...
of perfect soulmates...
being completed in...
a completenesses...
soul-matedness...
paired souling...
soul-mated...
wholeness...
complete!!!

Until again there comes...
a coming of longing into their being...
lurking stirrings of incompleteness…
creeping into those who mated for soulfulness...
depending on another...
for their wholeness of being…

Now finding empty holes…
so defying in soulful fulfillment…
the void of self does remain…
missing big parts in heartbreaking pain…
from the painful perfection they endlessly seek…
to stop the pain in an empty heart…
beating out dinging hollow echoes…

At the inquest for the deceased soulmate…
held on the twelfth day in the month of Never...
death was caused by a mindless head…a missing heart…
a soul pulled apart...a life worn out of alignment…
foolishly questing after the wholeness of self-being…
in the fleeting attributes of another…

Too late…
they came to know…
the truth for self is deep within…
always self-aligning within us all…
and only self-truth grows wholeness…
and then from within your godspark shines…
shining brightly ever aglowing!!!

Love wanes when relating falls away into dingy discords…
once joyful exchanges succumb to enduring encounters…
whenever greedy expectations are painfully enumerated…
histories of shared experiences respun in rewritten bias…
now twisted to tell sorrowful woes done against them…
recounting darkened shades of hurtful love done 'em…
in endless dull litanies of distorted *I said's* dialogues…
of now turned about *you said's* mismatching *I said's...*
their recollection is clouded by their hurtful anger…
angry frustrations in their deep rooted insecurity…

Echoes from yesterday's you-done-me-so-wrong-songs…
aborting singing in joys of blissful present reverberations…
all mixed-up with unfulfilled ever dangling expectations…
as impossible to satisfy as were all those promises made…

Vowed when courting waxing shinings were being done…
carefully exploring ways for being mutually accepted...
what was jointly acceptable while doing fun wooing...
now brings about only harshly snapped put-downs…
once joyfully offered places for open fun sharing…
are crudely remarked, now being put off limits…
lines drawn in the sand as *no-go-there-zones…*

Venturing near keep-away areas only begets…
abruptly pulled-away and pushed-off no go…
extending their punishing insecurities anew…
echoing from deep within their pining past…
usurpingly turning back surging ebb-tides…
encompassing more not going to happen…
never ever to be done again any more…
then come demeaning sad echoes of…
angers in possessive greedfulness…
controlling non-doings undone…
all with blame and jealousy…
looking ever elsewhere…
when their problems…
linger within them…

Echoes do rumble afar…
clouding out shinings…
in the nowness today…
all blackened with…
pinging pines…
greedy echoes…
thunder bangs…
so far behind…
enlightening…
delighting…
lightning...

Oh, to be...
bright in the light...
to grow sparks of joy!!!

Weeds of not so pleasing sameness do creep in waning ways...
clouds of discontent form to block enlightening knowings...
lashing words snapped in frustrating anger sting deeply...
recanting stings by explaining them as nothing more...
than yelled in the heat of anger doesn't lessen hurts...
stinging hits kill dead all touched by raging angers...
posting anguish areas with zaps of warning wrath...
danger mine-field big explosions occur frequently...
snipping shots hit as slanderous put-down slams...
guilt gets laid about to place blame elsewhere...
rank with stinks of insecurities and jealousy...

True security only comes from self-worth...
imposing guilt isn't going to do nothing...
but make a yucky non-relating void...
guilt is guttless and self-demeaning...
and controllingly so very selfish...
jealousy is possessively greedy...
driving painful pointed stakes...
into another *being* to show...
their claim of ownership...
marked with repellent...
jaded greenish colors...
where no one shall...
ever venture into...
never again...
never more...
not again!!!

Strangle-holds of jealousy do drain away...
vital life flows into stagnate cesspools...
all that's left from jealous possessing...
is nothing more than an empty shell...
made hard and brittle from battles...
fought over jealous entanglements...
perceived to be very threatening...
forced to be sacrificed far away...
to try to save an ill-fated *love*...
biased by greedy insecurities...
fabricated to possess control...
refueled by fearful guilt trips...
imposed forced expectations...
trust tarnishes from infighting...
entrusted sharings get trashed...
tossed away into deep space...
controlled cold non-relating...
the remains of *selves* are...
only lingering memories...
from a bygone time...

All so regretfully sacrificed...
into securing a false union...
now empty of life's joy...
overwhelmed by hate...
inbred of greedy gluts...
unhallowed mating to...
possessive jealousies...
enraged expectations...
promises disclaimed...
forgiveness goes fleeting...
fleeing from fighting again...
foul, most foul fighting for love...
fouls love way most foully...
trying to keep trust lost...
in hateful fighting is...
like screwing for...
virginity!!!--one...
prick all gone!!!

Forgiveness...
is the first victim...
to fall dead away...
in each new raging fight...
those weary dying words...

forgive me...

are now unheard...
that absolution thingy...
didn't work to repair...
all the harmful hurts done...
the quick fix acts of contrition...
failed to bring continuing...
the fight is won by one...
the love is lost in both...

Unforgiven...
the relating dead gone...
love done all gone...
end of fight...
bell dings...
bye!!!

All alone...
wrapped in...
a tear stained...
blanket of insecurities...
so very cold...
so alone...
alone...
gone...

Love...
is for...
giving...
free in...
flowing...
knowings...
growing of...
awarenesses...
life experiences...
for sharing in kind...
with kind sharing folks...
alike in sincere openness...
aware of the truthfulness of...
their godsparks shining with the...
pure honesty in shared inner glowings...
free of guilt and free of possessiveness...
free of lines drawn upon the sands of time...
free of masks and chains that blind and tangle...
free from imposed expectation fulfilling sacrifices...
free to let you be you and me be me in loving flows...
free to share with life experiences from along this path...
free to trust that no harms be done between one another...
free in true feelings of self-esteem that are self sustaining...
free of rendered judgments as to approved good and evil...
free to live loving ways for giving and knowing kindness...
Love is also for...
your being accepted...
as you are right now...
in the here and nowness...
of you being freely flowing...
along with your being accepting...
of folks you are befriending with...
free from your imposed conditions...
save honoring each with self-truths...
No expectations for making changes...
free to be truthful with fluid openness...

Awesomely aligning...
Blissing in balancing...
Creating good cheers...
Dining on deliciousness...
Enjoying enhanced energy...
Flowing freely with freedom...
Gleefully growing so gratefully...

Happily humming in harmonies...
Inspired indeed in our individually...
Joyous accepting you just as you are...
Knowing we are all works-in-progress...
Life learnings are constantly changing us...
Moving with us begetting more experiences...
Naturally by knowing increasing awarenesses...
Open minds accepting and open hearts cherishing...
Pushed along with the ponderings of life happenings...

Quivering with the quintessential vibes of attunements...
Rejoicingly refreshing feeling sweet music reverberations...
Self-secure in discovering self-esteem comes from within...
Turning away from troubling strife, guilt and greedy hurts...
Understanding humankind's true uniqueness is differences...
Vibrations vibing differently do indeed mingle in harmony...

Woeful wrongs eventually are rebalanced by rightful flows...
X-raying for hidden agendas isn't a need--no hidden agendas...
Yearnings do become a joyful reality when shared with friends...
Zipping off the pulling strings and Zooming free in loving life...

There...
you have...
a different...
A B C's...
of doing love...
in ways of loving that's alive...

Love...
is for...
living...
joyfully...
aligning...
together...
accepting...
openness...
attunement...
forgiveness...
realigning to...
try again with...
more feelings...
free of harmful...
guilts and greed...

Love is a natural...
gifting of glowing...
godsparks' beauty...
shining reflections...
no smoke & mirrors...
nor judgment making...

Such attempts restrict...
and bring about harms...
heavy weights of chains...
to drag along their ways...
being watchful keeping all...
steps taken within the lines...

Love flows free beyond lines...
in enlightening gentle touches...
comforting with caring hugging...
tenderly blowing clinging grains...
of sandy grit from lost time-lines...

Love expands free of expectations...
security is built upon entrusted ways...
of honoring with the truth of godsparks...

knowing there isn't refuge in telling lies...
weaving sticky webs entangling everyone...

Yielding into freeing flows of truthful ways...
love is forgiving hurts done along the paths...
forgiveness is often bitter and sweet doings...
sweet be some of the fruitful learnings shared...
bitter when seasons in the sun bare no growth...
time for plowing under and seed the soil anew...

Loving flows are constantly waxing and waning...
forever aligning with fatefully eternal movement...
in the vastness of universal balancing interactions...
of dynamics between inflicting harm or sharing love...
differences between good and evil are so judgmental...
but harmful ways become known when wrongs be done...
and enjoying be known when comfy love is caringly shared.

Take care and enjoy often . . . John

CHOICES

Once upon a time,
a once upon friend had a heavy choice to make,
between the first path she played a part in creating and planning,
and an eclipsing second path with harmful ultimatums attached,
if not the one and only path she selected.

At times, life is like a series of twisting potential paths
of mixed-up experiences we learn from,
based upon the choices we made,
or sadly, we had some of those choices made for us.

Too often, with those choices made for you,
you discover too late, that the vital deciding phase
has long been done decided without your input,
especially with real or assumed ultimatums
slanting the deciding process that you're not involved in!!!

I've never had much use for doomful demands
because they have such a final ultimate ring to them,
containing those deadly stipulations that zap relating
into a fading history, if *this* or *that* expectation isn't fulfilled,
or *these* conditions aren't met just so.
When toys get gathered up in anger, there's no more joyful
playing together, and the shared joy has been rudely taken
away—dinged away in fits of funky anger!!!

Together choices, once reflecting commonalties of mindflows,
now go discoursing far away, in opposite courses
and following differing sets of values.

Viewing those choices from your perspective, you try to see be-
yond your frustrations, looking through the smoke-screen,
to ascertain where those differing paths of difficult choices
might take you—or leave you.

Pondering what reshuffling your values will cause to happen,
or will cease to be.

The question is: to yield to choosing the seemingly easier path
of least resistance—or not.
Having to carefully weigh which choice brings the least amount
of guilt and anger is a real bummer,
along with anticipating the hurt of your pain when the ultimatum
is rejected—especially when you've tossed the ultimatum.
Or the loss of self when the terms of deadly entrapment
are concededly acknowledged out of frustration,
and then parts of yourself start getting sliced off,
becoming mere bargaining chips in the gamc of love.
However, once surrendered, those missing parts of self are very
difficult to win back—the game is fixed.

Now some foolish folks expect and accept
surrendering of self as absolute proof of love,
mistakenly believing their *proving* self-sacrifices
will set their true course for loving together forever,
as more of the parts making up the uniqueness of self,
are tossed into the melting pot.
The bubbling brew cooking away to make an *'us'*.
Slowly the *'me'*, who once was a so alive *'me'*,
in the crazy so wonderful courtship phase is gone,
chopped, sliced, and reshaped to be fitted into an ensuing *'us'*.

Each imposed *proving* choice
snaps more possessive ownership locks into place,
once meaningfully chosen values fall by the wayside,
self-esteem goes slip sliding away too, and all too soon,
your zest for the choicest joys in doing life goes too,
except for *those approved gladness happenings,*
deemed acceptable to *prove* your *love.*
The structure of your relating isn't a relationship of living in love
with each other, but rather,
of having to always *prove* your love to the other,
or deal with their stinging anger in scornful funky screams.

Knowings of friends from your past,
once those friendships held values for you, are written off.
History gets rewritten to reflect that those now valueless *others,*

must have read way more into your once upon a time friendship.
Now they're nothing more than hollow hauntings,
things going bump in the cold night.

Fading memories are eclipsed by non-relating ultimatums,
much easier to believe there wasn't much of a loss
when previous choice devaluing is done,
making discarding whatever once had value, easier to toss off!!!
Good-bye to you my trusted friend . . .

Oh sure, lip service is given to retaining *special* friendships,
but sadly, those are only shallow words,
now so lacking in meaningful actions,
just as chance contacts in passing feel so vacant of substance.
It becomes clear that once dear friends are now only impositions,
devalued by obscuring creeping darkness
from your dinging ultimatum based choices.
There's no dancing in a buffalo herd, as the herd shuffles off.

A few lingering friends might echo back empty words
of happiness about your newly formed union,
echoing again all those choice trite phrases, so easy to say,
and so longed for by you to hear.

While true friends will continue to try to be expressive
without making judgments of you,
about their sincere grave concerns
of an ultimatum launched *love* relationship.

These common sense words are far harder words to say to dear
friends, and sadly, the pleading words are rarely ever heard.
Because, they aren't the confirming praises
for your new found relating that you want to hear.
Only friends who care enough, will say otherwise
about your self-destructive choices—but you hear them not.

Once a lady professed to being deep in a thoughtful place
for pondering her many frustrations about choices,

and from her tormented place, she did ask to be whacked upon
her cute blonde head,
if she ever got into such a negative way of being again,
that caused her not to be thinking clearly
about what she was really doing to herself.
But whacks on the head really aren't the positive course
for finding clear thoughts within ones self.

And hitting, even metaphorically,
smacks with the force an ultimatum, with a judgment being rendered about how she is or isn't thinking clearly.
The thinking needs to come from flows within,
breaking the shell to get out.

Sort of like a fertile egg evolving to hatch a fuzzy peep into life,
whack the shell from the outside, and the peep will never be.
But wait for the little critter to break the shell from inside
and then a peep coming into being you'll see.
When the time is right, then the peep inside, will come free.
Whacking only forces the here and now into premature being,
and the instant *ready or not* is deadly to the peep's well being!!!

Too often folks look to others to make hard choices for them,
collecting a committee's collective concurrence,
or at least to give their approval as an endorsement
to what's already been decided.
Just in case the new relating doesn't work out as planned,
then there's another—and perhaps others,
to share in the blame casting sing along,
with the choice gone wrong done wrong song. . .
somebody else, who once upon a time said,
that was the *right* choice for *you*.

Those who you wanted to say, *'I'm so happy for you'*,
now they're watching you cry in your beer,
because back then you didn't hear what all had been said,
and you wonder what they are doing here . . .
play me a song, piano man . . .

Here there is also the risk
of empowering the *collective* to say, *'I told you so!!!'*,
which is so unfriendly, unkind, nasty,
and way stingingly harmful, when what was shared in open trust
comes zapping back at you with cutting scorn,
because you didn't follow their offered counsel.
Their *I told you so* advice,
is now boldly highlighted in the harsh back-lighting of hindsight.
And in view of your disappointing non-relating outcome,
they may have been wiser then, but now their dumbness shows
with all their ego self-stroking unkindness.
Repeating once again, their generously given advice,
that wasn't followed as they said for you to do.
Woefully, they forget that you are the one—the only one,
who has to *do* the *doing*—not them!!!

The choice you *do* choose,
is the choice you believed was true for you—at the time.
Right or *wrong* 'tis hard to say and doesn't apply
to your choice—only what choice *fits* true for you.

The unique thing about choices is, there really aren't any
right or *wrong* choices—only choices!!!
What makes the joys or hurts happen with the flow of choices,
is the composition and consideration involved in your choices.

If I make a choice to buy a novel to joyfully escape into the adventure of the woven fictional plot,
I'm going to compose my time with due consideration being
given to reading the new book,
thereby enjoying my choice fulfillment.
Indeed a rather simple easy kind of a choice 'twas made.

Gets a wee bit complex when I make a choice to befriend you
for now the choice involves another,
another given consideration to my offering of befriending,
wondering about the ramifications entailed in being friends.
The success of your choice depends in part on another,
do they shine with you in growing a friendship,

or do dishonoring by breaking your offering,
tarnishing the roots of your extended trusts,
making once glad eyes sad.

Sad indeed is the loss of a trusted friend,
a choice gone astray in complications,
the complexity of changes . . . changing choices.

True, some choices are easier to live with than other choices.
Those choices filled with good feelings all the way around,
with no harm being done, accepting the balancing and harmony
that comes from combining positive choices—that's easy.

However, some choices cause sleepless nights,
not fun kinds of tossing and turning all night,
but as hauntings of harmful doings done as poor choices
flooding the near reaches of your unsettled insomniac mind.

From many broken choices hopefully comes helpful,
insightful awarenesses, to learn from the injuries
that came from those harmful choices.
Then, when the time comes again to reflect upon what the
choices you may have made, you might not be so quick
to make such an ill-fated choice so soon again—or not.

With other choices, there is the feeling of falling into an abyss,
plunging into the grim bottomless pit of ceaseless torments.
Thusly, when you find yourself spinning in such as endless fall,
you do have the perfect opportunity to try out all those sky-
driving moves during your long free-fall!!!

Some choices show you clearly who your true friends really are,
and who were phony friends, only befriending you for long as
you do exactly whatever they tell you to do,
and you believe everything, as they lead you to believe is so,
also, as long as you don't make any waves!!!

At times you find you do have the ability to rethink,
and kinda undo some of your choices.

While you can't turn back time, and change what's been done,
sometimes, you don't have to continue enduring a choice that's
turned into a major bummer,
a choice no longer ringing true for you,
nor do you need to carry your self-imposed burden of guilt
with you when understanding amends,
are perhaps possible to free you from ill done choices.

Guilt is the self-harming burden—lingering left-overs,
spoiling away with yucky green fungus growth and nasty stuff,
hidden in the back of your icebox of feelings,
chilled bristly cold hurts from ill-fated choices.
Everyone makes unwise choices now and then—'tis human.
And sometimes, you are able to just pick-up the pieces,
and take your shattered choosings to the *'re-choice department'*,
satisfaction . . . amendments . . . refunds . . . exchanges . . .
with proof of purchase and two forms of valid ID!!!

Here's where you may wisely learn from your mistakes,
your proof of purchase is the hurt you're feeling from
the harmful guilt you're carrying,
from your feelings of done others wrong stuff.
You *own* your fucked-up choices, you have proof of purchase
and you can sure as shit identify the hurts your choices did to
you by your broken heart . . . your stretched and worried gray
matter . . . the knot in your stomach . . . your shackles marks . . .
your nailed to the wall bloody guilt.

Letting go of your guilty is part of the learning the exchange
value for refunding your choice,
truthful amending may mend harms done, and mend yourself.
Crazy glue fixes broken hearts,
wrinkled gray matter betells wisdom earned,
knots and shackles have ways of working free.

Sometimes the choices of others produce very harmful actions
that are impossible to make amends for,

because they made their hurtful choices so very clear through their accumulated wrongdoings loaded with their inconsiderate ways of interacting.
Their wasteful choices have produced the heavy consequences that they now carry with them,
and the only one they have to blame, for the damage they've done to others, is themselves—the *devil* didn't make them do it, they did the all harm to themselves.
The hurtful harm they've heaped upon others will surely be their undoing, because those hurts are within them as bad karma.

Satisfaction gets confused with revenge and perfection,
there's no satisfaction in revenge,
only bad karma and more shit getting dumped.
True perfection is a myth, and questing faithfully for perfection never brings satisfaction—only more distress!!!
There's no satisfaction to be found in an illusion.
If your choice was to chase after perfection,
'twas a fool's errant—like trying to save time in a bottle.

Satisfaction is a settling of sorts,
an acknowledging that your choice didn't fit right,
the fit was wrong, too big or too little,
or the imbalances of values drained off way too much energy.
The joys and the hurts eventually will settle out
with an acceptable satisfaction of refunds.
Sure you got a lemon, but now you got your life back, and
the learning values from your blundering choice, plus interest!!!
There's a substantial interest penalty for early withdrawals!!!

There are two kinds of choices—not between *right* and *wrong*,
what's *right* for some is *wrong* for others and vice versa.
The difference is between what you *need* and what you *want*.
You *need* fresh water to survive and flourish with life,
but you *want* sparkling spring ice water from a pitcher!!!
The basic choice, is what you *need* to sustain your life and how those *needs* are fulfilled, are often defined by your *wants*.
Too often, the greed of our *wants* overwhelms our *needs* or the *wants* become a fixation of wanted choices usurping needs!!!

What blows folks away, is feeling they have no open options,
like having stupidly painted themselves into a corner,
caught in a trap of their making with nowhere to turn,
and no way out of those greedy *I want* choices.
The choices they've made or just went along with,
or choices made for them, under the guise of *for your own good.*
Sort of like *eat this, you'll like it*, when in fact, you won't!!!
Ugh!!! Yucky yellow snow!!!

The problem is, each choice imposed upon you takes away parts
of you being you, as you change to conform.
They reform you into the reformation of you,
being changed—changed into the befitting ways of others.
Changes happen that takes away the essence
of the uniqueness of your very being!!!
The *unique you* gets lost as you change to appease—appeasing
choice changes for the pleasures of others,
and they're not at all pleasing or pleasant choices for you!!!
More and more of you is slip sliding away,
surrendered in favor of being *loved—appeasing*.

And now, the once pleasing sameness of doing a loving life to-
gether, feels as empty as the shell you are becoming!!!
Your zest for joyful choices fades away.
Your options start to expire, your once bright ways of being you
are replaced by a darker shade of gloomy black,
and not the beautiful midnight blue kind of black either!!!
The *you* who once was *you* at the beginning of the relationship,
has been changed—changed by all those imposed choices,
choices made in the formation of the *us*,
and now the *us* that is—isn't an *us* containing much of the *you*
that once was—once upon a time in the west!!!

How ironic it is, when the one imposing their changes upon you
finally bemoans, that you aren't the same person they once knew
way back when you first met.
And now they ask where have your once active passions gone???
Where have all the flowers gone???
They ponder and wonder why—why have you changed so much,

becoming so strange like you are now!!!???
Who are you???

They never seem to understand that all those changes in you,
that they now find so very objectionable,
are all the changes they forced to happen by their imposed conditions . . . their commanding demands . . . their taunting funks of anger . . . their remaking!!!

Condemningly, they cry out in anger about how totally different you are—and so quick they are, to place all the blame for each of these changes upon you—you changed!!!

However, they have reshaped you into the illusion they wanted you to be for them, reforming you into their vision of you,
based an image of their own making that really wasn't you . . .
only an illusion in their mind of how they wanted you to be,
and what they wanted wasn't you as you were—or are!!!
Their fantasy doesn't fit . . . they must quit!!!

They slowly discover the empty you,
and they no longer want you anymore like you are.
Maybe they'll leave you—as they've threatened so many times before, in so many ways, about so many things.
Or maybe they won't leave—because of appearances . . .
for the sake of the children . . .
because there's no place to go . . .
because of what people will say about them.
Or maybe you just go on existing unhappily together,
out of the fear of being alone—alone is so scary!!!

Whatever happens, those flowing exchanges that once were,
are no more—nothing much is happening.
You aren't interacting in positive ways any more,
all that's left of you is a changed and reshaped shell,
and nothing more, nevermore.

Those long ago glowing passions have gone
into the cold deep void of non-relating—non-being,

mere figure-head couplings going through zombie like motions,
the once alive inner beings have gone elsewhere.
All that's left are empty shells, blown upon the winds of fate!!!

Alas, at least being blown by the shifting winds of fate is a wee bit better than getting fucked by the fickle finger of fate!!!

Sometimes, we foolishly make hasty choices based solely on
what everyone else is doing—or seems to be doing,
wiggling within wakes from chosen choice chasers,
following rushing tides—rushing to embrace the latest fad,
before what's the rage today turns into being so common
tomorrow—or the day after,
yielding to empty traditions found to be somewhat harmful,
but still we continue to follow . . .

So sad, when the only choice to do something or other in the same certain ways, is simply because, *everyone* else does it that same certain way, or because, that's how it has always been done forever and ever—and always will be done!!!

Oh my, just because that's how *its* always been done doesn't
make the doing *it* just that way right—or right for you,
especially when the doing becomes so trite,
only empty words of empty doing,
done that way so long in so empty ways!!!

Then too, we live in times of increasing choices in many areas,
as choices upon choices get compounded and expanded upon
into a vast array to select from,
with so many choices to choose from that the mind gets boggled
deciding with all the choices to decide about—rehashing which
of all those choices is the most perfect choice for you...???

That endless quest for attaining an illusive state of perfection,
impossible to achieve because, perfection is a myth!!!

Seeking perfection often leads to having seconds thoughts about
your decided selection.

A choice made in haste is often a poor choice.

Wasting lifetime, pointlessly pondering,
if a different favor or another style or a variation,
perhaps a different shade, would have been better for you,
so undecided about what choice to decide upon.

Slowly, the self-esteem of selecting for yourself is given away,
as you give way to doing what's popular to do,
doing whatever is faddish—you know, the *in* thing.

Eventually, you exhaust yourself by trying to run with the trend
setters—those popular famous people of momentary fame,
who decide *in* fads at a whim of their fleeting fancy,
when their endearing endorsement of almost any fad,
may be bought for cash in hand—and of course,
a percentage of gross sales!!!

Fleeting fads feel so phony and plastic,
way lacking in substance—but so *totally rad!!!*

Then today's *rad* choice becomes *un-rad* tomorrow,
like I said before—something else is *in fad* the next day,
and then gone too, just as quickly, as if it never came at all!!!
The cycle continues on and on, greased with slick marketing
plans . . . introduced with a scheduled release date,
all chosen to made a big splash, and fleece folks out of their cash
with all kinds of cons and ploys—skillfully crafted in fashions,
to attract the trendy pop-pack to the newest passing fad!!!
Always cycling one rad fad into the cycle of another fad,
like snakes eating their own tails, there is no ending . . .

Choices are always evolving within flows in continuous cycles,
bringing about countless changes in the courses of your life.
Some folks learn from the experiences their choices bring,
Such are the offensive ways of inconsiderate people who end up
eating their own tails—choking on their bitter bile.
Alas . . . beyond their foulness . . . life goes on.

A positive approach for trying to do relating choices,
is to let choices be freely made,
and not imposed with threats of ultimatums.

To see choices for their positive benefits,
and not something done to do harm to self and others.

So much self harm is a perceived fear that comes from greed,
from ingrown insecurities spinning into jealousy,
fearing all those choices made by other folks which don't involve them until they butt their nose into their business,
these actions are self harmful and very restrictive!!!

'Tis far more loving to come from an accepting place,
accepting the fact of life that we all have choices
to make—big and small ones.

What makes all the difference in ongoing relating,
is how needful choices are made,
and how the fruits of those choices may be shared with others.

Those *others* need to understand that not all choices are sharable,
and those non-sharable choices aren't nasty . . . or selfish . . .
or harmful to them.

'Tis fine to express concerns when a *free* choice feels like it is being imposed on you.
Win, lose, or draw, the final choice is entirely up to you!!!

'Tis you who lives with the choices you make,
you know the karma you take on and give off with your flow of choices made.

The *right* choice for you comes only from your being truthful
with yourself—others can't define self truths.
Deep inside your gut, you feel when your choices are flowing true for you,
and not an imposed childish choice that is being made for you!!!

At times, 'tis fine not to make any choice at all,
status quo is often a so far so good place for keeping your options open for giving ongoing consideration about what's happening—along with your open mindflows.

Looking with the applied focus of your developing mindflows
brings your choices into a positive perspective,
from your viewpoint of considering what you need
and how you see things to be,
then the choice you make from an informed and aware place
is truly your choice!!!

May the all of the choices you make do no harm,
and enable you to enjoy often!!!

Thank you,
for making the choice to read my long ramble,
take care, my friends,
and enjoy often . . . John

MATCHES... Light & Love

'Starry, starry night, paint your palette blue and gray...look out on a summer's day...' those words from the song *'Vincent'* by Don McLean, sort of brings to mind the contrasts that seems to happen when we quest for love mates. Those blues and greys are seen as so many of the negative vibes that we've encountered and felt so painfully, while trying to find our one true *love mate* who is *perfect*, as perfect as a beautiful summer day, for us to couple up and be together with forever and ever and ever after.

Questing ceaselessly, we search for the one twinkling star that shines brightest with a true love for only thee and thy. In the richness of the night, the midnight blue from the blended hues of blues and greys, are nothing more than the celestial background for trillions and trillions of sparkling stars. Each and every star does sparkle with the potential light of love for you, waiting to be known by you, and you, and you, and perhaps you too. However, all too often in our quest for that *one-and-only-forever* person to bring love into our lives, we begin to see *the beloved* as the only sun up above—bringing all of the sunshine in life.

With your beautiful loving sun radiating so brightly, the rest of the stars seem to fade away, yielding to the blinding sunlight. Until the heavenly shades of twilight are coming again, and once more stars glisten in the night sky. Starry, starry night comes into sight, with the enchanting light of love sparkling brightly once again at twilight time, when the setting sun surrenders its dominating light, and yields to the vast eternal beauty of the twinkling night.

Methinks that lots of *one-and-only-forever* relationships are like the sun . . . *'you are the sun, I am the moon, play me'* . . . says a Neil Diamond *love* song and *'Play Me'* is the title too. *Play me* is what the sun does do, focusing loving rays upon you—stronger and stronger in those seemingly wonderful ways of *one-and-only-forever* tides. Until the harshness of the sun burns away your flesh—bleaching your bones pure white, as the brutal rays reach into your very centered core, consuming all of your energy flows, and blinding you from seeing that there are lots of other stars all about you. *You are the moon*, ever in changing phases of reflecting back nothing more than second hand sunlight.

Play me as the moon, a never turning sphere of barren rocks is locked into a restrictive orbit devoid of life as you know it—once knew life. And life isn't as romantic as it once appeared to be back then, when you first gazed upon the luminous body in the bliss of your young love. Back when you thought you knew that *soul-mated* love would come into your life. Makes no difference if you are the sun or you are the moon, the entire scope of your relationship experiencing is now confined to repeating the same orbit of a steadfast boring course you've fallen into again. You are locked forever in the gravitational pull of the sun—yet knowing the ever so gentle touches of star light where the sun doesn't shine. Shine on harvest moon. The more things change, the more they seem to stay the same.

Now, the sun doesn't like facing the fact that no matter how brightly this merry old Sol does shine, some of that star light also illuminates the moon, especially behind the moon—on the dark side—where the ever probing rays of the sun don't shine at all. The blue moon could be said to be joyfully *mooning* away with the stars. The not-so-merry old Sol doesn't like that you're knowing illumination from other sources. Rather befitting that you seem to still be in flow with your *seventh root* charkra at base of your behind--your bottom, ah, your *mooning*. Ironic, that the escaping flows venture into the currents of the universe from your back to basic seventh, when the other charkras are opening and closing with this *moon madness* of soul-mated love stuff you're experiencing.

So the sun blazes brighter and brighter with a burning fury that only an omnipotent sun can do—sending out roaring rages of solar flares and lots of massive eruptions, certain that its blinding brightness of raw force will overwhelm the starlight. It's obvious the sun is madly in love and acting like a lunatic, and the moon and stars sure have pissed off the sun, because those tender touches of well traveled light from trillions of ever twinkling stars, peacefully continue to find the circling moon.

When you get to the bottom of things, you are at the *root* of the matter. You're overwhelmed with the rush of sunny rays you're feeling, some feel good, and others feel bad. You're sort of sorting out your shit before there's no *'you'* left to sort. Some of what you're feeling isn't as you first experienced those feelings from another caring about you. Their caring now feels like the pulls of controls, pulling you more and more off center. That *head-over-heels love stuff* gets you out of balance with yourself—not to be confused with the *head-over-heels erotic enjoying positions* where the balancing is natural and very fluid. *Wake up little Susie, it's 4 o'clock and we're in trouble deep!!!* Your *seventh* is still open and you are in flow--*'7'* has always been a magical number. And those reassuring stars continue to twinkle on and on unabated by the sun.

The big sun is big time angry—major pissed. In a funky raging fit of lunacy the sun snarls, *"How dare those stars still sprinkle sparkles of light on my moon!!! I'll show them who the boss is!!!"* From very deep within its molten core, the pissed off sun lashes out more and more with awesome furious power. Still, all the stars continued twinkling, just as bright as ever before. Of the stars, the sun says in heated anger, *"Nevermore!!!"* Of course, you know what comes next—BOOM TIME!!!

Caught in the horrific nuclear chain reaction of its own making, the sizzling sun violently explodes in one final blustering blast of voluminous brightness, ending in total and complete self-vaporization. Gone in an instant flash is the quick-silver planet Mercury and the *Women from Venus* quickly become crispy-critters. At times, the flows of the universe do align the stars and planets in most fateful ways.

While writing this, six planets and a waxing crescent moon did beautifully align to be viewed from earth in the twilight sky of early December, 1997. However, in the telling of this ramble, Mother earth was graced by the good luck of having the two inner planets closer to the exploding sun taking the brunt of the sun's blast, and that lucky old moon was safe in the shadow of the mother earth—the protective magic of a total earthly eclipse of the moon. Those eternal flows of the universe saved the moon's ass—so to speak. But the *Men from Mars* didn't fair as well, being all exposed—they became just as crisp as the burnt *Women from Venus.*

The orbits of the earth and moon did shift along with the changes of the universe. All that remained of the sun was a powdery trail of dusty sun specks swirling across the universe, now being bathed in the gentle caresses of twinkling starlight. The *"Nevermore"* foretelling of the old sun came to be. Change is constant—even for the sun. *Twinkle, twinkle, little stars, how I wonder where you are, up above the earth so bright, bringing light into the dark of night . . .*

You are a star as bright and as sparkling as the countless points of light on a starry night. For deep within you, your god-spark dwells . . . the very soul at the core of your being. That special place where you center with yourself...where you balance and center yourself . . . where you come to know the truth of truths for yourself . . . here's the source of love & light for the garden of your heart where all your loved ones grow. The source of those growing friendships comes from the light of their stars, which flow with you as you come know the glows of others godsparks. Those are the truthful loving friends that you nurture in your heart, as they bask together in the specialness of your radiant godspark.

The garden of your heart is a wonderfully magical place where there is always good, and plenty of room for everyone you invite in and welcome them to stay in the beauty of your heart place. All your sparkling connectivity with your friends originates and sparkles here. Each mind blossom, sharingly created with friends, glisten as lovely stars, the *forget-me-nots* of your soul. Here in your garden, sparkle the lustrous fruits of memories, of the connections from your exchanged and mingled energy flows. Each time you bring thoughts, smiles, good feelings, and sharing lovings into being with such becoming friends, a wee bit of your eternal star dust flows with each of your free flowing words and actions. Your friendly star dust does mix and mingle together, and germinates to grow mind blossoms, forever after to be rooted in the gardens of your heart.

Energy flows nurture and grow your mind-blossoms. They come into being with gentle touches from twinkling stars that move in orbits equivalent to yours. You enjoy these fabulous flows as orbits align with you. There is no blinding light to fade the stars away and no scorching sunny rays burning down upon you. Your orbit is entirely of your own making. Gardens of your heart accommodate all of your orbiting friends who you accept as they are, and who you welcome to come and share with you as you are. The only provisions that you look for within your invited friends, are that they come into your garden open and honest, and being themselves with you—and you are thusly totally free to be yourself with them and they are likewise free to be themselves with you.

Mind-blossoms are best shared opened and opening together, and open minds are much nicer and more becomingly beautiful, than the closed, restrictive kind of mindsets so set in their ways of non-being—non-relating. Peddles of the mind-blossoms spread outward in a glorious array of true colors. Here in your garden there is the truthful loving acceptance where truths are exchanged and cherished between trustful friends. The air is alive with the honest ringing of thousands of tingling chimes, vibrating in harmony is the joyous music of countless godsparks matching with the twinkling of starlight.

Godspark matches sow seeds of *forget-me-not memories* you cultivate in the gardens of your heart. The gardens of your heart are as eternal as your soul, and unique to you. There you will always find the lingering starry growth forms planted by becoming friends of here and now, and those merry parted friends from long ago—before their and your physical orbits moved kindly apart. Their spirited remembrances linger in your garden as waiting touchpads to your heart, and you know those special dear friends are always welcome in your garden when orbits once again come into heartfelt alignment. Like all things, orbits are constantly changing with the flows of the universe—sort of like a *universal drift.* In the far reaching shadows of time, cherished memories of friends may fade from view, as their mind-blossoms drift off to the edge of your expanding garden. However, a wee bit of shared star dust, sprinkled with dew drops will refresh them into sparking anew.

Just in case you might be wondering, *sparking* is an old Pennsylvania-German term for *making-out*—that up-close and personal fun kind of enjoying friendly folks do. When you are *godsparking* with friends, you're *making-out* in lots and lots of ways—in addition to sharing up-close and personal joys!!! Your thought matches enlighten ideas as you play them back and forth with each other, floating them about as a feather upon the gentle breezes of your expressive banter. With this kind of sparking the greater the flames of creative passions—the better!!!

No moths are flying about the flame of the enticing allure of their enlightenings. There's no such thing as a dumb question or a stupid comment between friends—here you can share the secrets of inner truths as only friends can do. These open utterances are very different than thoughtless remarks that sometimes happen as dumb utterances—those types of stupidly said careless remarks that do happen to come out utterly ugly even between gardening friends. Shit happens, but in accepting each other as is, you also accept the ability to fuck-up—all of you are free to fuck-up—and free to unfuck too!!! heheheheee Those bumps and stings are indications of more of life's lessons you need to learn from. As accepting friends, you look at those bumps together and work out the harmful prickly parts.

All of the energy sensations around and about you influence the ways your energies flow with you. When you start to get in touch with alterations happening in your energy flows, you instantly start pondering how you are feeling with those variations. Reach out and touch a hot stove and the burning hotness causes your energy sensations to ouch your hand away—your reaction to this kind of a hurt is a no brainer!!! When a tooth has a hurt, the nerve painfully throbs to announce the attention demanding ache—another no brainer that often brings a headache too. Ugh!!! On the other hand, when your body is responding to pleasing erotic sensations, those tender tingling touches often bring a softly spoken response of *more please*, or merely the marvelous merry murmurs that speak in volumes—as your brain brings a positive reply to what you are enjoying. When you watch a beautiful summertime sunset and a gentle night breeze carry the fragrance of flowers in bloom, your senses are enjoying the natural beauty that abounds, and your sensations delight with these joyous awarenesses.

Those same energy sensations are just as fluid when you interact with friends. If those interactions don't ring true with you, and your godsparks seem to fall flat, and those honest connectivities aren't matching with where you are in the here and now, then you start feeling your energy flow being prickly or nasty kinky—you know those goose bump feelings warning of ominous things to come. Your brain begins to respond with messages of ouch time—a big bummer is brewing!!! Whatever the dynamics of your exchange are, it isn't feeling like you're having your thoughts connecting with your friend. Your feelings are in a dinging funk, and most likely so are your friend's. Your usually smooth flowing exchanges are feeling like a discourse that's pulling you off center—swinging you out of balance. This isn't merely a mood swing—these major fluctuations are happening in diametrical directions.

Ah, 'tis all a matter of energies being in flow. Like sex!!! Sexuality is energy hopefully in awesome alignment and in fun flowing connectivity that's joyful. Copulation is how humankind reproduces. Sex is also the source for extreme erotic pleasures and profound pains—ironic that there is the possibility of knowing pain while having sex, and pain from not having sex too!!! Depending entirely upon which sexual mind games that are coming into play!!!

The difference between pain or pleasure is how you experience the flows of what's happening with you. If you're feeling used and abused and like you're being fucked-over, then you're experiencing pain. On the other hand—or in hand as the case may be, if you're feeling in balance with each other, and what's happening is in sync, and sensations are surging together with tingles created from shared enjoying, then you're knowing symmetry from your pulsating pleasures. Such are the open, honest exchanges between caring friends—and most certainly no nasty games are being played.

Pain comes from lies. It hurts in two major ways when you aren't told the truth, hurt from feeling that you aren't seen as a friend to whom the truth may be told. That bridge of friendship shakes when the untruths try to slither across. The hurt from looking inside yourself to seek the answer to what you've done to cause your friend to believe they can't be truthful with you. Oh, 'tis most easy to cast all the fault on the other—they told the lie. But for some reason the *liar* believed they weren't able to be truthful with you as a friend. Sad to say, that this realization is often more painful than the lie that was told by a friend.

The other part of the major hurt comes with the shadow of doubt that is now cast over your relating. Lies have the ugly ability to spin on and on. For once a lie be said, then the odds are that at least two more lies will be told to cover-up or support the first lie. Both of those two new lies beget two more lies each, to keep the original falsehood in place. On and on the told lie spins around and around, begetting more lies, like a crazy spinning tornado wildly sucking the truth away. Thusly, the lying has the potential to continue on forever, for a lie told today can come back to haunt the liar for a thousand of days, and in just as many ways.

Additionally, when you learn of the lie that was told to you, you might also find yourself wondering about what else they told you that might also be untrue too!!! All this ongoing wondering about what's true, does have the power to pale friendships and cause flows to wane away in what's been taken on in the backwash of worries about what to believe. Missing matches and the potential for enjoying are quickly fluttering away, and that's a sad bummer!!!

In the garden of your heart, those lies they told may cause peddles to fall from their blossom. Weed-lies creep in to grow in your garden, and these weeds have to be pulled out, roots and all, or they'll spread like wildfire—and not the pony kind of *Wildfire* she was riding when she rode down from Yellow Mountain!!! The weeds are like the killing frost. The accepting of each other isn't as open and honest as it was becoming or had been. It's kind of hard to be accepting when there is weeding needing to be done. The freedom of being yourself and being accepted as is has been tainted by the darkness of the deceitfulness that was regretfully done.

Lies ding away with lingering reverberations saying, *'I don't trust you enough to know the truth.'* Or they might say the lies were told to *'protect you from knowing the truth'* about something or other that they didn't think you could handle knowing about, or that they were only telling you what *'they thought you wanted to hear!!!'* Lies and excuses to explain the lies seem to go together like shit and piss. And shit and piss will really stink up your garden and make a mess—a big yucky stinky mess!!! Attracting buzzing flies too!!!

Lies have a way of spreading the hurt you're feeling. Your family of friends in the garden of your heart soon tune into something being very amiss with you. Yes, they'll ask you what's wrong. Now, you're faced with being up front and telling them truthfully what's happened to you—the depth of your sharing with them depends entirely upon you and your relationship with your friends. Friends have a unique way of knowing when not to try to pry into an area where you aren't ready to go into just now. They also know to accept that some things that occur with other friends just don't involve them. They'll also honor your saying *let's not go there* when there's a topic that's not ripe for discussion just now.

You surely don't want to compound what's happened by saying that everything is *fine*, because everything certainly isn't *fine* with you—and to say *fine* has the dratful dink of another dinging lie!!! You're hurting—and your friends know you are anguishing with pain done to you. It's impossible to conceal when you've been kicked in the balls!!! That's why they've asked you about what's wrong. They aren't asking with the typical *hi, how ya doing?*, that a politically correct society seems to *have to ask* in passing disinterest. These are friends who are sincerely interested in how you are doing. They need a bit more than a reiterated *fine*, so redundantly tossed about to answer casual acquaintances.

Now is not the time to become a martyr and do a pity poor me because wrong has been done. Nor is this the time to get curt with a cutting, *'my problem, not your problem!!!'* While that may well be true, this is not the time to play problem identification games. Your core friends can't change what you feel has been done to you, but they might be able to help ease some of your hurt with understanding and empathy for your plight. The shit will still be there, but they might help you with a bit of nonjudgmental sorting out of some of the dynamics of the mess—as only friends can do!!! Also, they wouldn't be asking the question if they couldn't handle the answers. There is an acknowledged truth that what is shared isn't going to be twisted around and tossed back at you by helpful friends—there won't be echoing comebacks and no *I told you so's*.

There's no shitty greed or pissy anger allowed into the garden of your heart. Strife strangles flourishing growth and does lasting stressful harm in scaring marks. The only kind of *harm* allowed in the garden is the kind found in *harm*ony!!! Enjoying the harmony of the good vibrations is what happens in the garden of your heart. No discords are allowed. The only meanness permitted is the dude blowing a *mean* horn, and the only beating that heard is from the drummer's wicked beating on the drums.

Lies are devastating because they are control devices. Lies are used to manipulate you, because you believe what you are told by a friend to be the truth, which in reality isn't at all true. It sort of feels like the lying fabricator is being greedy about you, and needs to control what you know about something that directly involves you. Their lying governs the false domain of what information you are allowed to know. On the flip side, don't go believing that everything that happens has to involve you, because the reality is that various happenings will surely happen that don't involve you. That's not to slight anyone, nor is it done to cause harm by you not being included, 'tis just the course of the orbits in flow and nothing more.

Maybe their greed is the jabbing jealous kind. They do harm to another friend by telling lies about them to you and perhaps to others too. Then too, they could be lying about one of their friends to you, they want to be greedy with controlling your time while they slip away to have fun. Of course, they didn't want to tell you because the lie would hurt you. Hurt you!!! Right, and those hurtful lies are nothing more than love-*taps*!!! Ugh!!!

And the *'taps'* that's being played on the lone trumpet is for the *gone is the sparkle* from your once friendly bonds of trust. Tarnish shows when the day of truth is done. No glitter comes from the dull dink of damaged good times—gone by the wayside, done and gone are all the possible enjoyings that won't come to be. The fun frolic from your once friendly flows sadly trickles away into the pit of nothingness. Oil spread upon troubled waters bursts into a raging fire, as the friendship bridge over those troubled waters burns away. Those roaring rages incinerate even the possible potential from passions that might have come again to be. Only you can decide how much of you those flames from the burning bridge will also destroy.

There's no room in the garden of your heart for hate, anger, or harmful doing. You are feeling betrayed by what has been done to you by one whom you once welcomed into your heart. You feel the pulls of temptation to lash out at them—to strike back at them so they know heavy hurts too. Give them a yucky taste of the same foul shit they've dumped on you!!! You want to cause heavy rain to fall on their parade—fuck-up their life just like they've gone and fucked up your life!!!

However, anger doesn't belong in your garden, and hate is an all consuming emotion that will kill your garden deader than dead and cover you with shit. You know that whatever you put out that does harm to another, comes back to you many times over. Harmful happenings do have ways of befalling those who bring harm to others. Thusly, 'tis not your job to cause the befalling to fall upon their heads. Now is thc timc to keep your head, and embrace your belief that for all things there is a season—nope, I'm not gonna burst into song!!! Ain't your job to plow the furrows of revenge across their empty field of life. Some will say that revenge is a dish best served cold. And so it is when the serving of that dish is done by the universe. Those doers of hurtful wrongs still have shitty yuck on their plate to learn from the consequences of their harmful actions. Eventually, their shit will be confronting them. Then they will be up for relearning life's lesson about all the harm they've done to others along their path in life.

You do some relearning of life's lessons' too. You reflect on how you interacted with them as a friend, that surely contributed to them succumbing to lying to you!!!??? You need to do a real assessment of your hurt that those lies caused—was it a sharp slap on your ass cheeks or a royal butt-fucking without kisses or KY??? Did your reaction to what happened come from your insecurities contributing to what went down??? Is it possible that you've made much ado over nothing??? This making much ado out something that really isn't a wrong doing, does lots of folks in by what they assume happened, when nothing harmful was done. And you ponder where forgiveness begins, and how far does forgiveness reach before forgiveness finally comes to an end!!!??? This turning the other cheek stuff only goes so far, and 'tis hard to turn anything about, when you feel as if you've just been crudely reamed a new anus.

Love is for giving, and you've given love to your friend, now you've been hurt by giving of your trust. Do you still have love for them beyond your hurts??? Does your heart continue to be open to accepting them as they are??? Does your love and acceptance flow in a course of forgiveness to them??? Does the essence of your flows that still remain, provide enough of a basis to transcend beyond the muck that's happened??? Is the value of your friendship enough to try to allow your flows to flow anew again??? How many tries do you try before your trying times are done and gone??? Will light & love bring about the peaceful solace found in finely woven weaves of friendship again??? Or will that light & love be sucked into the black hole that's been created between you??? Alas, all these are questions for you to ponder deep within yourself, for only you have the answers for yourself—those inner truths that only you may come to know.

With very few exceptions, I still have love lingering in my heart for once upon a time friends that have done me wrong along the way. The sting of those hurts have long gone, the impact from their hurtful actions has long ago been lost in the eternal sands of time, but continuing with me is the tenderness of loving flows once shared, along with the harshness of those hard life lessons learned. Maybe 'tis human nature to have the good memories remain after the badness has faded away with the passing of time. Could be that the lessons to be learned shine strongest with the positive, and that sheds light on the negative stuff that happened—and sometimes the negativity is so great that the best that can happen is to totally avoid them and be done and gone from their life. Time passing has a unique way of providing you with a fuller perspective of what the dynamics were that went down back then. Just don't go falling prey to the trap of trying to rewrite history.

This doesn't mean that you keep the good memories and black out those bad ones. Everything that has happened in your past is with you—both the good and the bad. I've never found a *selective delete* brain button that allows me to delete only those bad memories and keeps the good ones. Helpful folks might urge you to look only at the good parts, but you really have to look at the bad parts to learn from them, and then allow those bad parts to depart only after the lessons have been learned. My heart continues to be open to them, because only through a heart-to-heart understanding can what was done be looked at and learned from together. The problem with lots of folks is that they are often too blinded by the hurts they perceive as having been done, to be able to look for understanding when real understanding is what's needed the most.

Sadly, with those *one-and-only* soul-mated togetherness couplings, those who do indeed do wrong to others, see no need to seek understanding in the dynamics of the bad that was done. They believe that what's happening with them and their *mated-one* is all that really matters to them, and then tough shit to any others who get hurt along the way—including *their soul-mated one!!!* They have an ill conceived vision of how life will be for them ever after, and that's all they're interested in knowing of life. They're so certain that by being inconsiderate to others, and always appearing to be considerate of their *one-and-only,* that they are securing themselves in the *one-and-only* relating of their making. Thusly, they fail to see the hurt they do to others who once upon a time were friends too, and now those friends are tossed away—as they toss away parts of themselves too. As they see it, they really don't need friends any more because they have everything, or so they believe, in their so-so wonderful *soul-mated one-and-only relating.*

Godsparks indeed sparkle most brightly when *soul-matches* are happening. There's no reason to be into playing those self-serving protective *one-and-only* games because you're considerate of *one-and-all,* and there is no pull to tell lies about what's happening. *Soul-matches* are like a cluster of individual stars glistening with your godspark. Some have an orbit that brings their star closer to your godspark, and other stars have passing orbits that come and go with the ways of cosmic flows. Indeed, some friends are known to other friends and are into befriending too, and all is natural and unforced, as friends come to know others as friends, as they make the choice to become friends, and the friendship circle grows with no fear of loss from the friendships that are happening, and brightly glowing within the orbits of your godspark.

Any harm that is done with greed, guilt, and jealousy has the potential to mess-up those orbits, so no harms may be done. The flows of differing needs are always changing, and adjustments happen with no judgments being made about the alignments happening as no harm is done. The *soul-mated* ownership stuff and possessiveness and insecurities are gone from all interactions and the light from the matches sparkle with all enjoying. Territorial range wars are usurped with everyone enjoying the green, green grass of an eternal spring. Each and every star orbiting is unique in their own being, and being in orbit doesn't mean that all those orbiting stars are going to all mix and match with all the others—some mixing just won't occur. Like all things, there's constantly changing growth along the way, as more and more of those adjustments and realignments continue to happen, a core cluster of stars often stays near and dear.

There are also gifts from the universe that come into your orbits as the path of comets swoop near you, with once in a lifetime types of experiencing for enjoying. Those fateful fasting fine friends fleetingly flowing fast with you. Ah, wonderful by chance encounters for an instant of knowing another kindhearted godspark, graced with the good fortune of sharing ever so briefly, and then the comet flows onward leaving a lingering trail of star dust from the linkage of shared joys. Perhaps, the far and wide reaching paths of these comets will once again return in passing another time, or not. Regardless of whatever else occurs with the flows of life, godsparks did briefly sparkle with sharings once upon a time in passing, and those glows shall always remain joyfully aglow with you.

Those eternal joyful glows of sparkles are the best kinds of forever, because they glow endlessly with your godspark. Sparkles are glows that are indeed endless, while pledges of *love forever* from a *one-and-only*, seems too often to be a rock-n-roll kind of love, where *forever* gets swamped when the *love boat* gets rocked, and the young lovers haven't yet learned to roll together with the flows of life. Thusly, they abandon ship, instead of jumping with each other and rolling into the dynamics of what's happening. When there is abandoning happening, the empty ship is soon adrift, floundering, and eventually sinking into an angry rocking sea of greed and jealousy.

Godsparks shine out bright loving light in all directions, dancing about as shining moonbeams upon the ever flowing waters, casting light upon potentially dinging rocks, and rejoicing with the rolls as they go dancing upon always moving waves. And the godsparks from endless stars twinkle and sparkle across the eternally changing universe. Oh, 'tis so egotistical to believe that from all those zillion upon zillion stars that there will be only one star that will align and orbit perfectly with only you. Because all those zillions of stars do indeed align and twinkle with you already. Not as a controlling sun, keeping you locked into a tight chain-like orbit of the sun's making, but as the joys of orbiting about so beautifully with all the planets and stars and comets and space junk stuff surrounding you.

Once upon a time, long before telescopes, humankind was led to believe that earth was at the very center of the universe, and the sun and moon and stars all went about orbiting around the earth. Some of those heavy religious dudes got all bent out of shape at the notions of Galileo, studying and measuring the movements of the heavenly bodies circling about earth with his telescope. But of course, the druids had done lots of the same measuring and concluding many centuries before. That star gazing dude, Galileo, had the balls to proclaim that the spinning earth went around the sun along with all the other moons and planets, and only the moon went around the earth. Such blasphemy!!! This news was indeed a major bummer to those faithful believers who had been told *from above* that the God-created perfect earth was the center of the entire universe. Thusly, that pope guy did a number on Galileo by hitting him with a major put-down and locking him away for heresy. But the truth of Galileo's discovery was eventually found out. Because no matter how hard those restrictive mind-controlling-dudes of religious ways did try, they just couldn't control the expanding thought flows of all humankind, and the ever increasing proven knowledge those flows did bring into open awareness.

Jingle this about your mind and try these thoughts on to see how they fit with you. Each and every one of us folks, has at the very core of our unique being, the godspark of creation from the universe. The same kind of godspark as all the many twinkling stars and such glowing living things from all across the vast universe. Some of what's orbiting about us, has us included within their starry orbits, and some orbits are beyond us for now. But even with what's orbiting beyond us, there is a pulling flow that brings a yearning to some of us adventuresome folks, to ride upon the waves of curiosity to discovery and learn from what's just beyond us and be touched by the light of distant stars.

Thusly, we are at the very center of our personal and individual universe that we share with all those other stars, because in the vastness of the cosmos there's plenty of space for every one. And it is a universe of our making in some ways, and in other ways, we go with those fateful flows. We are able to acknowledge alignments of orbits about us, and free to ponder, with natural mindful questing, what is beyond those orbiting cycles of sameness—slipping free of self-imposed mind-bondage, and stretching outward from our godspark center to joyfully venture about the celestial body looking for the wonders of creative discoveries found within all those possible new orbiting alignments to experience.

From our birthing day, we are at the center of discovering our newly expanding universe. An ageless, yet virgin universe that's ever increasing with us, about us, and for us. Some folks find that the fate of their birthing has locked them into a narrow universe, and they need to push themselves beyond the restrictive place imposed upon them by the geographical fault of where they were born. Others find they are a branch of a royal kind of a tree, and thus, one day they too will be doing royal kinds of doings—such a bummer it is to be born into the curse of all those heavy stately expectations. Lots of folks are born into a place of limitless opportunities that are vast beyond their seeing, if they just have enough gumption to open their eyes and look at what there is beyond their nose. In many ways, what you see and do depends entirely on what you do or don't do, and what you see when you look out upon a starry, starry night sky. Do you feel like you are being dwarfed by the vastness of the universe, or do you feel a marvelous tingle that shouts with joy, *WOW, I'm part of all this!!!*

Yuppers, 'tis sort of like that *is the cup half full or half empty* question. If you see your cup as being half full, there is lots of room for many more life experiences for you to come to know. However, if you see your cup being half empty, you're missing lots of life experiences that are being drained away. No one can do life experiences for you. All of life knowings are very unique and up close and personal. However, those selfish restrictive others can sure try to keep the sparking matches of life brightening experience from being experienced by you!!!

Like the young lad born to be king is cloaked in a majestic robe with the imperial demeanor of how he is always expected to act and be. And when he becomes king, he then sadly finds his kingdom is often so very small, boringly restrictive, and being king isn't fun at all. While young common folks can freely look to the stars and feel the true grandness of their being and an endless universal kingdom all spread out for them. *WOW, I'm really part of all this!!!*

Take care and enjoy often . . . John

S P A R K S . . . love or harm

Please take note...
The following ramble is about sexual attitudes,
and so as not to offend anyone, in these days of full disclosure
and political correctness please take heed of this note.
Read at the risk of having your sexual awareness expanded
about the major differences between *good* and *bad* sex.
Is what you're feeling a good enjoying loving exchange,
or does it have the demeanor of a harmful encounter???

Attitudes are acquired from your life experiences,
feelings constantly emerging from reflective mindflows.
Attitudes are way different than imposed belief values.
Values carry expectations and judgments from others,
kinda like one size is supposed to fit all with similar values.
The problem with decreed values are differing belief meanings
even among folks who believe they have the same beliefs.
Differences happen, values shift and change over time
causing folks to feel like they are often at a loss and sometimes
out of sorts, as they try twisting to conform to doing what's
expected of them to be doing, while other folks are less stressful
nonconforming to the values of others that don't fit them.

Attitudes are more up close and very personal
when guided by the belief of *'do no harm as thy will be done'*.
'Tis a way positive attitude of consideration for one and all,
and from that *do no harm* place, sexual attitudes take on the
noticeable contrast of becoming either *helpful exchanges* or
harmful encounters, depending on where you are coming
or not *cumming* from!!!

That *'do unto others as they do unto you'* is a hot bed
of potential nasties just waiting to happen.
True, extending a helping hand is helpful in doing,
and the return of the same in kind is good and neighborly.
However, equally true is the potential for a smiteful and mighty
return that's harmful, not at all helpful,
and plow the barren course to revenge,

seeding revenge upon the ill-seeded fields of retribution
in endless cycles of pay-back retaliation,
soiling the soil of the heart's garden,
tainting the earth red with blood spilled in vicious vengeance,
sowing bad seeds for countless unborn generations,
undoing the humankindness once done
with the endless doing of hurtful unkindness.

The allure of *do no harm* interacting, is the freedom from
all the strain and stress of doing harmful doings.
As they say, *'for all things there is a season'*
and all the jazz about the changing of seasons,
the whole cycling thing is karma,
that *what goes around comes around* in redoing transitions.
Those who do harm to others in the flows of the universe
will have harm coming on back on them,
hopefully enabling them to learn from the hurts.
Thusly, when no energy is wasted on harmful doing,
more flowing energy is free for enjoying,
enjoying more of the marvelous joys of life
with a more becoming attitude and free of frustrations.

Methinks there are only seven sexual attitudes which encompass
all motivational mindsets whenever intimate activities come into
sharing and knowing all the lustful joys of the flesh.
Nay, this isn't a *how to do* whatever with whomever, nor a
what to do or *what not to do*, which so is moralistic judgmental,
and 'tis really no one's business about who does what.
But this is offered as a potential expanding of where
your active mind is most likely sexually playing
whenever sexual feelings come into interactive playfulness.
Also, those yucky ways that sexual attitudes are harmful
to folks will be explained, as well as the good attitudes.

BANANA SPLIT is a most playful sexual attitude
for enjoying lots of openly erotic fun.
These are exciting exchanges where everyone-wins
in these merry games of sexually delightful treats,
as long as your enjoying is open and trustingly honest,

mutually shared in the making,
and completely free of the strings of conning promises.
Honesty about the purity of safe ingredients is vital,
and most sensual with lots of good feelings exchanged.

You can make a mouth-watering BANANA SPLIT
anyway you'd both, or more, would like to make the treat.
You don't even need to split the ripe and ready banana,
but peeling is indeed highly recommended,
joyfully scooping up the refreshing ice cream flavors.
Those yummy flavors don't always have to be
the same traditional vanilla, chocolate, and strawberry.
Be deliciously daring in the fixings,
and try raspberry, coffee, vanilla-fudge, peach, etc . . . et al,
pouring on lots of thick sweet gooey toppings
that slowly drip all over everything and are lots of fun,
syrups of chocolate, butterscotch, cherry, and pineapple,
and rich hot chocolate fudge too—not too hot!!!
Walnuts in syrup are yummy too,
but 'tis wise to avoid chopped nuts—ouchy painful!!!
They all blend together into a super special deliciousness,
with lots of whipped cream, which is naturally creamy fun,
with no pain or marks come from this fun kind of whipping.

Alas, the whole concept of BANANA SPLIT joys,
is a lot of mutual tasty fun being openly shared
with no hassles from painful knowings happening.
Nor are there any lingering marks to later bring those nasty
pangs of dinging guilt after enjoying your shared tasty treat.
There is also no need to worry about gaining weight
from your happily hedonistic feasting joys, because those
possible extra pounds will surely burn away in the pure sweet
passions of your mingled energies zestfully enjoying freely.
BANANA SPLITS are pure fun!!!

VITAMIN C is a very healthy sexual attitude,
the friendly pepper upper that's so uplifting at anytime,
chasing off headaches and depressions with refreshing joys,
bringing relief from stresses by just knowing good feelings.

Of course, sharing is certainly encouraged
with your mutually healthy minded friends,
having a marvelously sexy work-out and working-on-in,
with passions purging open pores for flowing perspiration
while doing nice and easy aerobic heart pumping actions
in a wide variety of stretching positions.
There's no challenge to look at a stop-watch because this kind of
exercising is wonderfully grand when pleasingly prolonged,
doing extra innings and overtime—free of sudden death!!!

Exercising together way up close and personal,
is so joyfully enhancing when shared.
'Tis perfectly fine to take needful matters
into your own befriending hands too, as you enjoy doing what
comes naturally in your knowing masterful ways for enjoying.
When you get right down to it, you know best of all what feels
good to you, and way healthy to show just what and where too!!!

There's no need to keep scores in VITAMIN C exchanges,
everyone who comes and plays full out is a sure winner
when they are enjoying playing here.
This isn't a contrived competition for scoring points,
nor is this a spectator sport with cheering fans.
The locomotions in motions are what matters now.
Paying close attention to follow through
really does improve greatly upon stimulating strokes,
and keeping balls in playful movement as long as possible
is much more important than keeping your eye on the balls.
Lay-ups yield to lay-downs, and free-style is just fine.
There's no need to shoot from the free-throw line,
because there are no lines for anyone to stay within!!!
No flags get thrown by whistle blowers,
but some clothing will surely be tossed freely about.
There are no loss of downs,
and going on down is indeed mutually encouraged,
Here, kneel downs aren't being done to run out the clock!!!
On this merry playing field of super joys,
touch down passes are never blocked from end zones,
and no one is ever thrown out at home plate!!!

No foot faults are ever called
because you are on the sure footed path for natural joys!!!
Upon these courts a love game is never one-sided playing,
and everyone has an equal advantage.
Indeed, making two point conversions are a sure thing,
not that the telling of tallied scores has any relativity,
because with these kinds of healthy exchanges
everyone is a winner, and comes out ahead of the game.
You know, of course, that play most certainly continues
long after hitting the refreshing warm showers.

VITAMIN C is indeed a very healthy way for enjoying
doing what comes so naturally into being in playful ways.

MOUNTAIN HIGH is the rarest and
most quintessential of erotic experiences.
If death be the final chapter in departing,
then these aphrodisiac awarenesses are the zenith
of enlightening brilliance in your passing along the way,
coming as momentary glimpses of spectacular light, and love,
and peace...in gracefully fluid flows balancing with all the
movements of changes vibrating in ever moving harmonies.
Play it again, Sam.

MOUNTAIN HIGH is when all linking interactions flow
extraordinarily together in synchronized sharing.
Surging godsparks unite, as passions mutually ignite,
combining marvelous movements with each sincerely shared
tender touching, linking lovingly together into a joyous mode
of being both giver and receiver.
You're into gleefully giving, and thankfully accepting lots of
good erotic loving, tunefully aligning in spinning revolutions,
launching into lifting-off with the flow of your energies,
taking flight to shed the pulls of gravity and climb high,
flying higher and higher in unique blissful union,
passing high above sparkling snow capped peaks with wondrous
winged ease, far, far above majestic mountains so high,
soaring to where the air is rare,
and such created energy flows are even rarer.

Leaving earthly bonds far behind as you rejoice together,
relishing taking off in amazing astro-flight.
Through the open portal you go . . .
joining in the eternal energies of universe,
cumming together in the pure ecstasy
of your brightly shining beautiful blissfulness,
and cumming again and again and again in fluid joys of
reverberations, as lightning flashes, and orgasmic thunder
rumbles along, roaring in rejoicing volumes,
pulsating from combining created energy rushes,
zooming onward to the attainment of the very zenith
of this quintessential threshold of being.

Godsparks glow ever so brightly
in the unique unconditional acceptance of love;
love as perfectly pure as the heart flows
growing true in the glorious gardens of your hearts;
love cherishing the momentary created gift of completeness
in this briefly shared universal passage;
love unscorched by demeaning sacrifices
and untarnished by entrapping expectations;
love in the boundless beauties of accepting
what is being shared in the here and now;
love freely felt in all ways, and always,
far beyond the vagueness of forever;
love freely fluid and undefined
by tainted taunting chains of demanded bondage;
love shining effortlessly and endlessly
in the reflective afterglows of your godsparks;
love lingering long with you everafter,
as elated exhaustion eases you from your high flight,
lovingly floating your beings, ever so smoothly,
back to awaiting earthly pulls,
continuing long after to gently cradle you
within the rarefied warmth of beautiful afterglows,
shining with your glowing godsparks evermore.

MOUNTAIN HIGH is more like a marvelous experience,
an extraordinary experience grown from grateful attitudes

aligning in time for an astonishing linking together.
Many strive to attain this shared experience
taunted as orgasmic perfection, by romance novel writers,
who write of the myth of those bell ringing orgasms,
and their readers only seem to know dull donging dings
that aren't doing much to ring their chimes!!!
Flying high is indeed possible to experience
when your attitudes lift free of all the guilty gravity,
soaring blissfully beyond all harmful pulls.
MOUNTAIN HIGH doesn't happen via stressful striving efforts
and plotted planning for having everything be just so perfect
to make the experience happen on scripted cue.
This is one of those mysteries of life that just happen
very naturally while you are enjoying,
and part of what makes it happen
is the not trying to make it happen,
not trying for perfection in planning,
not trying to capture the moment,
not trying to force growth and just allowing yourself
to be free flowing and unhindered by the stress of taxing efforts.

At times these paramount experiences are a unique unfolding in
recalling reflections of the joyous highs of previously flows,
projected transparently upon the here and now of enjoying,
not as some transference fantasy mind game,
but as a freely enjoyed focusing with shared joys,
a feast of familiar once upon a time joys . . .
feeling the merry mantra surging with joys . . .
enhancing the current rushing flows of joys . . .
reawakening the sensual touchstones of joys . . .
delighting with mounting passions of pure joys . . .
arousing within discovering new touches of joys . . .
circling all around the fire pit flaming with hot joys . . .
transcending beyond the comparing of known joys . . .
more opening the floodgates for all enhancing enjoyings.
The greater the wealth of experience from enjoyings . . .
the deeper the shared lake is to swim in,
the more expansive the variety of joys for recalling . . .
the smoother the ease for flying freely above the peaks . . .

enjoying more . . . enjoying even more!!!

MOUNTAIN HIGH is alive with the awesome energies
of resounding echoes tingling the air with very fine flows
of the rarest array of sounds in beautiful sparkling harmony
so very gleeful in melodies uniquely blending together,
soulfully sparking the music of joyful bliss evermore.

CHILD is the deadly double edged sword of the seven attitudes.
This is marvelously joyous when filled with loving light,
when mutually enjoyed together
to procreate a new loving godspark
into a welcomingly desired growing life form,
freely agreed upon by both
as being a jointly endearing sharing for their lifetime.
Their openly known purpose for blissful coupling is now
especially for creating new life.
Truly, their love-child is a welcumed gift from the fruitful union.
Painlessly the sharp blade cuts the newborn offspring free,
free from the nurturing mothering cord,
now the caring comfy love of both nurturing parents continues
ever on as parenting lifelines,
lifelines linking this child with loving parents
in a most joyful joining together creating life anew,
free from the imposed command to go forth and multiply.
For all things there is indeed a growing season,
and that time only comes into being
by their joint deciding and agreeing,
and not from the selfish nagging urging of others
expecting grand-offspring!!!

On the flip-side . . .
this pointed sword can also prod an unexpected, unwanted,
unwelcomed, unloved child to life
into an abusive lonely cold existence,
with the unborn child oftentimes being wielded
as a most hideous nuclear weapon,
harmfully swung as a means to entrap, to control,
and to manipulate the fates of others!!!

They spin a web for entrapping another into a loveless wedlock
with the first indication of pregnancy!!!
Ensnaring results from not using birth control methods is done
with telling lies . . . *I'm on the pill . . . I had a vasectomy!!!*
misleading one to believe everything is safe to enjoy!!!
Concocked controlling pregnancies . . .
keep'em pregnant and barefoot and down on the farm...
knocked-up with another one in the oven . . .
for an unwanted even half-dozen!!! *Ugh!!!*
However, 'tis not birthing a new welcomed life into being,
that's *not* the focus of their controlling kid hatching plays,
what's being done is deceitful entrapment!!!
A child so ill-conceived by their encounters,
may long carry the wrongdoings of their warring parents!!!

Some self-invested religions impose dictums
prohibiting the use of any birth control methods,
selfishly wanting their flocks to multiply via birthings
from continuous inbreeding, to increase their faithful holdings.
Sad too, when these anointed leaders make all the rules,
but they sure don't get into playing the procreation game!!!

Such an ugly bummer, the miracle of child birth becomes,
when reduced to an entrapping and controlling device
in a society continuing to use children as ensnaring traps.

OLD SHOE is a sexual attitude that's all worn out
by being taken for granted for so long,
deep in the grave of a rut of their own digging,
locked in a dull sameness that's not pleasing nor pleasant!!!

Their contrived sexual encounters and their morning eggs
are generally the three minute kind,
neat and tidy and always the very same style,
conveniently scheduled during a TV commercial break,
or while the VCR is remote controlled onto *pause!!!*
Usually on Saturday night, they do a very little bit of *balling* . . .
so they can at least say they did *'it'*, but *not doing 'it'*,
except for *'that time' of the month* when they do nothing at all,

and sadly nothing at all is missed, by their not doing!!!

The sorrow is that what might have been
so joyful once upon a time, just isn't joyful for them any more!!!
Now, enjoying sexually really doesn't seem to matter,
trashed by their collective put-offs and push-aways
as they continue to only go through empty motions,
mostly reacting to irregular notions,
ever so briefly pressing flesh together . . .
while thinking of repainting the ceiling, *beige—perhaps,*
pondering about doing this or that thing later,
or maybe an egg-shell white would be nice,
while they are again enduring doing their expected duty!!!

Once burning playful passions
have been long ago put out with so many put off's,
fits of raging anger piss passions out, making stinky smoke,
pushed aside so easy in passing,
and soon what doesn't happen is so devalued,
so contrived and so slopped over with nasty blame games
that what's passed over now, isn't even missed in the passing!!!

Ugly lines get drawn in the sand about what to, where to,
and how *not to go to* any more are painfully defined.
Their previous enjoying freely together there is nevermore.
Once known joys from life experiences are off limits for sharing,
and less and less enjoying is available
within their reduced non-relating and not knowing,
as jealous ways of gossipy gaming usurp
all those flows that once were, but are now pushed away
like old shoes tossed in the back of the closet,
they've seen better days and are still useful,
and they have a nice comfy fit at times.

The happenings in the lives of others are now seemingly
way more important than their dwindling away sex life,
which is very sexless!!!
However, the bedroom ceiling has recently been painted.
If and when they ever have sex, that's okay,

and if not, well *'it'* really doesn't matter,
because 'tis become so very joyless,
and most unbecumming too!!!
Sadly, it seems as if everything and everyone else matters more
than their once lustful enjoying.
What sex there might occasionally happen
feels so plastic and phoney and not at all real to them,
with so many other happenings happening endlessly,
that happen to matter more than their enjoying being happy.

So they are left with just slipping on in
going through the empty motions,
if and when there's a common notion,
and when the notion ain't common,
then faking *it* isn't at all uncommon!!!

Thusly, enjoying sexually goes slowly slip sliding away.
Shuffling off to Buffalo,
and you can't roller skate in a buffalo herd!!!
All the self-imposed stresses and frustrations of life overwhelm
their dinging on empty encounters,
as dull repeated dings of depressing drudgery
drain away all those once upon a time joys.
Where have all the flowers gone???
Gone to the wilts of guilt, long time passing . . .
Gone too is the expressive *'oh, my!!!'* that once spoke in volume.

The color of the ceiling???
Oh, that's a nice powered puff blue . . . for the time being.

TAXATION is a costly sexual attitude
that coldly converts sex into a bartered commodity!!!
Bought and paid for sexual favors
lukewarm willing human flesh for sale,
in any desired size and flavor, for a price.
Anything at all is available to buy—everything has a price,
and the asking price is always negotiable!!!
When the hour is late enough,
even unreasonable offers are considered,

help me make it through the night!!!
The sexual encounter is nothing more
than a simple business transaction,
a matter of this amount paid for that arrangement,
ding-dong the deal is agreed,
ding-dong the deed is done in no time,
and the fat lady with big tits sings off-key for everyone
but no one notices—*her singing!!!*

Yes, these purchased lays of lustful play
come complete with ego boosting lies,
because the cash and carry deal on social intercourse
includes some of the best professional acting ever done.
The rumpled bed is but a stage
upon which we all must play our parts,
and the audience-patron-payer is always said to be,
You're so wonderful, honey!!! and *Oh, you're the best!!!*
whatever you want to hear you'll hear from them,
all scripted lines are included in the price paid *to play.*

They are all fleeting fucks, only bought and paid for sex,
and the *fuckee* is into doing whatever you want them to do,
and so willing to say all those lies you want to hear!!!
As long as you've got the money, *lots of money, honey*,
they've got your *good hot times!!!*

The method of payment isn't always cold cash, any legal tender
will do, major credit cards accepted, *sorry,* no personal checks.

Sometimes the payment is not at all legal,
nor tender—such as with rape!!!
Rape is high priced dominating TAXATION, taking another
sexually by crude assaulting force, forced to deliver whatever
style of sex is demanded, forcing the raped one to get on down
and start doing or risk loosing your life to the threatening knife.
Rapers are an ugly low-life scum of society's foulest ills,
very lacking in self-esteem, even with their over-bloated ego!!!
Often, *rapers* are only able to *get off* at the high expense of
forcing themselves on another, in their mean taxing control!!!

Promises of things to *'come later'* . . .
as a promised reward for sex is TAXATION too!!!
Likewise 'tis taxing whenever expected sexual favors
are the payoff for whatever is assured to be waiting!!!
You go out on a dinner and movie date, and later . . . well,
do you want to guess what's *expected* to *cum* next???
Date rape occurs when the sexual favor issue is forced,
force is applied to collect the expected sexual payment!!!
So sad when the basis for maintaining a friendship
is only for more and more sexual exploitation!!!
Run-around Sue might be a fun filled easy screw in private,
but 'tis darling Donna who gets to go out in public dates!!!
Bummer how many ways sexual tax collecting gets done
in so many controlling nasty ways.

TAXATION is the demeaning manipulation of others
for meaningless sexual favors of imposed expectations,
insignificant encounters that are endured just to get whatever the
often empty payoff might be!!!
Sexual blackmail for sex once done is also TAXATION that
could be collected later, and far, far into the future, endlessly
paying a highly inflated price for an ever so brief knowing of the
forbidden flesh—could be the fresh was tainted with disease!!!
Woeful too, are those taxing teasing games, the *beg me for it* and
how much do you want it bullshit, the alluring teaser that goes on
and on without ever coming close to a positive outcum!!!
Teasing is nothing more than dancing to the old deviled tune,
the look-n-drool—but don't you dare touch syndrome
that's making for a frustrating taxing situation.
These teasing games sooner or later become so tiresome,
draped in the tattered shrouds of endless empty promises,
draining away any possibilities of ever sharing joys!!!

TAXATION is the attitude that's happening
whenever sex is used as a reward or punishment *thing.*
The painful punishment is on both of them,
as the happy potential for enjoying sexually
goes so quickly up in flames from the heat of raging anger.
The burning flames of spiteful fighting is a hellstorm

blowing out the flickering flames of passions.
This is the very nasty give and take fallout of fighting,
and although some may claim that the best part of fighting
is when they make-out, making-up is really a myth.
More often than not, their senseless battling has drained off so much energy that there isn't anything left to enjoy with.
With all kinds of fault-finding being done, self-esteem takes a grave taxing tumble, and not the fun kind of tumbling into bed!!!
When blow-ups and angry spats are likely at any time, about any thing, or over nothing at all, then lots of walking through mine-fields happen to try to avoid the deadly perils of more strife.

Way deep TAXATION shit is taxing someone into doing demeaning sexual doings, to prove their love—that isn't love!!! That's pure TAXATION, and if you're foolish enough to believe that paying taxes is an expression of proving love, then send the IRS your tax return on February 14th, with a beautiful Valentine articulating your undying taxing love—free of deductions!!!

TAXATION is also expressed with the misbelief of the taxer claiming everyone else does *it* this way or that way or whatever. That's nothing more than a comparing bummer, used to con another into doing something based entirely on what others are *said by them* to be doing, and most likely, they aren't even doing *it*, whatever the *it* has been said *they* are supposed to be doing!!!

Methinks more taxing lies are told about sex
than are told when lying about any other topic,
lies of doing *it* more often than they really are . . .
lies about not doing *it* when they really are . . .
lies about who they've done *it* with when they haven't . . .
lies about who they haven't done *it* with when they have . . .
lies told as promises about *it* that will never be fulfilled . . .
lies about how *it* doesn't matter when *it* matters . . .
lies told about how good *it* was when *it* wasn't . . .
lies told to themselves about how *it* will get better . . .
taxing lies never make anything better!!!

There is no love when a taxing force of will is imposed upon you

as an expected means to prove there is love!!!
Imposing one's will at the expense of another, isn't doing love!!!
All that proving *if you love me you'll do it for me* stuff is only
the insecure needy greed of TAXATION, and there will surely
be more unexpected tax collections being gathered later!!!

Sadly, their teasing taxing smiles are painted plastic,
their feelings are as hollow as their empty extortion promises,
taxing promises made during the heat of proving passions
in the lustful taking of the tariff the night before,
quickly fade far away and are soon forgotten
in the awakening rays of morning's first light.
Ransomed promises made of made-up love forever,
will wane, and nothing is left but over taxed emptiness.
These empty taxing teasing promising games go on and on,
leaving an endless wake of broken hearts and shattered dreams,
as lying cloaking darkness ultimately yields to the light of truth.

Indeed, 'tis the heartless ones who do the taxing until one karma
balancing day, they too are finally taxed by a more cunning and
insensitive tax collector, who out taxes them at their own taxing
game with no returns earned on their paid investments.
When their means to pay the tax is gone, the tax collector moves
onto new taxable situations, ready to be milked of all their assets.
Render unto Caesar what is due or thy will be done and gone!!!

Centuries ago, humankind was smoothly slipped into mindless
taxation without much representation, and that's not at all
becoming nor loving of one another.
TAXATION crudely converts sex into nothing more than a
bartered commodity, only a stack of *dry goods* waiting for a
buyer with the means to pay the asking price.

GUTTER is in the absolute lowest pits of the darkest sexual
attitudes, and so very painfully pitiful, because gutter dwellers
uphold and forcefully impose their Puritan beliefs that all sex is
always evil in every way, and that anything even remotely
related to sex is very dirty and nasty and yucky too!!!

The problem is GUTTER rakers feel so moralist righteous
that they impose their self-serving beliefs on all others,
deciding that everyone needs to become religiously saved
from the wicked vice of corrupting crass copulation.
They delight in pointing shameful fingers of blame at all of those
sinners who do profanely engage in any kind of carnal activity!!!
Most likely, they've never experienced such blissful joys and
most likely they never will, because they are obsessed with
draping the world in the dank darkness of horrible guilt
over disgustingly branded sins of the shameful flesh.
From their narrow gutter point of view, almost any form of
sexual expression is seen as a grievously sinful vile action!!!
They're devoted to their entrenched intolerant beliefs,
believing that only their beliefs are righteously right.
All other beliefs are wrong, untrue, unclean and ungodly.

Except for strictly dictated, correctly approved copulation,
sex is proclaimed to be wrong and off-limits for them.
Thusly it is, and so shall it be forever, that sex is very evil.
Henceforth, sex is exposed as wrong for everyone else.
All those yielding to the sexual temptations of the flesh
shall know their ceaseless curses of guilt and shame
befalling them with torment and hellish damnation.
The promise of burning hellfires shall await all who fall prey
to the sickening foulness of succumbing to sick sexual ills.
Those sexual ways of finding false delight within the unclean
flesh of another, are the totally wicked ways of non-believers.
Sadly, gloomy GUTTER-rakers attempt to inflict all others
with their pointed burning pains of their rigid religiousness!!!
From restrictive GUTTER doctrines, they set about finding fault,
shame, guilt and endless blame where *none* are to be found!!!
Except for all the evil they believe they see with their averted
eyes tightly closed to a world they'll never come to know.
All they seem to know is a fragmented fabricated life,
seen through the narrow GUTTER tracks of their mind.
Therefore, many of life's most joyful experiences
bypass them while bringing heathens enjoying,
unbelievers who are unclean of mind and body,
wicked in their self-indulging lustfulness of enjoying.

GUTTER rakers always seem to have a mad on, greatly angered, because everyone isn't as guilt driven as they are, and hostile too, because they see sin in so many things!!! From their all seeing, all knowing, biased perspective, they sit in self-asserted discernment of all those *they* have deemed to be wicked and evil, as they, the purely righteous, have so judged!!!

GUTTER rakers are forever seeking converts, those unbelievers who the rakers savingly turn away from the evils of the foul flesh to be accepted into their bleak cloistered beliefs, embracing their closed minded ways of non-being, trading away earthly joys and pleasures for the proclaimed promise of eternal salvation said to await only the very faithful in the afterlife.

When gutter rakers engage in partaking of the flesh, their *taking* might happen on New Year's Eve, which allows them to blame strong drink and celebrating for their wee bit of a slip in slipping into the forbidden flesh, and their annual dip into the flesh is most certainly very brief in duration and empty of feelings, with the blinds pulled down and the lights turned out, so they don't have to cast eyes upon offending flesh!!!

GUTTER is dangerous because those rakers take it upon themselves to poke their noses into the private business of other folks. This attitude is the most selfish and harmful, because the *rakers* expect and want everyone to believe and act just like they do. They constantly look for gritty dirt and nasty stuff everywhere and they continue digging in the gutters until they find it.

There are the seven sexual attitudes identified for consideration. The first three and a half attitudes *do no harm*, they're exchanges filled with joys, mutual flows aligning and attuning in caring interactions, and very openly sharing relatings, humming with heartfelt harmony . . . of good vibrations coupling together!!!

There is laughter and lustful enjoying, and beautifully erotic exchanges happening, and your omnipresent security comes from deep within your godspark, long enlightening you with inherent glows, you glow from delightfully being yourself!!!

Meanwhile, positive life experiences are created in cherished sparkling memories of your joyful knowings with friendly like-minded folks met along your path.

The second three and a half attitudes are indeed painfully harmful, and sadly spread by ongoing bad examples to the unfortunate offspring of future generations who continue on in these negative modes of abusive interactions.

These encounters aren't mutual, they play foul dinging notes of discord, self-esteem dwindles away with each piece given up, pieces of self tossed off as not mattering, while negativity clings woefully to those consumed by sexually controlled greed.
The heavy wet blanket of imposed guilt covers them over like stink on poop, taunting jealousies abound to blind and bind, and double-standards get dumped into place too.
Contrived appearances usurp meaningful substance, and lairs spin deceiving tales so cunningly told, boldly lying to tie up minds in twisted knots ranting to undo natural mind-flows.
'Tis depressing how these selfish undoings
pervert thought flows and prevent sharing joys,
turning people into possessions with no mind of their own.
The possessed have given up their heart and lost their mind
in doing the games of these negative attitudes.
Like the donor in a heart transplant operation,
the giver is a mindless dead shell.

We fill ourselves up with all kinds of expectations about mixing and matching love and sex, binding them together in tightly knotted ties of disheartening frustration and disappointments, all melancholy mind games of our own making, as we sadly fall into these sorrowful traps, making for some great song lyric material for those *'somebody's done somebody wrong'* songs, but blows us away when we feel the hurtful wrongs of being used and then tossed away, mere discards in the never-ending love gone wrong quest, and that's sure nothing to sing about!!!

Indeed, it is very harmful converting *loved ones* into possessions, dictating what may or may not be and how to be as expected.

And you know sure as shit that one of the *loved ones* always seems to be sacrificing so much more than the other, when one perceives more value in what they do than what the other seems to sacrifice and do. Thusly, relating imbalances happen, dinging everything harmfully out of balance, ripping apart their ways of interacting.

Whenever we've shared beautiful joys, there lurks the risk of expecting those beautiful ways of knowing together will *forever* be that way, but memories can't be saved in a bottle any more effectively than trying to save time in a bottle.

Cherished memories live as friends in the garden of your heart, always alive there to revisit and reflect with again and again. Unless, of course, they've been totally trashed and crushed and scrapped, as in done and gone--banished away forever. Ah...'tis the ways of remembering life that memories will never be recreated like before, because that time before is gone into the here and now energy of yesterdays, and into today goes the now of creating new growing joys, hopefully free of harmful guilt and greed and nasty stuff.

Indeed, we get locked into possessiveness, thusly, living a loving life suffers when the focus of life is the craving of possessions. Sadly, 'tis easy to slip into mindless attitudes and dwell there. It is far more healthy and joyful when you are in mutual flows, and attuning with similar mindflows for enjoying often.

It may seem like I've spent way more words rambling about the negative attitudes, than expanding more on positive interactions. The reason is because more people are entangled in the negative attitudes, than are into the uplifting flows of positive attitudes. Many folk might have mindset of believing that what they are doing is good for them while being inconsiderate to others, because humankind has grown accustomed to all the negative ways of interacting as an accepted matter of course. The nasty sexual game playing continues by imposing self-serving controls on new generations, trapped into endless cycles of non-relating that are so demeaning and way unkind!!!

Eventually there comes a time when nasty double-standards turn full circle and come back at them, their offsprings have sprung into being just as they have been.

We look to others to bring us joy, wrapping our means to know joys in ways that are dependent on others to produce the diluted secondhand joys we might come to know.
By always putting our expectations for joys on others,
we've slowly lost our ability to self-create our own flows for knowing and sharing joys.

'Tis far better to plant flowers in our own gardens
than to look for others to bring us flowers.

Now is the time for humankind to get back in touch with our unique abilities for creating joyful ways of interacting in positive sharings pulsations that have godsparks shining anew!!!

Take care, and enjoy often . . . John

ODE TO A BIRTH CONTROL METHOD

I usually don't do writing requests, they seem too much like an
editor giving assignments to be completed by a deadline,
being grateful for those plums known as a *feature article.*
When I'm writing for sharing in this cyber-space media,
I just like my thoughts bubbling to the surface,
free of the struggling toil to milk an idea into something.
I like to see what's befitting for sharing from my mind quest.
However, a delightful lady friend gave me a topic . . .
asking that I let my thoughts flow about this subject,
as friends share with me, I share with them in kind.
Thusly, I am hopefully bringing her smiles and bringing you a
few smiles too with my *ode to a birth control method!!!*

Once upon a time being asked about such methods would have
caused me to break out in a cringe, but since my vasectomy,
I now flow with a grin as everything arises just fine in a timely
fashion . . . to enjoy in lighting passions most hotly raging,
knowing I'll never have to ask, *"You're what???"*

I first thought a rundown of sort might be in order
about the merits of the Liddy's Loop vs a Copper 7,
or the joys of bubbling foam and those cute sponges,
touch upon diaphragms, and jells so lacking in flavor,
of condoms, plain and ridged with collection nipples
that come in a wide array of bright shocking colors,
and for safety's sake, condoms are conveniently available
for purchase at all kinds of stores everywhere,
because it just ain't chic to forget the sheik!!!

Merrily, my mind ponders the many wonderful ways of huggles
and snuggles and tender touches, arousing oral joys and stroking
and probing delights, bringing mutually marvelous satisfactions
a coming, without sowing seeds in the fertile chamber within.
Knowing the shared blissfulness of being *right there,*
without assuming the risk of having those sperm
starting their long upward swim of unification,
to eventually unite with those waiting eggs.

Avoiding the unhedonistic way of *just say no*
as not being joyfully realistic and so unfucking restrictive,
just as is unbecomingly becoming a *born-again-virgin.*
For once, the first time fateful deed has indeed been done,
the sweet hesitativeness blended with eager anticipation,
the delicate flower is plucked forever away in an instant . . .
all done and gone forever more in a moment of passage!!!

The most important part of a birth control method isn't the technique nor the physical devices employed, and not what becomes of the white stuff that comes about, and what's in place here or there or somewhere detouring swimming courses of those wee willie wigglers—so set as they are in their way to make headway to become part of growing a new human being.
Alas, the part of the method that matters most is the mass of active gray matter between your ears that's flowing with thoughts about what's happening, attuning, revealing, aligning, relaying, and evaluating with all the rest of the unifying actions, reactions, and chain-reactions linking interactions together,
because the brain is the primary birth control method,
and not the genitals—they're only along for the ride.
But of course, the active involvement of the gray matter
plays a huge part in determining riding qualities.

The brain is the balancing point of all pivotal choices to bring a birthing idea into the nowness of action, or to prolong pondering the doing, weighing *what if's* with *if only's* and *what about's.*
Evaluations affecting evolutionary eventualities, as reasoning rings with recalled reflections of reality, parting hazy illusions with your truthful affirmations, plowing fertile fields to receive thought seeds, preparing places for germinating mind plants,
conceived by heartfelt beats mingling with mind flows,
free of warning gut feelings that *something ain't right!!!*
The beating heart alighting and aligning with an array of mind blossoms sparking into being, birthing energy surges into life.

Here too, is the ongoing conversion factory, where hopes and dreams are mixed and matched with reasoning acquired from life experiences, awash with awarenesses from life lessons learned

to convert budding aspirations into doable plans that grow you
into the future, for the future is you, and the future is now.
Now—in the nowness of your existence today, projecting the
future your vision focuses upon, bringing your focus into your
realness of being now as the uniqueness of you in the here and
now, and in the time span between now and then,
what once was your dream—now becomes your reality.

Such a fine world this would be, if making dreams come true
were as simple as making them happen between now and then,
but the more complex your dreams become, the grander your
plans and scopes of the makings, and as you dream others into
your envisioning, you assume the chancy risk of your dream
becoming their own concept, as they envision your dream to be,
as they apply their mind-drifts over your dream.
Then your dream drifts away, fading out of focus,
eclipsed by the cloudy imposed wants of another,
with no light to grow your idea seeds into mindplants.

Birthing controls are often self-imposed,
limiting doings with hindering perceptions of undoables.
Clinging to myths of false securities restricts reaching,
'tis very difficult to reach out when your hands are tied.
Then too, pangs of put on *guilts* prevent possibilities,
ugh, that guilt shit is such a major bummer of a killer!!!
Also, all kinds of variables controls come into play,
getting all tangled up causing dinging procrastination's,
putting off, and putting off with projected uncertainties,
frustrations increase while pursuing the perfection myth.
Over-controlling and attempting to force perfect growth
all contribute to controlling unbirthings, and the real secret to
birthing an idea is balancing—balancing controls what you know
and are learning to launch your dream into flight.

When I was learning to fly an airplane,
an old two place, bright yellow, L-16 trail-dragger,
with lots of jerky stick motions, I did lots of over-controlling.
My rough landings bounced Fred all about the back seat.
Fred was a great flight instructor,

he was a man of few words and easy on the stick.
'Let the plane do the flying,' said he wisely again,
'gently point the stick showing the plane the way.'
Fred taught me landings with his hand almost on the stick,
always ready to correct my heavy over-controlling ways
to keep me from crashing the aircraft.

Late one afternoon, I was landing and taking off, landing and
taking off—again and again, making what's known as *touch and*
go landings at the small private Garden Spot Airport.
He talked me through each one—always correcting some,
at least I was learning to over-control less and less,
proving in some areas, that improvement is possible!!!

As the sun was about to set in a clear western sky,
Fred said, *'one more landing--make it a good one',*
and indeed, my landing was as smooth as a floating feather,
no correcting, no bounces, not a word from Fred,
except for him saying, *'that was a good one'.*
I was taxiing to the hangar area when he had me stop.
Fred got out of the plane saying two words, *'solo time'*,
quickly closing the door on any discussion!!!

Mixtures of dread and joy assailed me as I positioned
the plane at the end of the runway and checked for traffic,
checked the instruments and another look for traffic,
all done in preparation for my first solo take-off roll.
I wish I had been as certain of my abilities as Fred was,
with a feeble, *'Oh, fuck, here I go!!!'*
I increased power and released the brakes to take flight,
rolling down the runway with increasing speed,
letting the lift build nice and easy like,
easing back on the stick to bring the tail up nice and easy,
feeling lift increasing as air moved faster over the wings,
then experiencing that one special moment of lift-off,
lifting up from the passing runway,
and flying solo free of the bonds of earth,
climbing high and higher into the just dusting twilight sky,
'Oh, WOW!!!', overwhelmed my earlier, *'Oh, fuck!!!'*.

I was flying,
I was flying free, on my own,
really flying free of my imposed self-doubts.
Such glorious freedom as I banked and climbed,
relishing the pure exultation of finally taking my solo flight,
loudly singing, *'off we go into the wild blue yonder,*
flying high into the sky'
way off key, but with lots of joy as I banked again, orbiting
around the small airport to make my solo landing approach.

'Ohhh, fuck!!!', again with a *fuck* of possible pending peril,
landing . . . *ugh* . . . my first *solo* landing—like, all alone,
with no Fred talking me through to a safe landing.
His skilled hands weren't on the other stick this time,
my whole fate was entirely in my own young hands,
rather frightening since I was almost sixteen!!!

With ugly visions of pancaking, groundlooping, or worse,
filling my head and a clammy cold sweat happening,
thinking I really have to pee,
I started to ease the plane into my downwind leg.
Fred's voice started talking in my head,
'ease off on the power' . . . 'a little more' . . .
'coming in too high, ease on down' . . . 'bring the nose up more'
. . . 'more to the left' . . . 'stay on center' . . . 'nose up a bit' . . .
'less power' . . . 'let the plane land nice and easy'.
Again, my *'Oh, fuck'* became an *'OH, WOW!!!'* as the wheels
gently kissed the runway with that wonderful squeal of rubber
meeting concrete, that very sweet sound of a safe touch down.
Oh, so very smooth was my first solo landing,
marvelously beautiful—at least that's how it felt to me,
and in my blissful moment of relishing my safe landing,
I almost forgot to brake!!!

Alas, I was all set to brake before taking-off,
but Fred wisely knew I was ready for my solo-flight,
even when I wasn't certain I was ready to do it.
Now I can sort of relate with those young birds,
pushed out of their comfy nest to take first flight!!!

So often we put our brakes on prematurely,
never seeming ready to fly free and high on our own,
coming up with a delaying host of pragmatic reasons
as to why we aren't going to do something,
lingering over a long listing of *why not's* not to try,
why the risk appears to be so great.
All those many things that could be lost in trying now,
putting off until tomorrow, and tomorrow . . .
what's in the here and now to be enjoyed today,
if only all the *why not's* could be done away with,
to make trying become a possibility.
If only . . . if only . . . if only . . .

Oh, sweet bird of youth, take flight and know the joys
of flowing along with the freedom that awaits,
free of all the self-doubts that hindered so harshly,
shedding earthly bonds, soaring high,
far above the mountain peaks,
climbing higher and higher to play tag with drifting clouds,
to dance about with the twinkling stars.

Once we experience the joys of free flight,
it really isn't a wonder as to why we often forget to brake,
because we want to prolong our freedom,
delighting in the pure joys of freely enjoying life!!!

Aha,
braking,
coming back
to our earthly pulls,
for now this free flight
is over for this span of time,
as plans birth to fly soon again,
again and again. For once the flows
of freedom to be free come joyfully to thee,
those exhilarating feelings linger long with you,
awaitingly so ever ready for enjoying some more,
and even some more, and more to the center—ah, there!!!

Too frequently, we over-ride our birth control center,
not trusting in ourselves to accept the offered risks,
clouding over potential doings with those *what if's,*
pondering endlessly, trying to balance *this-n-that,*
caught in the spinning rounds of indecisiveness,
whipped with whirlpools of self-wonderings,
sinking into quagmires of personal quizzes,
seeking our seemingly elusive inner place
to explore centering truths of one's self,
where your godspark glows brightly,
and balancing truth of self be known.

At other times, we are way too quick to act,
taking big leaps of faith without establishing foundations,
forgetting the advice: don't play leap-frog with unicorns,
extending trust in others when so little is known,
about who and what is being trusted in.
So coyly they cunningly say smilingly, *'trust me',*
and the pretty wrapped packaging is so alluring in pink,
but so lacking in real sustaining substance to trust in,
and the hasty actions taken are premature in coming,
the doing is still-borne in mistrust, lost in the rush to birthing
for the mere reasoning rush of doing something,
and the hasty doing is damaged by dinging dinks!!!

Woe too, be upon those who try to control,
imposing upon others with birthing idea in flows.
'Tis way nicer and much better all around
to align truly helpful influences without controlling,
this is indeed the art form of rare interpersonal interactions.
Really great teachers are thusly talented with the gift,
in ways of teaching without painfully teaching down,
while the student gains in self-worth while learning lessons.
The learning becomes so joyful and lots of fun when students
understand what the lessons are all about, and how lessons
learned now continue to bring benefits long after graduation day.
Wise teachers are also lifetime students, because in the quest for
life learnings, we are all forever cycling and recycling
between being the teacher and then a student again.

Some parents are wise in such teaching ways too . . .
by interacting with offspring in ways for assuring
positive flows and lasting humankind values,
not from doling out endless presents of things with strings,
nor by cleaning up their endless inconsiderate messes,
but with beautiful gifting of helping in meaningful ways,
learning the value of their efforts related to a dollar
by earning for themselves the means to fulfill their wants,
learning respect and consideration of others
by cleaning up after themselves in a most timely way,
learning that everyone is different
and to be considerate of the differences of others.

Showing ways for the child to slowly discover
the uniqueness of being truly themselves,
to grow naturally free from long reaching shadows cast
by the ills from their forefather's past,
free of the insecurities that well meaning parents tend to
protectively project upon growing offspring—in fearful efforts to
save them from haunting ghosts loitering along with the parents,
impeding parent/child sharings of learning how to be true and
honest with their deeds and doings in the present.

Balancing birthing methods for considering:

Amassing affirming affections,
avoiding assaulting anger . . .

Beautifully bouncing beyond boundaries,
banishing bullshitting boredom . . .

Crafting creative courses,
closing contriving controls . . .

Doing delightful deeds,
dropping dulling dumbness . . .

Expanding empowering energies,
exiting entangling entrapments . . .

ENJOY OFTEN!!!

Freely flying free,
flinging fright faraway . . .

Growing glowing godsparks,
grinding guilt gone . . .

Honoring heartfelt harmonies,
halting harmful hazards . . .

Investing in innovative imagination,
icing imposing impatience . . .

Joyfully joining jammings,
jinxing jaded jabbers . . .

Knowing keepsake kindnesses,
kaputting karma knockers . . .

Living luscious lovings,
losing lurking leeches . . .

Making merriment memories,
mashing messy monsters . . .

Never-ending natural nicenesses,
naying needful nastiness . . .

Opening opportunities often,
overting overbearing ogres . . .

Pondering pleasing possibilities,
purging pulling pouts . . .

Quickening quintessential quivers,
quaking quacking quitters . . .

Relishing rejoicing raptures,
rousting rank rudeness . . .

Savoring succulent sweetness,
suing slithering serpents . . .

Trusting tillable truthfulness,
trashing troubling terrors . . .

Unbridling unique understandings,
undoing uncaring ugliness . . .

Vibrating vigorous variations,
voiding violent vamps . . .

Winging wildly with wonderment,
wilting whimpering whiners . . .

Xeroxing Xanadu,
X-raying xerosere . . .

Yearning yummy yeppers,
yanking yelling yucks . . .

Zinging zestful zooms,
zapping zone zealots .

Thusly, my friend's request is now fulfilled,
my promise to do so honored with my above rambled thoughts,
having become another birthing for sharing.

Take care and enjoy often . . . John

FUCK REDUX

Early in 1972, I was having a breakfast meeting with a marketing consultant friend, when he tossed me the creative challenge of trying figure to out how to market *fuck.* I laughed and explained that the world's oldest profession has been selling *fucks* for centuries—even before there were centuries, *fucks* were a medium of exchange. He said he wanted me to figure out how to sell *fuck legally.* Again, I explained that selling *fucks* is legal in parts of the state of Nevada. Also, there are some municipalities in the United States where laws prohibiting prostitution are not enforced. He said he wanted me to devise a way to sell *fuck* legally in any state in the union. We agreed to the terms and conditions of the challenge and made a wager upon my creative ability to successfully market *fuck.*

My creative problem solving process is to take a legal pad and start to list what I knew about *fuck* and what I needed to find out about the subject. I boldly printed 'FUCK' at the top of the blank page and started writing out the different ways *fuck* could be used in a sentence. I'm sure I'd have surprised a few of my former English teachers that I actually remembered that there are various word usages. Then I started writing some of the common applications of the word *fuck.* With a bit of rewriting and editing I discovered I had created a brief 305 word essay all about *fuck.*

Almost two centuries earlier, my ancestor Ben Franklin had taken a goose quill pen in hand and written an essay *'On Passing Wind'* as part of an address of introduction he delivered to the French National Assembly, while he was serving as the first United States' ambassador to France. The French National Assembly was notorious for their rudeness of sleeping through speeches being delivered by visiting diplomats. Ben wrote *'On Passing Wind'* as a creative endeavor to hold their attention and to keep them awake. When he returned to Philadelphia, Ben had his essay set in type, printed as a *broadside,* and then circulated his very funny dissertation about farting to his many friends and associates. Ben had a way with words and self-publishing.

I did my essay as an illuminated manuscript page using an old style of calligraphy. I then arranged with a small job printer, Harold Herr, to print my essay on a heavy natural parchment stock. I filed for a copyright with the Library of Congress. I wasn't sure if my self-published essay would be granted copyright protection because of the subject and the title of the essay being *'The Immortalization of Fuck'*. However, the Copyright Office cashed the check and sent me a certification of copyright.

Next, I placed display ads for the manuscript in several popular *men's magazines* to sell *fucks* by mail order for $3.00 each or 2 for only $5.00--*fucks* at affordable prices delivered to your door. Soon, orders with cash, checks, and money orders started arriving from folks all over the United States. I made photo-copies of the orders and checks as hard proof of selling *fucks* legally throughout the US. Then I called my friend and arranged a breakfast meeting so I could collect on the bet we had, which he agreed I had certainly won. What did I win??? Well it was a very big payoff, he paid for a huge country style breakfast at the Lancaster Hilton!!! Winning the wager was secondary to the solving the creative challenge of selling *fuck* legally—and having fun with it!!!

Regarding the legal aspects of my *fuck* essay, I wanted to see if my testing the waters with this essay got any attentions from those who rant and rave about the use of this abused word. I didn't receive a single complaint, gripe, or bitch about my essay. I received lots of reorders and *thank you notes.* What is ironic over 26 years later, is that my original draft had, *as a political statement-- "Fuck Nixon!"*, however, upon the strong recommendations from friends who reviewed my essay, and then suggested changing *Nixon* to *Washington*, I made the change. In 1972, then President Nixon was pursuing anyone using his name in a disrespectful manner, and prosecuting would-be *Nixon* bashers with the full force of the federal government. I figured I could make an interesting case for my use of *fuck* in a humorous essay, but "*Fuck Nixon*" could have gotten my ass in a jam. The irony is that Nixon *fucked* all of us with the whacky Watergate mess and having to resign for his abuse of presidential power!!!

The following is the original text of my infamous essay:

"The Immortalization of Fuck"

Fuck is perhaps one of the most interesting and exciting words in the English language. Fuck is the one magical word which just by its sound can describe pleasure, pain, hate, and love. Fuck comes from the German word "frikon". In language, "fuck" falls into many grammatical categories.

Fuck can be used as a verb, both transitive (He fucked her.), and intransitive (She was fucked by him.). It can be an active verb (He really gives a fuck.), or a passive verb (She really doesn't give a fuck.), as an adverb (She is fucking interested in him.), and as a noun (She is a fine fuck.). Fuck can also be used as an adjective (She is fucking beautiful!).

As you can see there is a whole lot of real versatility with "fuck". It pops up everywhere. Besides its sexual connotation, this lovely word can be used to describe many situations: Fraud--"I got fucked by that crook!"; Dismay--"Oh, fuck it!"; Trouble--"I'm fucked now!"; Confusion--""What the fuck?"; Aggression--"FUCK YOU!"; Despair--"Fucked again!"; Philosophy--"Who gives a fuck?"; Incompetence--"He's a real fuck-off."; Numerology--"Sixty-fuckin'-nine."; Rebellion--"Fuck it!"; Displeasure--"What the fuck's going on?"; Satisfaction--"Fuck me again . . ." Also, as: Descriptive anatomy--"He's a fuckin' asshole!" To tell time--"It's six-fucking-thirty."; As a prediction--"Well, I'll be fucked!"; A political statement--"Fuck Washington!"; Incestuous--"Mother fucker."; Governmental affairs--"Fuck the IRS!"; A poker hand--"A royal fuck."; To start a relationship--"Let's fuck now."; As an acceptance--"Fuckin' A"; Enjoyment--"Fuckin' WOW!"; A closing--Fuckingly yours."

Use Fuck in your daily speech proudly. Fuck adds prestige to any conversextion. Put this colorful four letter word to work for you today. Tell someone today "Fuck you!"...or "Let's fuck."

CREATUS was my weekend have fun with creativity company to which I assigned this copyright. CREATUS is Latin and means *to create.*

I was familiar with the postal regulations about what constituted *obscene materials*, but I also had a friend in the U.S. Postal Service Mailing Requirements Department review the essay to make sure there wasn't even a slight violation of some obscure mail regulation. He laughed and said he didn't see any problems with the essay, and then he bought several copies. He believed this essay came into the area of being considered a *scholarly work*, explaining the correct usage of a commonly used word. The physical act of sexually *fucking* is secondary to the widespread usage of the word. The use of this old word is internationally familiar, but folks continue to attach a shameful breach of conduct to the mere utterance of *fuck.* The spin that gets attached to *fuck* makes it a profane word in certain kinds of uses by some people.

There are many words that are profane and describe obscene actions that are freely used every day with no one pointing fingers and yelling *bad words*!!! *Hate* and *hatred* in all forms are very offensive words and actions in common usage. Along with the words *war, fight, kill,* and *rape* are way monstrous acts, and yet, these deadly words are freely spoken, written, and acted out and even played with. In more customary usage, there is *shut-up*—as a turn-off and *never-mind*—as a push-away. They are destructive phrases that are certain to disrupt interactions and are disrespectful. Of course, being respectful and considerate of others seems to be out of fashion for many people. Not to mention disrespectful words that are ethnic slams and dirty digs. I won't foul my ramble by including a listing of all of those disgusting words—they don't need any more exposure than what they already get. Also, all those demeaning descriptive words that are voiced about regarding unknown people so casually—often based solely on judgmental appearances: *fatty, skin-n-bones, dumb, lazy, ball-less, plain, homely, ugly, tease, too young,* and *too old.* All nasty words of put-downs that have the power to sting deeply and offend muchly. *Liars, lies,* and *lying* sting deeply and offend muchly. *Liars, lies,* and *lying tattletales* are most offensive words and harmful actions too.

Sadly, society has empowered the word *fuck* with the dishonor of being able to usurp all those obscene words and damaging misdeeds. *Fuck* continues to be a taboo word that *nice people* don't usually use—or at least not in mixed company. It seems strange that *fuck* is considered to be so profane, while ugly *'hate'* inflames and hurts in a socially acceptable fashion!!! *Fuck* gets referred to as the infamous *four-letter-word*, but *'hate'* is an even more damaging four-letter word. The acceptability of the word *hate* opens the door for mean and *hateful* actions driven by *hatred* that will *kill*—another nasty *four-letter-word.*

Folks might subscribe to the belief that FUCK is an acronym meaning *Forbidden Unlawful Carnal Knowledge. Fucking* was considered to be a court-marshal offense in the British Royal Navy. This old regulation was used to punish seamen for *fucking around* in unacceptable ways. However, the Anglo-Saxon roots of *fuck* may be traced way back in time to long before there was a Royal Navy. *Fuck* was part of the language of the common folks, and often served well to express their joys and the imposed plights in their life. Their usage of the word *fuck* was frequently to be expressive about negative situations--as in someone being *fucked-over* or *fucked-up,* which is way different than *being fucked silly* or *having your brains fucked out* or *joyfully fucking into next week!!!* There wasn't anything forbidden or unlawful about *fuck* until controlling rule makers came along and made *fuck* into a naughty word.

During World War II, another acronym evolved that used the word *fuck*: SNAFU, meaning *Situation Normal All Fucked-Up!!!* Once again, on the receiving end of the SNAFU was the common foot soldier, who was really feeling *fucked* out on the battlefield when the situation went differently than the generals had planned. Of course *fucked-up* could be, and often was, interchanged with *fouled-up* to make the usage more acceptable for *nice people* and to appease ever present censors. However, those combat soldiers in the middle of a raging firefight, weren't feeling *fouled-up* because promised *fouling* reinforcements didn't arrive in time because of a SNAFU. They really were feeling *fucked-up—fouled my ass!!!*

Oh my, censors—those tireless tasters of mind food that decide what is permissible for mental consumption and what is spoiled or improperly prepared. Censors usurp the guaranteed First Amendment rights of the populace to enjoy free speech under the guise of protecting the well being of the ignorant public by determining what the *well being* of the public is, according to their point of view!!! Ever so quickly, these watchdogs of *our* morality impose their restrictive standards of what thoughts and actions are allowed to be expressed and in what moralistic manner. Regardless of how *fuck* is used, censors are sure to hit upon the word as being unacceptable and cut-out, crossed-out, and have totally done away with the word *fuck.* This is all done under the controlling directions of the protective censors.

These guardians of public morals plead that what is being expressed can be said in more socially pleasing and acceptable fashion that doesn't offend anyone. Somehow, "I got *fucked* by that crook!!!" just doesn't have the same sense of frustrated outrage as, "I got *sexually intercoursed* by that crook!!!" Aha, but "I got *screwed* by that crook!!!" is more likely acceptable—go figure!!! "Ohhh, yesss, dear, *carnal knowledge* me now!!!" said in the heat of lustful passion, fails to be as excitingly expressive and as erotic as, "Ohhh, yesss, dear, *fuck* me now!!!" I guess *screw* might work if the dude is named Phillip.

The purely enjoyable aspects of *fuck* have a delightfully resounding ring, "Oh, yes, *fuck* me!!!" has a joyful tingle that "Oh, yes, *do* me!!!" ugh—that *'do'* just doesn't have the expressiveness. However, there is merit in, "Oh, *do fuck* me!!!" Now that does have a welcoming ring. "I'm gonna find me some *good fuck'en* tonight!!!" is hopefully more positive, than saying, "Tonight I shall seek out some *good carnal knowledge*!!!" Or in other words, "I'm interested in exploring *good fuck'en* aspects of *carnally knowing* with you!!!" brings into being the merry potential for mutual learnings usually not found in the library.

The moralistic concept of forbidden and the restrictive limits of being unlawful, are the nasty negatives that put disapproving spins on the word *fuck.* Various cultures and societies have differing viewpoints on *fucking.* But all of humankind is like a huge *fucking melting pot*—we all have similar aspects of *fucking* in common and variations on *fucking* are not at all uncommon!!! Knowing how to *fuck* is what all of humankind commonly shares—however, some folk are more knowledgeable about the more joyful ways of *fucking* than some other folks. Methinks, those who are more comfortable with mutually joyful *fucking* have lots more fun *fucking* and enjoy more often!!!

Historically, humankind has been *fucking* and being *fucked* since long before the dawn of time. Without *fucking* happening there wouldn't be any humankind to have a history to record. Methinks when dawn was dawning into being, our primitive forefather's were way into more joyful *fucking* than we are able to enjoy from *fucking* today. Their natural surroundings were most hostile, and thusly, their enjoying the simple joys of life were more fully relished with appreciation. They were free from all the social restrictions that ensuing centuries of evolving civilization would possessively affix to *fucking*—and the *fucker* and *fuckee.* Perhaps in their early primal lustful couplings their utterings where most likely a resounding, *"OOOhhhh, ffffuuucckkk!!!"* Enjoying *fucking* and the mental discovery of the gift of fire, were perhaps the evolutionary process that motivated humankind to an interactive level above the beasts.

Enjoying *fucking* by the warmth of the fire, that kept the hungry beasts away, is what might have first jelled humankind into tending tribes. Each clan member tending to the common good of the whole, safe from wild animals within the safety of numbers and by the light of their fire. The birth of civilization was born out of lots of hot lustful fireside *fucking.* Those first exchanges between neighboring tribes were possibly sharing learnings of variations for enjoying *fucking* and the tending of the fire. I'd like to think that back then, humankind was in a very basic survival place for everybody staying alive—and not being eaten by the animals or falling into the hostile landscape that could gobble you up in an instant. Their informal unions were for the common good and well being for all of those evolving beyond the beasts. They shared the common values of food, fire, and *fucking*. The maintaining of food-stuff and controlling fire was their daily work, and their enjoying *fucking* was the fun part of their life. Everybody learned the vital skills and methods of survival, and freely shared with others newly found learning experiences for all to benefit from. Life was a lot simpler way back then.

Fast-forwarding several centuries, the common sharing dwindles away as the hungry beasts are now fewer and the mapped landscape is less unfriendly. The common survival bond slips into the bondage of harmful undoings from conflicting restrictive social beliefs. People got lazy and inconsiderate of others, looking for others to slave away to do their doings that are so undoing. Some clusters of people are more adventitious than others, their venturing forth was often in treks for acquiring more knowledge, expanding their knowledge base was the constant quest for the more daring tribes. A little bit of knowledge goes a long way, and some folks went a long way looking for more learnings about the ways of an expanding world. Other folks grew most restrictive and cloistered their clans off from the rest the of the world. As they saw life, from their narrow self-serving point of view, they knew what they knew and that's all there was to know!!!

The most significant leap that was made way back then, was making the connection that knowledge was power—that same belief is true today!!! Sadly, the power of knowledge held by only a few in the tribe, allowed those blessed with knowledge to become lazy, and they used their powerful smarts to enslave others to do the work for them. Early *fuck-overs* to control knowledge started to mess up the open exchanging flows of humankind. And the first differences were made between the nasty *fuckers* in power and those powerless ones who where getting *fucked*—and not the jubilant kind of *fucking* once enjoyed often beside the communal fire-pit.

Somewhere along the evolving byways, sharing knowledge about enjoying *fucking* got lost in the sands of time. The lines got drawn in the sand between the *haves* and the *have nots*. *Fucking* dropped away as a joyful value. Perhaps, the *powers-that-be* figured if folks are enjoying *fucking,* then they weren't keeping busy doing enslaved type things. Consequently, the *haves* started putting restrictions on enjoying *fucking* and started turning a few additional bucks bestowing *fucking* rights—equal rights for enjoying ceased to be important!!! Or maybe, the *have nots* got into focusing on getting what the *haves have*, and their enjoying *fucking* got devalued in all their bemoaning about what they *have not* compared with what others *have*. They were so busy trying to *have* what they *had not,* that they no longer had time for enjoying *fucking* as they often *had*.

For those into having power, knowledge became the torch of fire to be kept aflame with more learning—restrictions got put on who could learn what, and what could be taught, and freely shared learning went bye-bye. Their once flaming passions for lustful *fucking* were slowly forgotten in favor of their endless quest for knowledge. The learning of life experiences didn't really need to include lessons about enjoying *fucking*. Perhaps there were some cocky statements made about already knowing all there was to know about *fucking!!!* Gee, the more times change, the more some things stay the same in the foolish *know-it-all* minds of humankind.

Enjoying *fucking* went underground. About the time when those people, the ones self-empowered with expanded knowledge, started putting restrictions on joyous *fucking*. With the tides of the centuries of knowledge washing about humanity, there were times when the joyful passions of lustful *fucking* were almost extinguished. Dark ages, under the guise of being so morally enlightened, befell vast segments of humankind as more and more of the common folks took up those self-saving ways of enlightenment. Believing they've seen the saving light they turn from the bliss of enjoying *fucking*. All the gloom and yucky con jobs of guilt and sin came as gobbling cancers to kill joys, mangle merry, royally *butt-fucking* many, voided away good grace and floated in good grief, and put a dark cloud across the moons of june and july!!! The august worked easy cons under the guise of for the good of all, when mostly it was their own art deco joys that were their primary concerns. Come September, and the common folks were being royally fucked, and they sure as shit weren't enjoying being *fucked-over*!!! And to make matters *fucking* worse, they hadn't figured out how to go about *unfucking*. Thusly, so enlightened, they turned away from the ways of knowing carnally, and became more carnivorous for all knowledge of power to become all-powerful—omnipotent even. But in their abilities for enjoying lustful *fucking* they were becoming impotent. Thus came December, and the winter of discontent chilled a joyfully barren land.

The captured gift of fire that first sparked the torch of knowledge aflame was indeed a double-edged sword. It was a sharp sword with both the power to warm mind flows into growth, while destroying other mindsets by setting their mind waves into a fixed way of being. The glorious gifting of the shared flesh for mutually joyful *fucking*, ceased to be a gift of self that could be freely given, and became a control issue for those with the power to dominate and enslave those common folks. Power to the knowledgeable *royal fucker* over the hackneyed ways of the *fuckee* folks. Major bummers!!! Big change in the devaluing of humans who were different, and the self-valuing of the wise-guys who fixed the controls for the *fuckee* mindsets. Who are they you going to *fuck* before they *fuck you???*, became the ongoing question of the day. So uncivil!!!

All things considered, *fuck* has continued to do well with the common folks. Lots of the average folks went right on with their enjoying lustful *fucking*—regardless of whoever or whatever those royally endowed people in power were doing. Except of course, when those rulers in power got into doing wars and harmful actions—wars really *fucked-up* enjoying *fucking*. The regular type folks always seemed to be blown away with those nasty spiteful happenings. Those in power declared the wars and the common folks were forced to fight the wars. I wonder how many billions of times those compelled to do the fighting and dying asked themselves the question: *"What in the fuck am I doing here, and what the fuck are we fighting for???"*

Controlling all kinds of increasing powers, those ruling powers also raped mother earth—by stripping off her dress of trees, looting away resources with rapping scrapes plundering deep inside her, fouling the flowing waters with dangerous yucky dumpings, and even busting the ozone bubble!!! Pop goes the ozone top!!! Those in power were so slow to hear mother earth's woeful weeps, just as they were so slow to hear all the wailing for those lost in their contrived struggles in warfare. For such a very long time, our earth-mother was taken for granted, abused by each passing generation, and so badly royally *fucked-over!!!* Now some kinder thinking folks are slowly getting into *unfucking* mother earth—woefully wondering of too little too late???

When things in life get all *fucked-up*, then sometimes the magical nature of *fuck* helps to make *unfucking* possible. *Unfucking*, when feasible, done in amending ways to perhaps heal hurtful *fucks* done in passing. *Unfucking* is the mindful application of positive efforts in trying to straighten out shitty *fuck-ups* without getting nastily *re-fucked-up* anew!!! Lawyers often get a bad rap, but the really good attorneys are professionally great at *unfucking* when they aren't busy *fucking-things-up* elsewhere!!! In short, *unfucking* provides the active means for fixing *fucked-up* wrongdoings with hands-on involvement trying to straighten things out. A third party granting absolving absolutions doesn't *unfuck* what's been so *fucked-up* by human unkind doings.

The invention of the printing press in the 15th century caused a major shift in the ways of expanding upon knowledge power bases. One of the earliest uses of the newly invented printing press was to print up *certificates of indulgences*—almost like printing money. Buying these *certificates of indulgence* were like acknowledging ahead of time, that the purchaser would or might eventually *fuck-up* and do a nasty wrong *fucking*. However, those purchasers of *indulgent certificates* were allowed to do their indulging *fucking-ups*, because they chose to pre-pay for the special assurance of promised absolution to free them from the torments of having *fucked-up*. Therefore, those who *fuckingly indulged* would not have to feel bad about being a *wrong doing fucker*. Sort of like having some of the very first *get out of jail free cards*!!! For a brief time, selling mass printed *indulgences* was a real income producing venture for those running the con-game of selling these worthless certificates. These *fucking indulgences* contributed greatly to an increasing number of common folks getting *royally fucked* and *fucked-over* again and again, by those with the cash clot to get *indulgent* rights!!!

More lines got drawn in the sands of time to mark the battle-lines in the ensuing wars of the sexes. Some evolving cultures were now converting women into mere items of ownership with the sole purpose of serving and pleasing their male owner/husband. Again the *fucking* that happened wasn't at all enjoyable for the *fuckee*, as all kinds of *fucking* mind games got played by both the *fuckers* and the *fuckees*. Those once shared simple joys of *fucking* blissfully were washed away, lost in the ever turning flood tides of becoming more civil and less joyful.

Mutually shared joys by the fire pit were lost in the all consuming powerful flames in the mangling mandates of emerging societies. Those once burning bright passions of lustfully insightful linking in their safety of firelight—these once free primal joys—paled away in the imposed glaring harsh judgments of those leading society astray from the joys. Lots of folks, wanting to always be socially right and acceptable, were slow to notice the imposed heavy structure of guilt being dumped on them for simply enjoying the very human non-harmful acts of enjoying life!!! In their earnest seeking to become socially accepted, they put on made-up appearances to appease all those would-be power brokers. Those acceptable appearances were defined demeanors, which came complete with the approved put-ons for appearing to be enjoying themselves. However, the common folks could only enjoy in approved and accepted ways of enjoying, while all the time being *fucked* in brutal ways, by those in higher positions of proclaimed power, and those royal *fuckings* weren't at all joyful for the *fuckees*.

With all this nasty *fucking* not being enjoyable for so many centuries, you can surely see how the once most joyful *fucking* got to have such a nasty reputation, especially when there was nothing at all nasty about originally enjoying *fucking*—between agreeing adults and no barnyard animals please!!! Indeed *fuck* was perverted by those in power to be seen as such a very nasty a word. A word that nice people, so wise to the ways of acceptable society, they'd never want to admit saying, or own to the fact that they are at differing times both the *fucker* and the *fuckee.* The beautiful balancing passions of just enjoying *fucking*, get lost in the spin cycles of worrying about who's on top as the *fucker* and who's on the bottom as the *fuckee!!!* Thus, there was just way too much concern about *what's what* in trying to always be socially so very correct and placatingly acceptable that those untainted blissful joys are long gone.

Alas, and there are those who say but what of love??? Making love is so romantic, endearing, so lasting; and far nicer and smoother than the crudeness of just enjoying *fucking* beside the fire pit. Methinks there are many folks who are hung up with the over-rated, artificial Hollywoody concoctions of making love. Therefore, unless all those romantic notions are in perfect motion, just like they've seen in the moving picture shows, their *loving couplings* aren't going to feel like they've just had a plastic perfect love connection—but was rather yucky and very lacking!!! And not at all like the love shown in all those popular depictions of what they expected romantic love to be.

Romance puts all kinds of expectations on joyful *fucking,* and all those manufactured anticipations amass to crush all the juice out of enjoying. When their making love isn't making it as joyfully as they were so sure the loving would be—well, those poor *fucking* techniques are what gets the blame. Surely not their love, because their love is perfect, just too, too, perfect, and everybody who thinks they know them will tell you they have a real storybook romancing love!!! But rarely will anyone who is all caught up in the romancing thing, admit that their joyless love making is really faked and empty and lacking in every way!!! Of course their romancing isn't as passionate as expected, because their plotted interactions are carrying all those heavy expectation burdens of fantasy fabrications!!!

Oh for sure, there were all kinds of dream worthy fantasies happening for centuries. They were all avenues for spinning open the minds of the *have not's* to allow them to briefly escape the ever increasing applications of controlling powers by the royal *haves.* Dreamscapes of the proud prince riding in to slay the nasty dragon, and then carry the fair beautiful maiden off into the loving dreamworld beyond the sunset where they all live happily ever after.

At least that's how the fantasy romancing storyline is often told. But all too frequently, the proud prince turns out to be a real asshole, and pride goes tumbling before the fall. The belief that all dragons are nasty is a myth—only the ones that breathe fire and fart thunder & lightning are hostile and in need of slaying. There are many more average looking maidens than there are fair and beautiful ones, and unpretentious princes come in all shapes and sizes—some might appear to be bullfrogs. And only in their fantasy dreams, does everybody live happily ever after, because controlling powers come into play and enjoying blissfully gets all *fucked-up!!!*

Fuck redux, as everything cycles back to the systematic devaluing and eventual loss of enjoying blissful *fucks* by the fire pit. When those smart-asses started playing with the power of fire, their enjoying of life got *fucked-up.* The more control they had over fire, the less fireside enjoying was happening. Controlling fire brought freedom from and control over the beasts, while opening the hatching of primitive powers. The keeper-of-the-fire dude had the jive juice of control over the tribe.

The keeper kept warm by fire pit, while directing the tribe on how to gather wood for tending the eternal flame of the fire. The fire keeper would do his magical *fucking* hand jive keeping the fire alive in mythical secret ways. In some tribes the keeper of the fire was a smart thinking woman. Being keeper-of-the-fire came to those with the smartness of mind to learn of the controlling ways of tending fire. Enjoying by the fire, safe from the beasts was omnipotent. So being the tribe's fire-keeper was the first power play position supposedly done for the well being of all—but a major benefit for the fire-keep who didn't have to go out and gather fuel for the fire, and some keepers even avoided being drafted into the hunts for the savage beasts. A gentle *mind-fucking* of just evolving minds, in exchange for continuing blissful *fucking* by the fire-keeper tended fire.

Someone *fucked-up* and changed *blissful fucking* to *blessful fucking* and the fire-keeper got credited with bringing then the bright blessing of *fucking* by the fire-keeper's blessed fire!!! The original transcending of bestowed power to a smarter human being dude, was purely a simple matter of being blessed to continue lustfully enjoying *fucking* by the fire pit—providing the gathering of fuel for the fire were their pay-as-you-warm taxes. Naturally, fuel taxes were collected by the fire-keeper. Thus, the first bucks were exchanged for *fucks* paid to the clan's smart pimping fire-keeper!!!

I sold my *fuck essay* for *bucks!!!* In 1975, I got a phone call from a vice-president with Pinnacle Books in New York. They were publishing *The Whole Sex Catalogue* edited by Bernhardt J. Hurwood, and he was calling to request my permission to reprint my *"The Immortalization of Fuck"* essay in their soon to be published book. They had found me when they were verifying my copyright with the Library of Congress. The copyright assistant who helped them to research my filed and granted copyright was named John Wayne—not the same John Wayne from movie fame!!!

I quickly agreed to work a deal for them to publish my essay—selling *fucks* for bucks big time, but sadly not for really big bucks by today's big bucks standards. We made arrangements to meet in New York the following week to work out the details. However, I had to confirm the deal via telegram at once--like instantly. Thus, I called Western Union for an operator to take my telegram message to go to Pinnacle Books. Everything was going well until I got to the title . . . *"The Immortalization of Fuck"* . . .

"Excuse me, sir, is that 'buck' with a 'B'???"

"No, my dear, that's 'fuck' with an 'F'!!!" I said laughing.

"Oh sir, I'm afraid we aren't allowed to use *that word* in a Western Union telegram."

"Ah, then we have a problem, because this telegram is an interim legal document granting Pinnacle Books my permission to publish my essay as part of a book. And the specific title must clearly be stated as it is."

"I understand, sir. But *that four letter word* can't be used in a Western Union telegram."

Thinking letters, I asked, "How about 'F' '*' '*' 'K'???"

"Oh, good idea, sir, but I don't have an '*' on my keyboard!!!"

"Okay, how about 'F' '-' '-' 'K'???"

"Oh yes, sir, that would work. I like a *fuck* much better with dashes!!!" she said laughing.

I did have to wonder, if the contents of a telegram are private, then why couldn't the word *fuck* be used properly in the contents of the telegram??? Did Western Union have someone reading all the telegrams to purposefully check confidential messages for offending *four letter words*??? I still wonder about that, and about those people who today continue to take liberties with their review and censoring of private and personal correspondence—how much of that happens on the internet???

My deal with Pinnacle Books included doing some promotional book signing appearances along with several of the other contributors to the book. I met some really fun folks, but I discovered that fame stuff is grossly over-rated and involves lots of *mind-fucking*. All the *be here and do that* now in the name of just being sort of famous on the edge of things. The talk shows seemed more like cattle round-ups. Herding the ever changing bunch of celebrity cattle in and positioning them to make nice with everyone in front of the camera. Everybody smiling and saying plastic things that have no meaning except to swell their already swollen egos!!!

Having my essay published in the book also made for some interesting conversations on the usually rather boring cocktail circuit. I dare say it was kind of fun having cocktail party people trying to guess what my claim to fleeting fame was . . . and it was also funny seeing their feigned dismay or their increasing smiling interest when they found out I really sold *fucks* legally for bucks!!!

Yes, I know various folks have *borrowed* freely from my essay, and my early reflections on *fuck* have been used in lots of different ways. I like to think that my essay might have helped to remove some of the nasty stuff that has been unfairly dumped upon this word to mess with the minds of humankind. Perhaps my efforts have helped to have *fuck* used a bit more correctly in personal communications.

On the eve of the dawning of a new millennium, humankind is overwhelmed with assorted self-proclaimed keepers-of-many-fires. Enjoying by the fire pit is the lustful passion that has been lost in the shifting mind changes of centuries. The fire-keepers learned the ways of power, including the nuclear-fire that can surge forth to destroy us all. Enjoying the kind consideration for one and all, in the safe haven from the beasts, has in many ways become a zoo, and we are now the very same beasts we once feared. Monsters mashing around in harmful ways of *fucking joy* away. Would be rulers doing perverting power pulls that dismember the fragile fabric of humankind. Power plays conning away trustful considerations by converting once upon a time kindness, into a *fuck-you-before-you-fuck-me* mindset of grossly inconsiderate distractions, and tossing around guilt and greed and jealousy like party ill-favors laced with hatred. Bummer when the beast controls the fire, and the passionate communal fire pit has long ago been pissed out—gone with the yucky stinky smoke. The beast is within, grown from the seeds of our winters of discontent, bringing the coldness of winds most foul that freeze fast the flows of passion and chills the godspark with a mask of dullness.

Hopefully, my *Fuck Redux* ramble has produced a few smiles about the bad rap *fuck* has gotten over the centuries. Perhaps I've opened some mind-blossoms about beginning to understand the amending concept of *unfucking*, and maybe I slipped in a wee bit of renewed learning regarding *do no harm* to anyone—painfully nasty *fucking* is very harmful. And perchance, I've increased your awareness of extending kind consideration to be more considerate to others—hurtful *fucking* has ways of coming back and *fucking-up* those insensitive *fuckers!!!* And hopefully I've provided some insight into how passionate joyful *fucking* was, way back then, before the time clock started evolving humankind into the ugly ways of politically correct *fucking,* with *fuckers* and *fuckees.* Mostly I hope I've voiced a call for the regenerated growth of the basic primal freedoms for everyone to enjoy often by the fire pit—safe from the fear of the hungry beasts that prowl about and free from the raging dangerous beast within.

Take care and enjoy often . . . John

The Mystery of BC

BC arrived during a blizzard, the historical heavy snowfall
was measured in feet, stranding me in the warm home of a lady
friend, about a long snowy mile from my house in suburbia.

After the snowstorm finally moved on, several days passed be-
fore the main roads were open and my car was dug out from the
drifts and I could venture a return trip to my home.
Snow drifts surrounded my tri-level ranch style home,
the driveway was blocked with deep snow.
I parked off the road and waded to the front door unlocking the
door, I went inside the cold, quiet house.

This was one of the first electrically heated houses, and each of
the thermostats had been turned down low—the quiet was shat-
tered by an unearthly S C R E A M ! ! ! ! ! ! ! ! !
Suddenly filling my house with the sounds of horrible rage!!!

Now I have no fear of spooks, haunts, and those strange things
that go bump in the night, but this was a scream unlike anything
I'd ever heard—a long slow blood-chilling scream that went on
and on with grotesque changes in volume and pitch.
This had the sound of some kind of forbidden terror!!!
I went to the bedroom to get my pistol and flashlight,
and then started my search for the source of the screaming,
so shrill was this continuing earsplitting yelling.

I bluntly yelled, 'STOP SCREAMING!!!',
but the screaming only increased unceasingly.
So much for trying a commanding booming voice!!!
I loudly banged open the door to the basement,
the wailing seemed to fill the entire basement area,
as I searched under the pool table and behind the bar,
into the darkroom, flicking on safety lights by mistake,
investigating every possible space to no avail.

I couldn't find the origin of the shrieking.
However, the source now seemed to be overhead.

Back upstairs I cautiously looked in each room,
and found nothing but the ongoing screaming,
the howling seemed to be everywhere—and no where!!!

All that remained to be searched was the locked attic—the large storage area under the eve of the roof, and now the screaming was coming from right behind the tightly closed access door.

I rapped my flashlight on the door—the outcry stopped,
all was as quiet as a winter graveyard at midnight.
The only sound was a metallic click as I cocked my pistol,
now thinking a shotgun would have been a better choice,
then not, a 12 gauge could make a big hole in my roof!!!

I undid and slid my belt free from my jeans and looped my belt through the handle of the attic door.
Now I could stand back from the opening door swing,
with the flashlight and end of the belt in my left hand,
and my trusty Ruger single-six in my right hand,
ready to confront what awaited behind the green door.
From within the attic came the clattering and crashing of things being knocked over and hitting the floor, leading me to believe there was something of substance waiting there.

Just about then, I did have thoughts of calling 911.
However, with bad road conditions and fender-benders,
it would probably take a long time for the police to arrive.
Besides, I had been trained as a USAF Air Policeman.
I was also a SAC trained Airborne Ranger, holding a weapon I was most familiar with, and I was sure I could hit whatever was waiting there before any harm could befall me.
But of course, back-up would have been nice too.

Yes, I was stalling, pondering what it could be—what had enough mass to knock things over in the attic.
Perhaps the best course of action would be to just leave—leave whatever was there be, to go away in due time.
As they say, *let a sleeping dog lay.*

But this sure wasn't anything sleeping!!!
With my pistol trained on the door, I gave a quick yank,
and off to the side in the shadowy darkness of the attic,
two surreal eyes glowed golden reflecting the light,
disembodied glowing amber embers in the pitch-blackness.
I swung my beam of light and what I captured,
in the bright circle of light was a full grown black cat!!!

Thus begins the mystery of the black cat.
How did a mature cat get into my sealed house when the snow
around the house had no tracks, and end up in my cold attic???

I uncocked my pistol, closed the door, and went down to the
kitchen to get a can of tuna as a way of tempting the black cat
out of the attic under somewhat controlled conditions.

The fish scent brought a low screeching wail, and a bit of catty
licking the chops as the black cat slinked cautiously towards me.
Once again, seeing a means of escape from the attic, and yummy
tempting food in my extended hand, the starving black cat
stopped about a yard away, looked me in the eye and looked at
the can of tuna, and then looked at the floor in front of him
as if to say, *I see you . . . I see the food . . .*
Now I want to see the food here in front of me!!!
And that's what I did, but the black cat waited until I returned to
the door before starting to devour the canned tuna feast.
After eating some, I got a look of, *from a can???!!!*

This was the start of my strange relationship with BC,
BC . . . but of course, short for *Black Cat,*
hehehee . . . as if you didn't know that!!!

BC also became short for Black Creature, because the Black Cat
became very uncat-like, and more like a creature in the form of a
black cat, at least that's how he was around me.

Now I'd seen this kind of transference happen once before,
when Gray Dog changed into Gray Thing.
Gray was a silver-gray poodle, orphaned at birth.

He was about to be tossed into a bag with rocks, and thrown to a watery death in a pond, because Gray was a *party-poodle.*
He had a small pure white diamond on his chest and his size was wrong—too big to be a *toy*, too small to be a *miniature*.

I paid cash to save the days old orphan, and then nursed him from a baby bottle during his early life in Oklahoma.
Gray was a friend and constant companion for 15 years, a natural hunter and an ever alert guard *dog*, a real rough and tumble protective type, not the fancy image folks might have of a poodle, and not like most dogs either.
Thus, he became Gray Thing, he wouldn't respond to Gray Dog, call him *Dog*, and he'd go into a funk and sulk!!!

Gray was long gone, but never forgotten,
so BC was welcomed to stay with me, he checked out the house and prudently looked me over.
He decided he'd stay for a time, sprawling out in a patch of sunlight in the living room, fading quickly into a comfy *cat* nap.

BC's sprawled positioning caused me to wonder, if stretched out on his back wasn't a wee bit peculiar for a grown cat.
I thought cats were into curling up in a ball, his reclining spread in the sun struck me to be more like Gray's way of sun bathing.

I called around the neighborhood, no one knew of a black cat in the area, one lady hung-up me saying, *black cats are bad luck!!!*
My next call was to the local SPCA, thinking they'd be a clearing house for lost family pets, but they had no reports of a missing black cat, told me to place a *found cat* classified ad, if I kept the cat—to be sure to have him declawed and neutered!!!

Ugh, never having any experience as a cat owner, the idea of being neutered and declawed caused me pain, way cruel to do to the seemingly young but mature cat—now napping on his back in a patch of sunlight.

Now I tried to find out how BC got into the sealed house, searching all the places where he might have come in.

The garage door hadn't been opened in months, and the seal around the bottom of the door was so tight that not even a trace of snow had gotten in, all the doors were sealed air-tight too.
I couldn't find an opening where a small field mouse could have entered—let alone a full grown cat.

I went back into the attic looking for any possible way BC could have gotten in and escaped the raging blizzard.
Once again my visual inspection found nothing.
I had a candle with me, to see if the flame would flicker to reveal the signs of a telltale draft—however, the flame was all straight and steady with not as much as a hint of a flinching quiver, as I vigilantly circled the attic perimeter.

And to this day, the mystery remains as to how BC came to be in the cold dark attic of my hermetically sealed house???
As years went by, the plot thickened.
BC became a rather unique Creature of very uncat-like behaviors, while being cat smart, purring like a happy pussy, with nine lives.

Like Gray Thing, BC was a hunter—he'd stalk the cornfield next to the house bringing home trophy after trophy of field mice, standing over his prize until I paid him attention, bestowing praises on him for his fearless hunting skills.
I've been told that's a hunter-cat-like tradition, but not so cat-like is that when he'd be off roaming, my shouting *BC* would have him instantly running to me, just like Gray Thing would instantly come a running whenever I'd shout out his name.

BC was never declawed and he never scratched me, nor did he do any furniture scratching.
As for not being neutered—deballed!!! Ouch!!!
BC was into safe sex before it became popular.
I just couldn't convince myself to have his nuts cut off.
Anyhow, he never did that pissing all over the house like cats often do, marking their breeding territory.
BC didn't need to do pissy ownership stuff, indeed he was a most evolved pussy.

BC loved long hot bubble baths—I'm a Calgon man!!!
I'd bliss in the bath—*Calgon take me away*—while BC would stand on the edge of the tub, enticed by the mountain of foaming bubbles, but I knew it was only a matter of time until he'd fall. Thoughts of a freaked BC in the bath water flooded my mind, he could claw in my flesh—my very tender personal flesh even. Painful thoughts of BC's claws capturing my cockbird!!!
Therefore, I encouraged BC to play with the bubbles at the end of the tub where my feet were, kinda an assumed risk management safeguarding of my vitals.
As if my concerns where a foretelling, BC did slip from his precarious perch, splashing into my bubble bath with a surprised outcry—soon turning into a prolonged purring of delight.
Now I was once again astonished by BC—because everyone knows that cats don't do baths—no how, no way!!!
However, BC sat down in my hot bath water, seeming to be very curious about the surrounding bubbles and not at all concerned about being in the water, with no panic freaking and clawing to get out—and that's totally uncat-like!!!

I once watched BC playing kitty tag with a tiger cat, when the tiger cat dashed around a big mudpuddle.
Much to the surprise of the bigger cat, BC went plunging right through the puddle—tagging the amazed cat with muddy paws.
The tiger cat was totally flabbergasted seeing another cat willingly run into muddy water—somewhat like a vampire seeing another vampire going for a walk in the sunlight!!!

BC loved to take me on walks, he'd encourage me to *walk him* by bringing his leash—carrying his lead in his mouth was a clue.
Now was the time to go for a walk with him, and indeed folks would look rather dumbfounded at a black cat strutting smartly along on a leash—out for a merry stroll in the neighborhood.

Gray would also bring me his chain leash, plopping the leash at my feet with a clatter, or shake his head swinging the chain links hitting my legs to get my attention.

BC did tricks on command—the usual ones of sit, roll over, lay down, but he won't ever play dead—neither would Gray.
BC enjoyed leaping up and knocking down a Frisbee, anything sailing close to him was fair game, or springing into the flight path and then pouncing down on the gliding Frisbee.
Gray was both a Frisbee catcher and pouncer too, he'd pounce on almost anything--even big dogs.

Gray had a fascination with big dogs, always trying to get bigger dogs to play—BC tried to play with both cats and dogs too.
They definitely had a *don't mess with me* demeanor, but mostly BC and Gray got along with everyone.
Except for skunks!!!
Both Gray Thing and BC had tangled with skunks.
Gray came home covered in yucky skunk smell, that night, he was one tail-down, stinky dog, from mixing it up with a skunk.
Ugh, he was a mess and I bathed him in tomato juice—that really does work to get rid of the skunk smell.

BC also came home reeking of fresh skunk spray.
Now this was really very odd for a cat, because what self-respecting cat is foolish enough, to go at it with a polecat???
I believe horny BC was lustfully trying to get up close and personal with a skunk—because he reeked of skunk stink.
As soon as he came in the house smelling yucky, he raced to the bath room, jumped into the empty tub, waiting for me to turn his bath water on—BC stayed there while I went for tomato juice,
I thought cats knew not to fuck around with a skunk!!!

One Halloween, I had a carved pumpkin by the door, BC hung by the pumpkin as trick-or-treaters came by, he'd be sitting on top of the huge pumpkin or jump out from behind it surprising the costumed kids—I believe if it hadn't been for the burning candle, BC would have gotten inside the pumpkin.
He was way into the first day celebrating of Halloween, the great orange pumpkin was his costume, except the pumpkin wore him, black on orange—so to speak!!!

BC was also a fun trickster—as well as a treat.

Celebrating Halloween was over and the great pumpkin had seen better days, BC followed me when I put it with the trash. He just kept walking down the street, I guessed that he didn't want to see the trashmen take his decaying great pumpkin costume away, so he went off on one of his roaming jaunts. Later that day, I was raking leaves in the front yard, and I was carrying a bag of leaves to give to the trashmen who pulled up and were tossing my trash into the truck. One was picking up the pumpkin, when suddenly BC popped out of the pumpkin, much to the shocking surprise of the trashmen. They all laughed at BC's cat-in-the-pumpkin trick. As they drove off laughing I heard the one guy say, *Now, that's the real Great Pumpkin, Charlie Brown!!!*

BC was a lot like Gray Thing—the similarities were astonishing. Gray was buried in the backyard under a dogwood tree, next to my snowbound house where BC appeared. I was into my seventh year of knowing BC, when he passed away from heart failure too—I also buried BC under a dogwood tree, a strange combination of a *dog* in the body of a black cat.

While I was writing this as a work-in-progress, I drove to meet a friend for dinner on Sunday evening and I noticed the PA tag on the car ahead read 'PUPKAT', very unique how those gifts from the universe seem to happen when you need a smile.

I do indeed hope that my reflections from another time, have brought you a few smiles too, maybe even a laugh. I also hope you'll think kindly when you see a black cat, there's no bad luck attached to them, black cats need love and caring too—just like we all do.

Take care and enjoy often . . . John

USED SHIT

Listen my friends, and please kindly take heed, this ramble is sort of pointed, and thoughts expressed herein could cause some deeply buried and securely locked away places to be pricked open as you read.
This rambling mindplay, also 'tis a bit long for a reflective sharing, and some parts are primal and rather raw.
Thus, this disclaimer is provided so as not to offend you with my thought flows—read at your own risk.
I'm on a bit of a roll, roll along with me if you dare.

My intent here is to take self-imposed fears we humankind tend to carry along with us, and convert those fears into regular shit, because shit may be flushed clean away and be done and gone.

These shitty fears might be deeply entrenched, hidden in dark places deep inside.
At times you might feel that all those stashed away yesteryear frights are gone far from sight, but the shit from lurking fears continues to stay with you—popping out like a plopping load of dropping shit at the most inopportune times.

Indeed, 'tis most usual for folks to believe, that their fearful shit is way unique, really some kind of special fright shit!!!

However, the truth about that frightful shit is that the most horrible shit of all is nothing more than the plain old garden variety of shit—with just slightly different spins and slight variations in color and consistency.

The only thing special about that shit is that it's all *used shit.*
You're the owner of the shit within you, because that leftover shit is of your making, and only with you now because you've hung onto the shit—more correct the shit has hung onto you.

When you look at your fears up close, you'll clearly recognize all those fears to be your shit, nothing more than remaining waste matter left behind from passing life experiences that

you've learned painful life lessons from—forced learnings from attending the school of hard knocks.
The *would-be teachers* are long gone from your world.
However, you seem to be still hanging onto shitty souvenirs, and for the sake of your well being in the here and now you really don't need shit covered keepsakes.

You've known the pain and the torments in all the anguishing anger of those rank remembrances,
from the pungent ache of betrayals from broken trusts,
to the slashing cuts of promises plowed under in passing,
the freaky guilt of feeling that you weren't enough,
the self-doubts that dangle from haunting *if only's,*
and the continuing nagging fear that it will happen again . . .
and again . . . and again!!! Ugh!!!

Once you might have worn a blood-soaked,
bright red bandage as a perverted badge of courage showing all those who would care to look, the outward appearance of your wounds, but that's just the very tip of the iceberg, because the mass of the frigid frightening pain is the huge cluster of old shit locked deep inside you—very deep inside where no one can see.
With time passages, the bright red blood turns into the brownish colors of mud—so yucky your bandage becomes!!!
And when showing the world your horrible hurts no longer serves a pitiful purpose you finally cast those messy shrouds away, but the mass of fearful shit remains, still festering a raging fever in your mind, and tainting your heart with foulness.

Now, some folks come to know a most special place,
that's the garden of your heart.
Here's where your godspark dwells, surrounded with the growing memories of cherished friends you've shared life passings with.
Some are friends from long ago and far away, and others are as new as this evolving day, some have passed your way but once, and others visit with you more often, because you've welcomed them, and invited them into your safe enchanted garden.

No harmful doings of any sort are ever permitted in the garden of your heart, no lies betold, no greedy doing, no bemoaned woes, no jealousy of anyone, no envious comparing this with that, no guilt tripping expectations!!!
Here only nurturing beauty grows with each one sharing in the sparkling delights, happening here in your most special place.

Here is where all your used shit becomes fertilizer, rich deep dark humus enriching your garden soil, here's where all those self-imposed ugly fears decompose into the seemingly nothingness of taken for granted organic fertile loam—fertile soil supporting blooming life blossoms.

Now, some folks will be quick to over-react to that expressed *self-imposed shit* concept, bemoaning that their shit isn't the *self-imposed* kind!!!
Explaining their shit is from wrongs done to them by others—others who have done wrong and dumped *their* shit—and there's nothing *self-imposed* about dumped shit!!!

Oh, not so!!!
Sure, you might have gotten dumped on,
but their shit just washes away as they go away!!!
However, the shitty way you were left feeling,
is caused by the clinging shit that remains with you.
All those hurt feelings that shatter you to your very core,
are where your fears, worries, and self-doubt come from.

'Tis true some dumpings do indeed get thumped on you,
with no warning given!!!
There's no foretelling the brutal dumping was gonna happen
upon you just then—shit happens!!!
With a zip and a ding you're covered with their shit,
and you feel so completely violated and totally abused
with primal feelings of being hurt way bad.

Perhaps you were just in the dumping grounds, one of those nasty ill-fated occurrences of being in the wrong place at the wrong time, or maybe a trusted friend dingingly turns away from you, or takes advantage of your friendship and does you wrong.

Regardless of why—the dumping is befalling upon you!!!
The shit being dumped all over you is clearly coming at you from someone's anus!!!
Major bummer, because you're on the yucky receiving end, and that sure has you feeling very shitty!!!
You're caught out in the open, without an umbrella, during a raging shit storm!!!

But, all of that external shit they are so unkindly dumping washes away with plain soap and water!!!
Oh sure, there might be a bit of stain for a time, but that too, eventually wears away—*self-imposed shit lingers.*

That's the hardcore shit that clusters into shit-stones, making up those heavy duty fears that becomes the shit you carry!!!
They're the burdensome milestones marking shitty life experiences you've known, all those jagged pieces of your broken heart get mixed in with those yucky shit-stones, and they get all fused together inside of you.
But the sharp pieces of your shattered heart still bring you searing pain everytime those cutting parts slash open the innards of your being—once more you experience the shitty frights of being dumped upon, again!!!

You fear how their dumpings left you feeling with shitty stings that caused your self-worth to be trashed by their yanking away of nurturing trustful bonds with another.
Those links have been uncaringly stripped away from you, gone forever is an important part of your world, taken away by someone leaving while their shit remains behind.

Now, part of the lingering shit could be your frustrations of believing you've somehow pushed them away, or maybe the interactions were such that they just finally ran quickly away from all those shitty interactions trading bemoaning put downs!!!

And now, you are stuck with all the shit they've left, in the wasteful wake of their leaving, abandoning the bitching hassles behind them, leaving you with the shitty remains of the day!!!

In the measurements of time,
those shitty actions done to you
might only take but a mere fraction
from the entire history of your timeline,
but the heavy burden you are left to toil with
stays with you as a dinging resounding echoing
of the depressing discourse that messed over you.

Now, some folks do take the path of trying to resolve ills,
seeking some form of meaningful closure with the dumper
as if to glean remaining understanding from the dynamics that
have left you all alone and carrying such a shitty heavy burden.
So noble you are to try to find a sort of resolution
when all of the solutions seem to gush on by
leaving you covered with a shitty mess,
feeling like your efforts to mend
are going nowhere fast!!!

Some get into a place of trying to vainly hit back at the dumper,
zap them back *good* to bring them hurts like the achings they've
brought to you!!!
Alas, you know well that old bit about *hell has no fury,*
like someone who's been scorned--dumped on!!!
So tempting it is for you to lash back at them in raw revenge,
cunningly crafting your twisted plot for tormenting retribution,
smiting them back with endless shitty hurts!!!

There is no tribute to anyone in revenge, no honoring of your
self-worth that's trashed all over again in doing vengeance,
nor any sense of value in doing a payback on them.
Ah, 'tis hard to feel value in the perceived shitty hurts you're
feeling from laying in the pulsing pains of your broken heart.
Seems like your remaining life's energies are rushing out of your
bloody wounds, there's just no value in scorning back—that
would wastefully drain more of your energy away.

There's no worthwhile gain in venting back at them, they've
shown you their heartlessness by dumping on you!!!
Your choices are really rather simple, you either burden yourself
by accepting their dumped shit—often a heavy load to bear,
or pull yourself out from under their pile of smelly shit.
The choice is entirely yours to make, to carry their shit or begin
to crawl free of their shit!!!

'Tis okay to believe that somewhere along their path—the person who dumped upon you so badly—will receive their just due with the passing of time when they are being dumped upon by another, because you remember that thingy about the only constant in life is change, and those life changes will circle around and around until they receive a heavy-duty dumping in due course—when their lesson in learning about life and the harm they did returns many times over for them to learn from.

Sadly, many who do dumping harm have never learned, and in
the inter-play of life's flows they become a mere shell—empty
of meaningful life's energies.
Because they exhaust lots of energy in all their shitty dumps,
becoming more and more burdened by all the shit that they too
must carry, haunted in the deep dark of night with worries of
wrongs that will never be forgotten, never really put to rest,
because they know that what they did to others will sooner or
later be done to them in kind.
Perhaps, in those *kindnesses* they might eventually learn
from those nasty shitty harms they once did to others.
Alas, the greatest harm of all they've done,
is the harm they've done to themselves.

They have cast their die by being so insensitive to you,
betrayed you with lies of unfriendly deceitful doings,
misled you by spinning tales of untruths.
They had a hidden agenda you got dingfully zapped with,
so they sure aren't going to be mindful to anything
you might have to say to them—such a waste to try.
But you do try offering an olive branch to make an amending
peace between you, only to have them ignore the offered

kindness, or have the branch taken and used as a bloody whip to beat you away from their closed door—they don't want you near them now as some ghoulish reminder of a tossed away person they've used and abused to get to where they are now.

Thusly, your effort to reach them is like pissing into the wind, your piss is just gonna come back at you, and have you continuing to feel yucky—even more messy!!!

Some might call this a bit of over rationalization,
but sadly we often do tend to create what we fear.
We are also taught to fear like some are told to fear the night!!!
Thusly, they miss knowing the beauty of the night.
Some are told not to touch fire, however, they often need the experience of burning hurts, because there's no perception of fire hurting—until their first hand burning ouch happens!!!
Then they know from their doing that touching fire does hurt!!!

Some will venture into the mystic veil of night, and instead of the expected fright they discover the many beauties of the night. Nothing to fear here except for the implanted fear we carry with us, and the awareness that what we often find isn't always as expected—the hungry beasts that once prowled the night have long ago gone away with the changes of time.

Lots of fear is spun in all sorts of expected expectations, the anticipated acceptance of being found unworthy of coming to know another in open acceptance, the apprehensive allure around acceptability, worrying and wondering and pondering potential areas of aligning accepting, fear of not being acceptable, fear of not being heard, fear of being called out—before even getting up to bat, fear of no alignments, fearing loneliness, fearing all alone, fearing fear, friendless, all alone, so alone.

Once planted, seeds of entangling fears grow ever so quickly as all weeds do—feeding upon doubts begetting more fear, spreading outward from your core of being, surrounding actions in the clutches of self-doubts, breeding unchecked with greed

and jealousy and guilt, producing a big fearful mass to cope with, and every doing is done in consideration of your ever present *fear factor* being applied.
Strangling fear comes into play, and kicks self-worth away into a spin of tumbling self-doubting fears.

Fear—the yucky shit that gums up the doings of having a more joyful life, of living a fuller life, of enjoying life's benefits, free of fearful frights and open to delights.

You have the ability to learn from your fears, and those fears aren't so overpowering when those lessons learned are converted into caution signs—reflections of life's learnings.
You benefit from those warnings carved into milestones left behind to mark your passage—operative phase *'left behind you'*.

Healthy cautions are positive uses for those shitty milestones, and sure you may create a reflecting pool deep in the garden of your heart—a place to recall and reflect upon lessons learned. Methinks milestones are great stepping stones when positioned around the edges of the reflections pool—feels befitting to walk upon those laid bare bones of once frightening fearful mind monsters and learn caution from their tempered experiences.

Some folks overdue caution, their caution becomes a means to avoid doing joyful things.
Oh, for sure they'd enjoy doing something—perhaps!!!
At least their spoken words seem to say so.
But then they come up with a thousand and one *excuses* not to do it—regardless of whatever else they say—excuses rule!!!
Their over cautiousness keeps their desires firmly in check, and they're so into checking caution flags that their yearnings soon wane away blown upon the breeze that flutters the tattered flags. Their would-be doings are lost forever in those over applied cautioned avoidance—so insincerely they always seem to say,
'I'd love to but . . .'
Oh my, way more honest to say what your worries are now, now in the here and now of being free of past ghosts!!!

What hauntings cause your caution flags to flap about rethinking through what keeps holding you back, and talking openly about your applicable concerns.
'Tis better than coming up with lame excuses—excuses are so draining of your energies!!!

Because those excuses have the power to spin the fabric of your fluttering caution flags into the tight binding ropes of fear, ugly fears of your own making tightening all around you, preventing you from enjoying more joys, and from trusting in yourself to enjoy more life.

Some worrisome folks put their perceived fears on others, imposing upon others the fears they have continued to hold.
Maybe they've learned of these perils as they passed along their pathway—they become alarmed for you, sensing where they fear you're heading when you fail to heed their alerting pleas, and nothing they could say will alert you to the dire straits they see you entering—there's no way to change your headstrong course.
Alas, you must remember, 'tis the course of your choosing—you are fixed on the star you follow, and they can't worry now about unfucking what you are into doing your way.
The doing is all your doing, so they don't need to burden themselves by being fearful for you.
When you eventually discover you're in deep shit, hopefully they won't go compounding your plight by meanly snapping,
'I told you so . . . I told you . . .!!!'

Some fears just sort of creep up on you,
or you get freaked watching the coming fearfulness!!!
Such as showing outward signs of age, those increasing telltale frustrations with each stress filled wrinkle, the sighs from each new sag, fearful your new glad rags won't hide the extra bags from life's dings of nags, slowly creeping appearance changes, fearing transitions happening, feeling the reaching grip of fear about no longer having an acceptable appearance.
Fearful of how others will really see your outward shell,
so fragile, so overly susceptible to thoughtless comments.

At the same time, you might also be growing within, as you come to know from life learnings the wisdom to see beyond outward looks and behold your inner beauty sparkling true, reflecting life's glow from within you.
That's your ageless godspark glowing, and that beauty abounds far beyond all your put on shrouds—in the garden of your heart, the unkind stresses from time passages, fade away from you.
Here, the essence of your being is all you, being you, accepted as you are, today, tomorrow, and everafter, all ways, always.

Always, your truth will overcome the clutches of fear, even when you cycle into opening and sharing more of you being you with another, which is better than clapping closed, pulling in tight in anticipation of more shitty new dumpings all over you!!!

However, within you, your godspark glows centering with your being, spreading outward as a beacon.
A light guiding you to safe harbors when you trust yourself to take the risk, your sweeping beam of light chases fears away.
When you apply the *Trisk Factor*—
Trust yourself enough to take the Risk!!!

Forget about heartthrobs, go with the feelings in your gut, have the gumption to trust yourself, to accept another knowing you as you are, as you accept coming to know them as they are.
'Tis far better to evolve into *so far, so good* relating, than discovering your bleeding heart has trapped you into a fatal attraction—same old shit, on another day.

Myths often create fears that are stressfully frightening at times, not those made up olde tales of vampires, nor the pot of gold at rainbow's end—*I always seem to be at the wrong end!!!*
But rather, the myth of perfection, fearful you'll never find that one perfect person—that one who fulfills your shopping list of expectations with their hair just so stylishly perfect, and wearing the right kind of shoes, with charm and wit to keep you laughing.
But after the laughter fades away, their no longer great looking shoes get all scuffed, you find their perfect hairdo was really a wig, and the myth of what you thought you'd found as perfect,

is blown away on the winds like the remains of a vampire, caught in the light of the rising sun.

Perfection is such a shitty fright, the tiresome quest to achieve perfect perfection, and then, after that lofty goal is at last seemingly reached, the ongoing fear sets in, of not being able to maintain those airs of flawlessness, in an imperfect real world.

Perfection gets frightfully costly, all that just too, too, cute shit has a high price, taxing your resources to make the best appearances, cutting off and closing down parts of yourself, those parts that could be perceived as being unattractive, and you fear being seen as unacceptable as you really are!!! Then you fear the changes you've made won't be enough—fearing those changes you've made to try to appease the illusions of perfection, will slowly fade away to show others faults in you. One day you wake up with the frightening realization that you miss the parts of you that you've surrendered—sadly you begin to wonder if you will ever be real again, able to shed the perfectly painted plastic shell that doesn't fit you anymore.

Perhaps, the greatest fear of all is being real, sure you might try to play the game of fooling some people for some of the time. But deep inside you dwells the truth of the real you, waiting for you to find the realness of your goodness there, not the made-up person the world sees, because you only let the world look upon the person *'they'* expect to find you to always be, and the real you, might be way different in lots of positive ways, free of your used shit, but not being the ways *they* want you to be!!!

The real you inside is a gardener of life, tenderly tending the garden of your heart, your hands get covered with soil and you smell earthy, and within your self-worth you find the inner strength to overcome fears of not being accepted by some, and find far greater and lasting values in those regular folks who accept you as you are, as you accept them in the same kindness, in the here and now of today.

And you reclaim yourself from the battles for phony values,

yielding the field to fools who chase plastic perfection,
avoiding those who are more concerned with shoe styles than the stance of the person wearing the shoes!!!
Alas, 'tis the cut of a person's demeanor that matters far more than the tailored cut of appearances, a liar in a thousand dollar suit, is still a liar even in a new suit!!!

Acknowledging that you don't have all the answers,
often you don't even understand the questions,
but ever so slowly you're learning what rings true with you,
and that might not make sense to anyone but you,
however, those clear tones of truth are right with you,
and start to move you away from the pulls of used shit.

There's no fear when you let me be me, and I let you be you.
There's no fear in giving, nor harm in accepting.
There's wholeness aligning accepting, free of painted shells,
fullness of beings, free of used shit, openly enjoying,
enjoying lovings, doing more life, enjoying often, enjoy often.

Take care and enjoy often . . . John

PADDY'S REQUEST

Greetings be upon one and all this Saint Patrick's day,
the day in March for honoring the patron saint of Ireland,
the Emerald Isle—snake free,
but sadly, still with religious killing strife.
Ireland—where the wee magical folks could once be found,
back when Paddy was roaming about the island
around the early 400's—AD of course.

Back then he was on an early popeful mission, converting the scattered and diverse population of Ireland to a single belief!!!

He was way down on pagans, druids and wee folks,
snakes were often used metaphorically for heathens and pagans in conjunction with what Paddy was said to have done, but let's just suppose, way back then that history took a snakelike twist of fate as these two tales of my making will betel.
Both contain a thread of a thought about how the snake trick might have actually happened back then, 'tis the amount of conjured magic involved that makes all the difference between the two, and an eyeing honoring of divergences in flows, with both reflecting a differing level of attunement with natural flows.

One is done single-handed by Patrick,
the other is a collective effort of magical alignments.
Artistic liberties of creative expression have naturally been taken, leprechauns are said to do a selective application of *do no harm as thy will be done*.
At times, those wee little greenish folks can be very tricky, sort of hurtful, and so resourceful.

Thusly, my tales are presented for your kind consideration, with perhaps a few smiles of enjoying, free of any offense to the honored memory of Paddy.

Alas, I knew Saint Patrick not, but may my words honor his deeds and doings along his twisting God-set path,
forgiving him all the harm he unknowingly did

to those pagan folks who believed differently than he did.
Methinks, what was really behind his way cool snake trick back then, was how he befriended one and all of the common folks from the foothills to the highlands.
he touched everyone with his gentle ways of being.
He was gladly received everywhere,
accepting simple food and strong drink whenever offered.
Indeed, he seemed at first to be very accepting.

However, Patrick was well known throughout the land
for lashing out at slithering snakes,
perhaps with some lingering regrets, some left-over incomplete closure about the talking tricky snake in the Eden garden!!!
The snake who urged the biting of the forbidden fruit.
Any above average bullfrog will quickly tell you—ribbitt . . .
'tis major dumb . . . ribbitt . . . to listen to . . . ribbitt . . .
the self-serving . . . ribbitt . . . deceitful advice . . . ribbitt . . .
of a talking serpent . . . ribbitt!!!

What snakes have to say might be so tempting to hear,
and sounds so sweetly endearing to the ear,
but if you do as those snakes say,
you'll find yourself being just as twisted all about as snakes are.
You can surely bet those twisted snakelike ways of being
aren't the fun kinds of twisting, nor twist 'n shout either!!!
And there's no truth to the olde rumor that Eve was a blonde,
or so I've been told!!!

Patrick's claim to fame came from supposedly driving all the snakes out of Ireland.
Seems way back then,
those beautiful green isles were infested with snakes,
poisonous ones that would make you dead quicker than quick
with a mere prick from the nasty bite of those snakes!!!
'Twas well known back then, that an asp could bite your ass
almost any time you needed to bare your buns!!!
I do wonder if perhaps, that's where the saying,
'that's a real bite in the ass!!!' came from???

I have a vision of Paddy . . .
being sort of like an early Pied Piper,
only he did his trick with snakes instead of rats.
These days 'tis hard to tell the difference . . .
snakes and rats—both will fuck-you-over real quick!!!
The piper used a tooting pipe to play an enchanting tune,
Paddy used his resounding loud voice in song,
charming those nasty reptiles out of dark hiding places
with his hardy randy singing of reverberating earthy songs.

Perhaps he was also the inspirational source of some evolving
lewd lyrics for future limericks as a form of early expressions
by those poetic common folks living around the village of
Limerick, in the southwestern Irish province of Munster.

> There once was a young lad named Paddy,
> Who did the 'munster mash' most dandy,
> Finding nasty snakes where they lay,
> Vibrating them vipers to come out to play,
> Keeping up a beat with his feet quite randy!

It must have been quite a sight to see,
this long tangled mass of snakes slithering onward right behind
a singing loudly Paddy as he went stomping on his merry way.
Down to the beaches they came,
across the wet sand they wiggled,
right onto the exposed mud flats left by the outgoing tide.
Now the mass of snakes were way weary
from all that slithering, wiggling to get here,
so those snakes took to the invitingly soft mud flats
like hogs take to slop!!!
And yes indeed, all those snakes quickly fell fast asleep.

While they were sleeping,
the tide flows did come in from the sea again covering over
the sleeping snakes with salt water.
Then, with the eternal cycle of things,
the high tide—from the pull of the full moon—went out again,
and all those nasty snake remains,

well, they were taken away by the changing tide,
and the snakes were gone from Ireland forever after.
Nevermore could a single slithering snake be found
on those sparkling Kelly green isles.

Alas,
there be another tale of olde worthy of telling about Paddy,
ridding Ireland of snakes.
As the feat was told in folk lore back then, or so the story goes,
that Paddy came upon a wee little green leprechaun
all tangled about with a huge, nasty constrictor.
That ugly snake was totally wrapped around the wee folk.
The leprechaun was off the ground,
meaning the ungrounded cute pixie
couldn't evoke any of his self-saving magical stuff.
Sensing Paddy's heavy footfalls,
the snake swung about to see what was approaching
just as Paddy whacked the snake a good one right on the big
snake's horrible head with his ever-ready shillelagh!!!
That wicked huge snake,
who was squeezing out the magic of life,
got zapped out of his life via a crushing blow from Paddy!!!
Thusly, he saved the very life of the wee leprechaun.

Now, everyone knows
that when you do a good life-saving deed for a leprechaun,
they just gotta share their treasure
with the good deed doer—who was Paddy.
However, the fortune of the leprechauns
isn't the promise of a pot of gold at rainbow's end.
A pot of gold is such a heavy burden to carry,
and rainbow's ends are impossible to get under.
And when you apply Murphy's Law,
you'll always find yourself under the wrong end of the rainbow.

Nay . . .
the true treasure of the leprechauns
are the jewels of gifted knowledge from the ancients.
Their secrets of walking upon ladders of moonbeams,

magical ways to whistle down the wind,
wondrous ways to change the course of thunderstorms,
astonishing magic to make mere mortals ageless,
crafts to part the cloak of time to see into a distant future,
gifts of healing touches to cure ailing pains,
ways of spinning pure white light to ward off harm,
how to banish wailing banshees to far away places.
They even knew the secret of—or so it was said,
how to play safe leap-frogging with unicorns.

Well . . . as the story of olde goes, Paddy listened to the litany of magical knowledge offered from the ancients.
Many would enhance his ways of being and thinking,
making him smarter, stronger, etc . . . but Paddy asked if he might have the gifted knowledge of a very olde secret
not yet mentioned by the wee folk.

Indeed, this unusual request by Paddy did certainly cause the life indebted leprechaun to take pause and ponder upon the thought provoking prize Paddy was asking for.
All the other big folks who had earned such a special gift went for ever lasting youthful beauty or golden wealth.
A few even selected continuing good health,
and even a fewer number asked to be immortal!!!

With all the immortal blessings and curses of many loves,
growing together and dying off again, and again to grow anew with someone new, and the cycle continues on and on.
Unless the immortal loses their head, the immortal learns the true meaning of forever, and that's a long, long, long time.

Paddy was indeed tempted to opt for being immortal,
to live forever, never to die.
To travel the world endlessly . . . upon the shifting sands of time,
watching humankind evolving, gathering centuries of learnings,
and new experiences along the way—ah, 'tis tempting.
But a temptation not taken by Paddy,
who held fast to his original request.

Being befuddled, the leprechaun turned around three times,
patted his head and tummy, turned about another time,
and with a sweeping wave of his wee hand,
a congress of leprechauns did magically appear in a circle,
surrounding an amazed Paddy.
They sat down and started smoking their wee pipes, while
jabbering amongst themselves about Paddy's unique request.
Never before had a good deed doer asked for anything like this
from the wee people.
Thusly, they assemble to carefully contemplate
how Paddy could rid Ireland of all the sneaky snakes???!!!

However, leprechauns are guided by one constant rule:
'do no harm to any living being'.
But that rule didn't really stop leprechauns from having good fun
being tricky—heheheheeee!!!
Zapping snakes away did pose a *do no harm* problem, since they
were living beings, dangerous and disgusting as they be,
and no harm to those snakes could they bring.

Yet they had to honor Paddy's request,
for a debt of honor is a debt of honor,
and leprechauns have always honored their debts—until now,
now, until this perplexing snake dilemma!!!

They tried to do a bit of let's make a deal,
and sweetened the being immortal offer by including the unusual
ability that once a century, Paddy could bestow immortality upon
another mere mortal—a most generous offering.
Oh my, once again Paddy was tempted with such an alluring gift
to offer to loves, and sharing ever evolving experiences too.
But Paddy again held fast to his original request,
to find a way to rid Ireland of all those yucky snakes!!!
Perhaps Paddy was thinking about another gift, and the snake,
and the temptation that had been taken, along with all the grief
that had happened way back then under the tree.

Just then, a gathering of druids were passing nearby,
attracted by the pipe smoke aroma and bantering wee voices.

The druids joined the assembly considering just how to go about offing the snakes without doing them harm.
This discussion really interested Paddy, he knew that *'thou shall not kill'* was one of the *Big 10* carved in stone.
Paddy also knew that those graced rulers of ordained power were always finding ways around that no killing clause, saying things like doing God's work, which made the fighting, hurting, and killing okay for the true believers to do differently than the *Big 10* commanded, and brought a righteous death to the non-believers!!!
Those in controlling royal power usually choose to pursue the ill-logic, that *'might makes right'*, or so those true-believers wanted to believe.
And sadly, emerging humankind often defines, and makes right, with the smiting power of their higher might!!!

Paddy was very into following the pagan discourse occurring, as they talked and considered and reconsidered, then talked and reconsidered some more about all the various ways to *do no harm* to the snakes, and at the very same time, rid all of merry olde Ireland of those creepy slithering serpents.
Around a blazing fire, they sat and smoked in powwow, and talked and talked until dawn slowly crept in to bring a new day.

With dawn's breaking light sparkling as jewels from the fresh morning dew, mother nature's field of free diamonds, and they were blinded by the reflected light.
The light of a brilliant idea came to them from the dazzling glittering dew, as to how to go about dealing with the snake problem, and yet, *do no harm*.

At the very core of the solution was the natural pure sweetness of the morning's dew.
Now they talked in ernest, and very frankly of the most graceful solution their mindflows bubbled with, about how this would all come together with the right kind of timing, to rid all of Ireland of each and every snake in a single night!!!

They had a plan—a plot even—as odd as the scheme may be to honor Paddy's unselfish request, his bequest made on behalf of all the folks living in Ireland.
Of course, they all did party hearty and enjoyed good food and drink . . . while they carefully crafted their moonstruck magic, because 'tis way good to make merry, and be most joyful while conjuring together the unique blends of marvelous moon magic.
Size matters not to the wee folks, 'tis the realness of the person inside that really matters more than anything else.
Those leprechauns did indeed include some special magic . . . especially for unselfish Paddy!!!

And so it came to pass in olde time folk tales like this,
that by the light of the next full moon Paddy did walk alone into the very middle of a field of growing green grass,
known to be infested with asps, vipers, etc!!!
He raised his hands to the night sky, and mystically drew down the moonbeams that flowed to his glowing finger tips.
Soon he was aglow with the bright moonlight as he waved his hands across the entire field, and the beams of this special golden light spread out from the field, and magically all over the land.

While the snakes did silently slumber, the very tip of their tails glowed bright yellow from being painted by moonbeams dipped in the sweetness of the morning dew.
Everywhere Paddy looked, he saw coiled sleeping snakes with their golden yellow tails gleaming!!!

High in the northern midnight blue sky, an astonishing aurora borealis did appear, bubbling and boiling with cosmic energy.
What a celestial spectacle to behold, this night of moon magic assuredly was sensational, as those lustrous northern lights danced in colorful concert with moonbeams.
Then came an instant flash of bright lightning, followed by a strangely muted thunder, more like a prolonged rumbling roar than the booming clash of thunder, like the slam banging of mother earth's cellar door!!!

Paddy felt the flowing surge of the sweeping sound vibes more than he could hear the rambling rumble thunder.

All the sleeping snakes awoke abruptly, aroused after feeling the earth born tremors shake and wake them from slumber!!!
The snakes were all very hungry, as if awaking from a long hibernation, and now they were starving, famished even!!!
All the snakes saw a wiggling glowing yellow meal worm right beside them.
Oh how wonderful, room service—breakfast in bed!!!
In their collective cravings for food they went right after those glowing treats, so sweet and yummy was what they were eating, they quickly ate and swallowed more and more!!!
In an feeding frenzy, those snakes ate themselves up and down yielding to their gluttonous greed to feed.
The snakes where so full of themselves . . .
that they all collectively choked!!!
Asphyxiated themselves, they did,
and croaked dead right where they had eaten!!!
Done in by their greed and their own foul poison!!!

Paddy watched in awe as the dead snakes started glowing yellow, and then, turned into a colorful orange.
Then, in a moment, the orange changed to a rich green, eventually blending into the grass.

The leprechauns had explained to Paddy that he had to remain in the field, until the sparkling fresh dawn of day broke free, from the enchantment of the magical moonlight.
Then the magic of this purging night would be done and gone, and all of the snakes would forever be gone from Ireland.

Paddy must have dozed-off, because when he awoke, the sun was high in the sky.
He was sprawled in the middle of the field on a soft lush bed of bright green shamrocks.
Oh my, yes, all those snakes had twisted themselves into loops that were now the leaflets of beautiful luscious green growing shamrocks, that now covered the Irish countryside.

Paddy looked at the shamrocks with three leaflets—thinking
'three', the power of three, and then he made the link
to what he knew to be the trilogy.
Trinity, aha . . . Paddy made the bond with the shamrock.

As they say about such events, the rest is history.
Indeed, Paddy did ascend to being immortal by his deeds,
because his unselfishness freed Ireland of all the snakes
in a single fateful night, and for that he is remembered and
honored to this day.

But of course, Paddy was later cannoned . . . ah, canonized into a
sainthood slot as the patron saint of Ireland.
Which gives him an edge in being remembered,
but long forgotten be the magic done by the wee people upon
that fateful night so long ago in another time.

Now, you may think this is just a wee bit of the blarney,
and such is often the way of dusty tales of olde.
As always, my hope is to bring you a smile or two,
perhaps a few happy thoughts, and no offense is intended.

Aye . . . may Irish eyes be a smiling brightly.

Bright blessings upon you, and happy Saint Patrick's Day.

Take care and enjoy often . . . John

PINBALL GAMES

Decades ago, I was a pinball wizard of sorts—well, sort of,
back when you got to play a fun game for a mere nickel,
and players skillful at nudging and flipping,
could play a pinball machine for hours upon a quarter.

These days the cost of a pinball game is ten nickels
for five balls to play, and some games give bonus balls.
Much to my surprise the bonus ball will pop into play
when there is already a regular ball in play.
Suddenly two balls are rolling about and quick flips with the
flippers are necessary to keep them both scoring,
'tis most challenging to keep up with two balls in play.

With two balls bouncing around,
bumping and pinging points are all doubled,
as knowing fingers press buttons,
zapping balls off each flipper in synch,
sending them back into the scoring area,
hitting targets and back up the scoring maze,
while the clangs and dings and dongs,
betel a mounting scoring happening.
So tempting 'tis to advert thy eyes to quickly look and
see the rewards of higher scoring numbers showing,
but an inattentive instant will cause the balls to go off,
taken out of further play and the game is finished,
until more coin returns the balls for another game.

Methinks angled playing areas inclined over the years,
more slanted to roll balls faster making games quicker,
increasing the coins dropping into the flashing machine,
as feats of skills are tested against the biased monster,
so greedy to gobble up more and more coins.

Trooper was a friendly kid from my fun spent youth.
He was slow and a few cards short of a full deck,
but we never treased him because he was slow with thoughts.
He was younger but hung out with us anyhow.

He even got his turn at pinball when he had a nickel,
or one of us would leave a free game for him to play.

Now, a pinball wizard Trooper wasn't,
that eye hand coordination thing caused low scores.
Regardless of his poor pinballing skills we respected his sincere
efforts at trying because even without wins,
he continued playing and kept on trying without a bit of crying,
enjoying the fun of playing the game.
He'd never get angry and slam the pinball machine,
his fun was being part of the group,
as we gathered around the pinball game.

On Trooper's 13th birthday, we rigged the pinball machine.
With two guys lifting the heavy beastly game machine,
Eddie and I slipped pennies under the two front legs.
Thusly, changing the playing angle ever so slightly,
but enough to give Trooper the birthday gift of a playing edge.
With slower rolling balls, it was easy for us to win free games,
as we decorated the pinball machine in the back of the neighbor-
hood variety store with colorful birthday greetings
as our birthday celebration for Trooper.

Trooper arrived early in the afternoon for a birthday lunch of
chocolate cake and ice cream and to open his kid-to-teen gifts.
And of course, to play the thirteen free games we provided
as our two cents worth of birthday giftings.
He was thrilled that he'd get to play so many games,
more than his usual one game in turn.
The rule of the game is that the winner controls the play until all
the games won are done and gone, then the next nickel up plays.

Trooper played all afternoon, winning a couple and losing a few.
The uplifting penny shims made the tilt device more sensitive to
nudging the machine, and Trooper was a heavy handed nudger.
Then winning a few more and losing a couple less when he eased
off a tad on the nudging.
The slightly more level playing field slowed the rolling balls just
enough for him to make effective use of the flippers,

enabling him to run up some winning scores.
This made him feel like a winner on his birthday,
laughing and happy with his continuing pinball wins.
He was grinning from ear-to-ear.

We stood around the pinball machine cheering Trooper on with
his gleeful winning games, watching him mastering the flippers,
carefully aiming his flip shots as much as possible,
to get the bumpers lit up to give him bonus points.
We had never seen Trooper so happy.
When he finally had to leave for dinner, he raced home to tell his
mom and sister that he was a pinball wizard on his 13th birthday.

As soon as Trooper left, we removed the penny shims,
and never a word was said to anyone—until now,
about our birthday gift to Trooper that year.
When he played pinball the next day,
he didn't have the winning birthday lucky streak,
but he sure played an improved game from understanding
flippers and easy nudges more,
and perhaps he had a wee bit more confidence,
at least two cents worth.

We really didn't give Trooper self-confidence,
all we did was level the playing field for him a wee bit.
Maybe by shifting the game in his favor, he got in touch with
feeling like a winner, and discovered self-assurance in himself.
He really didn't need to ever know about the slight difference in
the lay of the game, from our helpful birthday adjustment.

These new fancy pinball machines of today, do indeed seem to
have more of an angle, making balls roll go out of play much
faster—way more difficult to nudge too!!!

The playing field of real life is more acute too,
angled more sharply to favor the corporate machine,
causing those who play the fast games of life,
to roll away completely out of play so quickly,
while trying to run up a high number score in big bucks.

Newer pinball machines suffer from gross inflation too.
The scores to win free games are now way into high numbers,
like over five million points to win a single game,
and there's no online help to explain the scoring,
or the fact that bonus balls come into play.
Also, some pinball machine now tauntingly talks.
A sexy come-on from a playful lady's taped voice,
invites you to slip another coin into her ready slot!!!
Telling you that her game is way hot to play,
if you're up to handling her flippers.
Oh my, a machine that jeers you to come play her.

The games of life are like pinball machines and you're often
playing into a stacked deck, because you know the field is tilted.
You often have no idea what your score is, not at all sure if
you're winning or losing, but the game continues on anyhow.
As long as you have balls to play, more tokens to drop in the
handy slots, the play goes on with perplexing scoring.
And in the middle of playing one ball, a bonus ball could pop
into play, taxing your attention with the task of doing some
horizontal juggling, and the horizon is artificially tilted.
The challenges before you keep increasing,
and two cents worth of penny slims aren't gonna do a thing to
slow the speed of your balls in quick play—and you still don't
have a clue about the complex scoring method.

But on you play, because 'tis the only game in town,
challenging the machine with your educated skills,
discovering nudges aren't what they used to be.
Those nudges that once moved the ball's path ever so slightly,
just aren't cutting it anymore.
The ball only seems to roll with gravity rules,
passing cleanly between the flippers right through the dreaded
dead zone, without a chance to flip the ball back into play.
Another ball is out of play, thumping dead—clanking to the rack.
After but a few moments of depressing play, you know the
scoring is way low even if you did understand the scoring
game—strange how often *scoring* becomes such a focus in life.
Those with the most toys win—nothing at all!!!

Now folks gather around to watch you play,
shouting advice and seeming to cheer you on,
telling you how to make your shots count,
urging you to keep your balls in the scoring area.
So often they're only restating the obvious,
over and over again as if you can't hear,
or don't understand what's being said.
It's like they believe their words will extend the play,
or change the rolling course of balls in play,
as if balls respond to what they say.
So quick to tell you how to score more,
when you're doing winning plays.
Just as quick they tell you what's wrong,
when you're experiencing losing ways,
ever ready with a litany of sarcastic *'I told you so's'*,
when you're done in by losing the game.
However, they're just as quick to take all their due credit for
directing your play when you win a game.

They also forget another rule of pinball,
'don't lean on the machine while I'm playing',
meaning that if the game ends because of tilting,
the tilting better be from the player's nudging,
and not from someone else leaning on the machine,
because only the player playing the game gets to work the
flippers and do all the nudging to try to win the game in play.

Seems like in the game of life many people have gotten into
being a Monday/Tuesday morning quarterback,
looking back at all those failed plays with their all knowing
stinging hindsight, about how stupid it was doing an end run,
when everyone knew a pass over the center could have scored.
So clearly they see everywhere you went wrong,
from where they see things to be.
They proceed to cuttingly tell you what *'you shouldn't'* have
done and what *'you should'* have done,
but you stupidly didn't do that when you could have,
from their enlightened point-of-view,
as they look backwards recounting your failed judgments.

Your ineffective flipping and lack of nudging moxie are all
betelling the shortcomings of your ill-fated plays,
as seen by those who only sit and watch for faults,
sitting up high on their non-player fat asses,
so often failing to see the faults within themselves.

Billy Jordan was a loud mouth watcher and he'd always have all
the flip answers, at least answers as he saw them to be,
about why players lost their pinball games.
He was always running his mouth about how to win,
but he'd never drop a nickel to run his own game.

Then one evening an older stranger came into the store,
made a telephone call from the phone booth,
and played pinball while waiting for a return call.
He won a free game with matching numbers at game's end,
just as the phone rang with his awaited call.
Being a nice guy, he gave the free game to Billy,
who'd been watching and running his mouth as usual.

Trooper was in the store drinking a soda because he didn't have
the two cents deposit to leave the store with the bottle.
We were down the street tossing a ball around when Trooper
gave us the secret *'come on the run'* yell.
We rushed into the store in time to see smart-talking Billy Jordan
hit the credit button to start his free game,
and we gathered around the pinball machine eager to see if he
was as good at playing, as he was at talking about it!!!

That was a fateful night for smart mouth Billy Jordan.
When each ball thumped dead from play he'd blame the lost ball
on whatever, like he wasn't really ready when he shot the first
ball went into play—*oh, sure!!!*
As the second ball went thumping down,
he bemoaned something had gotten in his eye!!!
When the third ball went rolling off the flipper and out of play,
without as much as an attempted flip,
because Billy claimed he had a finger cramp,
in his flipping finger—*oh, poor Billy!!!*

The fourth ball was just starting to roll points,
when Billy's frustrated nudging tilted the machine ending his free game with a very low score.
Then he blamed Trooper for leaning on the pinball machine.
Trooper was big for 13—but he sure wasn't a leaner.
'No one was leaning', boomed the voice of the stranger,
who had been watching Billy playing from the phone booth.
Then Billy blamed all the overwhelming pressure of us standing around watching and crowding his play,
making him nervous and throwing his game off,
blaming everything expect himself for not winning!!!
From that fateful night on, he was known as *Billy the Blamer,*
but we didn't see much of him after that night.

Sadly, people get so frustrated in the here and now,
that all they can do is bemoan about what isn't,
complaining of what's wrong with what there is,
endlessly bitching about what they don't have,
and grumbling about what they don't want to do.
In the meantime, scheming sinister scams to get what they want,
or to get more of what they do have, or tightly securing what they think they have!!!
In a foolish fleecing frolic that's so frustrating,
their life is liable to go tilt from always over nudging.

While those folks, more experienced with life, are frequently perplexed by the scheming blamers apparent lack of smarts,
in wasting so much life time in the here and now,
blaming, complaining, bitching and scheming such nasty plans.
The blamers chase shams with only plastic dinky prizes to win,
so empty in real value, so lacking in moderate pride,
so devoid of traces of personal satisfaction.
'Tis not a fun game they play, that eventually tilts out of balance.

When their scheme has spun foully and the last ball played out,
or harsh nagging pushes the game into tilt, scored numbers don't match and the last game is finally done,
then slammed scams all crash into an empty void,
and their enjoying of life gets buried in a pitiful grave,

covered over with the aged dirt of weary bitching,
an unmarked plot where only tangled weeds eventually grow.

Only your fingers are on the buttons,
it's your nudging makes the balls go or stay,
and win, lose, or draw 'tis your game 'twas in play.
Accepting both credit and blame builds confidence,
and provides your self-assurance to enable you to try again,
learning to better balance for over-plays and under-plays,
to find a centered equilibrium point that works for you.
Your focused balance of flows is what life is all about,
because when you get pulled and pushed off center,
you're frustrated out of balance,
and your enjoyment of life goes tilt.

You put the balls into play
and the longer you keep then active,
the better your score will be.

Take care and enjoy often . . . John

AWAKENING...

Early morning. The cloak of darkness gradually yields to daybreak's faint paleness, edging away the dimness. The magic dawning of light overtakes the lingering beauties of the night. Slowly opening my sleep heavy eyelids from slumber, I attempt to get a frame of reference to orient my being with these strange surroundings. Where am I??? The question jumps into mind. I'm not in my usual waking position—this isn't my bed!!! Where am I really???

My head isn't resting on my big soft feathered pillows, and I'm at an odd angle on this strange bed. Most likely a misconstrued placement of my body from having fallen into an exhausted sleep after a long playful night of enjoyment. In the tranquil gray morning light, my vision clears and slowly comes into focus, and I'm looking directly into a dark curly mass, nestled between creamy smooth inclines. My head is resting peacefully upon the lustrous inner slope of a lady's lovely parted upper thigh, and I inhale the glorious fragrance of a woman. So alluring to my awaking senses.

I'm in a warm mellow space, my groggy mind plays thoughts of maybe drifting back into sleep—close my eyes and just drift nice and easy back into the cradle of restful slumber; or maybe I'll come slowly awake and get into the needful doings of this new day. Apart from lifting sleep laden eyelids, I haven't moved, nor has she. So still she lays, in hopefully blissful sleep, enhanced by our prolonged couplings from a mere few hours before. By the dawning light, I see the wondrous folds of her womanhood right before my eyes. I gaze upon the pure simple beauty of her fabulous hidden wrinkles. I know how upper face wrinkles are perceived by society, and about all those vain efforts to conceal those earned mile markers left by life experiences from bygone times. These perfect pubic pleats appear ageless, and so invitingly arranged in a welcoming smile. Ah, yes, such an amazing sight to behold upon awakening. Yes, this is indeed a very rare insightful view of her usually concealed treasure of womanly delights.

Playing youthful games of *"You show me yours, and I'll show you mine"*, come smiling into mind. Quick fleeting glimpses, shared long ago by curious little girls and boys. Forbidden looks, when neither knew what we were seeing through the innocent eyes from an unknowing time. Now, decades later, I'm relishing a prolonged up-close view into yet another private jewelry box. Still curious, even with the benefits of being an experienced looker, etc. There are lots of variations in the special smiles those hidden lips convey. However, they never have the frown of a sour-puss, at least not those lips I've come to know. These lips almost always form a naturally knowing smile, but you need to look closely to see their beckoning welcome. And you clearly need to be very near, to hear the silent greetings these lips will so sincerely utter, to those who bring a listening ear. Purrring . . . Oh yes, such glorious lips of tingling treasures, I've helped spread them into joyous smiles in various ways. Each pair of lips is special, with cherished memories of those beauties as they were shared and known by me once upon a time. Now those variety of lips in my memory, all flow together into a blended composite art form that's representational of the kaleidoscopic personification of all womanhood right here in my face.

The possibility of returning to sleep diminishes for me, because the allure of her slumbering eroticism is so arousing. So near, just beneath my nose. I feel the first stirrings of my soft maleness, leaving passive limpness, as an awakening erection is growing—another part of me wakes. With her luscious lips so near, only an extended tongue touch away, there's a primal urging waiting to surge into action. Oh my, they are indeed very exquisite lips—so tempting, so inviting, so dear, so very near. Remembering our savory blend of tasty flavors, as I'm recalling more remembrances from our lustful night of sharing erotic passions. Those visions are now mindflows with me. And I recall her sharing with me, her once upon a time fantasy, now in the reality of her recently fulfilled desires, about how she wanted to drift into her exhausted sleep with my head resting so nicely between her open legs. Just like my head still is.

Yes, that's how I came to have my head still nestled between her open thighs. I wonder if she is perhaps enjoying an erotic dream of her recollected knowings from our sensual flows??? Should I awaken her from her joys of spiritual dreamscapes with a passionate kiss upon those exquisite lips??? Oh my, so invitingly near, as I mentally measure the mere extension of my tongue's reach away. Briefly, I ponder the merits of repositioning myself to permit my ponderously growing hardness to slide between her waiting smooth lips. Oh no, my repositioning movements would certainly be an abrupt intrusion into her silently sleeping place. I'd assuredly startle her awake!!! Indeed, the fortuitous position of my mouth, so close to her alluring lips, is the most direct approach to salaciously follow for gently awakening her from her peaceful sleep. She moved!!!

What was that motion??? Did she just move??? Was there the slightest bit of movement from her just now??? The merest hint of a stirring quiver in her sleep??? I'm sure she moved!!! Or was it nothing more, than seeing with my eyes, what my mind hoped to see—a clue as to how to bring her awake now. But there doesn't seem to be a hint of movement!!! Unless, she's enjoying a wonderfully wet dream. Now this wet dream thought, has some positive possibilities, and such a dreamfully enjoying hedonistic spirit, could perhaps gleefully engage her earthly being as well. Yes, women have wet dreams too!!!

Then it is possible, yes, really likely, that she is already very wet and wanting me deep inside her right there, in the here and now. From what I can see of her, I can't tell if she's excited in a wet way, because her secretly smiling lips tell no tales of her wetness. Cocks, by their natural need to swell with pride and crow, are so clearly apparent when turned-on. Her soundless sleeping pussy gives me naught a single purr of a glimmering hint. Nope, my perfectly delightful thigh-high perspective yields no trace as to the possible moistened state of her readiness, and I'm unsure now about how to know for sure by just looking. Ah, let's see . . . I need a clue . . . do I look for lip gloss???

Reflecting upon our nocturnal coupling, I'm tempted to just slip my aroused cock inside her nice and easy like, with hopes that she'll be welcomely wet, waiting and wanting me smoothly sliding joyfully deep into her. Then we'll start this beautiful morning by resuming our shared pleasuring from where we concluded in the middle of the night, before satiated exhaustion carried us off into the folds of erotically energizing sleep.

Wait!!! Hold that thought!!! When sleep came, as we also most assuredly did *cum* more than once, it was with my knowing tongue, delighting her with easy licks, while she blissed off into sweet dreamland, merging the sensations of our diminishing realities to ascend into the transition of spiritual flight. Transcending into mindflowing balances, where reality becomes the erotic dream most desired, and the longed for dream comes true for a brief time of factual knowing. If we'd continued our joyful knowing now, so long after last night's 11th hour, then my tongue should again be absolutely gliding between her ruby lips.

Oh, her sweet natural nectar is very enticingly near, just between her puckered lips. Waiting for me now, she's almost on the tip of my tongue. Just waiting, yes, in her sleep she is waiting for my lips to come kissing, kissing this sleeping beauty princess awake, and my tongue lapping through her poised lips into her renewed wetness, now, parting swollen lips. I want to fill my mouth with her marvelously aroused pleasure treasure clit, and dance the dance of angels with the tip of my merry tongue twisting and flicking upon the very tip of her aroused clit, feeling surging flows of erotic energies increasing with my face full of her sweetness in free flowing wetness. Feeling her joyous quivers when my puckered lips sucked upon her maidenhood, angel dances with flicks and licks upon her perfect pleasure pearl, energy rushes overflow from her sparkling jewel. I reach into her with merging energies as joyful licks consume her offered glowing gem, and feel her purringly attuning with her knowing, my touches, my knowing her naturally tasteful flavors, aha, recalling helps refresh the mind with previous happenings mind-flowing into the present. Alas, the present and what I want to do—indeed I do.

My watering mouth opens slightly, I lick my lips, my course of action is clear, because for the dilemma facing me now there is a clear solution, with repositioning concerns overcome with a most arousingly oral recall, that was both becoming for my mind and betelling of what to do. I want to lick her sweet pussy lips, feel her tingling purrs surge with my tongue tip. Ever so slowly and easy like, I extend my tongue into the delicate softness of her silky curls, sparkling in the first rays of a rising sun. Oh, those neatly trimmed hairs gently tickle my face and mouth in merry ways, merging with the hair of my flavor saving mustache, as the tip of my tongue glides right through, as each and every hair yields in silent tingles of joys to my slowly advancing tongue—WAIT!!! FREEZE!!! DON'T MOVE!!! STOP!!!

WHAT IF I startle her awake, and she's so surprised, and she's so shocked out of sleep, that she goes and empties her bladder!!! Ah, and with where I am, I'd surely get a face full!!! An unavoidable voiding!!! I freeze where I am!!! Perceiving in a halting instant, I'm in clear and present danger of being naturally watered—which is not at all like enjoying very, very wet!!! Wondering, in the panicking race of my alarmed mind, if my eager tongue making contact with her silky locks, might have provided enough touching to trigger off her uncontrollable awakening release. Oh, drat fuck!!! Frustration from another fucking dilemma, as I think about what I've gone and done!!!

Hopefully what I almost *did*. My tongue very slowly retreats, much more slowly than it had moments before been venturing forth toward her waiting lips. My eyes are intently searching for any hint of movement from her, a trifling twitch that might foretell an early warning and cause me to do an instant *Break-away!!! Break-away!!!,* and do a rapidly quick dive and roll free of the possible rushing gush of her ensuing jetstream. Alas, my tongue is free. I close my mouth. Yes, it has been known to happen that I do close my mouth at times!!! I've removed my tongue from harm's way and I don't move. Because now my poor Before Coffee mind has another fluid fucking point to ponder upon.

My erection reminds me that I'm only able to *cum* when I'm erect. Okay, depending on what's happening, at times I can *cum* when I'm semi-hard too. I know for a fact, I just won't *cum* at all when my cock is limp. I also know quite well, that I sure can't pass water when I have a full blown hard-on. Oh sure, if I really have to go—you know, those time when you feel like you're about ready to burst—I can forcefully point my hard cock down in a contorted bending way, and an unaimable stream sprays out to bring relief to my fluid filled bladder. Therefore, the truth is, that it is virtually impossible for most aroused, fully erect males to urinate, at least not without enduring some bending pain!!! And that's a matter of fact that has to do with this variable part of the male anatomy and its related release functions. It is also very difficult to get a hardon in cold water, and cocks shrivel-up into almost nothingness in anything cold. As a side note, I know first hand that having a vasectomy doesn't change a thing, except of course, to provide a positive male method of birth control.

When a guy is all hot and delightfully bothered, there is never a question if his aroused member is *cumming* or *going*--you can bet the farm and next week's lunch money that he's *cumming*—some *cummings* come sooner than others *cummings*. There's just no way pissing is gonna happen from a cock that's fully inflamed at standing tall attention!!! However, I don't know if the same *"no pissing during sexual arousal"* rule applies to aroused females. I guess this is just another mysterious question of life's meaningful awarenesses that my learning thus far hasn't taught me!!! Although, I've known several ladies who need certain private conditions to be happening before they can pee, some have to have water running before they can pee!!! Some can't use a public rest room. But most guys seem to be able to piss more freely whenever they feel the need to pee. Thus, I'm confronted with another discovery dilemma as I take stock of my fatefully positioned place, one more unknown aspect about women to learn about and hopefully benefit from.

If she awakens because she has been startled awake, and then she pees naturally and freely, she could get pissed-off for having shared a bit of the embarrassing moment of an unavoidable pissing, and I'd really get pissed on, which isn't something I feel a need to experience in this position. Not very erotic, her being pissed-off and me being pissed on. Of course, she just might pee a wee little bit, my thoughts muse upon that *wee little bit* possibility. What's a *wee little bit* of pee between friends??? Perhaps nothing more than a few drops of tinkle!!! Surely, I can handle that *wee little bit* which is barely a trickle, why I'm sure I can overlook such a small amount of her pee completely!!!

But what if it's a gusher??? A rushing raging torrent that saturates the bed—drenching the box springs from the free flowing spring running away above the mattress!!! You know how it can be in the morning—especially when you've had lots to drink only a few hours a*go* in the night—drat there's that word *go!!!* Maybe I'm really presupposing something that just won't happen. I don't know for sure that my tongue between her lips would astonish her and cause her to unintentionally pee!!! Sure, she might awaken and think my attentive actions are a continuation from last night. That's possible. Why, maybe she isn't in that deep a state of sleep. Could be she's only slightly dozing. Well now, there might be a possible solution—ahhh, need a better word that's less fluid—there might be a *conjecture* worthy of pursuing. No, daylight is a clue that morning is here, and she'd hear chirping birds and know she hadn't been dozing.

Enough of this encumbering fearfulness!!! I could gently bring her out of her sleep with my cock being slowly eased into her—ah . . . didn't I think this through just a few thoughtful moments a*go*—double drat upon that dratful *a go*-go word again! But I can't just slip my cock into her just now, I know how much she gleefully relishes all of our shared joys of oral adventures, why once we got together and . . . but then that's another story. Right now, there's a very rare potential offering for awakening her orally that's right in my face!!! A unique golden opportunity—ugh, drat, drat, drat on the *golden* stuff!!!

As I continue to consider the vital question of importance in the here and now: How often does a lady have the wondrous opportunity to wake up with the experience of her yummy sweet self being breakfast in bed??? One truth is positive and certain, she'd absolutely love being awakened with my tongue licking between her smooth silky lips!!! Hopefully, she'll gleefully remember her morning cunnilingus wake-up call for a long time to come as a cherished memory we shared together in passing.

If I were her, and she were me, positioned like I am right now, what would she do??? I'm sure she'd joyfully awaken me with her mouth lustfully filled with me. If I wasn't already erect, well I'm sure I'd soon be fully aroused from a marvelous multitude of pleasing sucking actions from her puckered lips and licking tongue!!! Yes, there's no doubt about it, she'd definitely arouse me with her all knowing awesome mouth!!! Would she also deliberate the feasibility, that I might be shocked into an accidental voiding during my brief transition from limpness to fullness??? Would her fear cause a delay in our shared enjoyment as she pondered possible outcomes as I have been doing??? No way, she'd have me aroused so quickly from her wondrous ways for completely delighting a male orally. Oh yes, I'd have a hardon long before anything else could be happening. Then too, I also know, without a bit of doubt, that she'd eagerly be repositioning herself most advantageously, for matching our merrily mutual oral erotic enjoying of each other so blissfully.

Yes, quick as a wink, we'd be joyfully positioned into the alignments for our glorious givings and rejoicingly receivings of sharing a beautifully blissful *69ing*. I know from experience, she's a very super sensuous lady who loves erotic sharings that combine so marvelously with the same delicious ways that I also enjoy freely and value greatly. She doesn't do those mindless games of teasing or using the bestowing of erotic joys as rewards or punishment like so many people seem to do. She's truly into enjoying for the pure pleasure of enjoying often. As my mind now races with these thoughts, I can almost feel her drawing my full hardness into her mouth. Slowly sucking me inside with her subtle pulls, while I covered her wetness with the open fullness of my mouth, once again discovering our many created joys, sharing blissfully, enjoying . . . more . . . mmm!!!

There is no question about what she would do if she had awakened in such a favorable position as I've been lucky enough to find myself in right now. Still, I hedge upon the fluid fear of what just might have an ever so slight chance of happening. I'm trying to throw caution to the wind, and get into a head place for enjoying what's right under my nose at this brief instant in time. My thoughtflows link *wind* with what happens when you *piss into the wind!!!* Makes good sense to always piss downwind. And it also makes equally good sense not to look up when you're caught in a downpour. I don't know for sure it would be a major cloudburst—perhaps a bladderburst!!! Then again it might only be a slight sprinkle, a passing April shower, or nothing much at all!!! Or nothing at all!!! Yes, it could very well be that I'm only delaying an exciting awakening that will have her greeting this day joyfully smiling with both pairs of lips.

Yes, she'd welcome my kissing her awake this way. Yes, she's very healthy in all respects, and she doesn't seem to be bothered by having a weak bladder—and we didn't really drink all that much last night. Yes, I know—or at least I believe I know—right where to play my licking tongue to quickly bring her awake and into the beginning raptures of magnificent ecstasy!!! And being in such a jubilant state of ecstasy, would surely put an instant hold on her possible peeing. Right??? Sure!!! Time to either piss or get off the pot!!! Oh drat, there has to be a better way to phrase that!!! Those who hesitate are lost!!! Bottom line is, that an exquisite opportunity could soon be lost forever by my own inability to move beyond my baseless self-conceived fears.

Oh my, and such an alluring bottom line she has. I don't know why I'm deliberating upon what to do about this sensual slumbering offering for so long. Doing all this prolonged speculation is so unlike my usual way of deciding what to do, when confronted with a fabulous found joy such as this right under my nose. I know I must soon seize this precious moment before me, or else this wonderful opportunity will pass away—silently slipping into the endless emptiness of *might have been's* . . . and those haunting *if only's* . . .

Another plan of action is coming together. Ah, coming together has a very nice ring to it, not at all like the empty ding of funky procrastination. The odds are very remote that I'll get a face full of anything, other than the sweetness of her naturally stimulated wetness, and our wonderful mutual pleasure in awakening her this way is worth all of the assumed risk. Yes, oh my, yes, I'll put my money where my mouth is, and put my watering mouth right where our enjoyment is going to soon be happening!!! Yes, and soon I'll be savoring the tasty delicious pleasurings that will come erotically into being with our renewed wakening into with this day.

I've never waited this long to consume such a choice treat so close at mouth. I usually can't wait for more than a New York second or two, at the very most, to fill my mouth with her while my tongue and lips make thrilling motions around, about, and within her special sweetness. I just love feeling her responding with wilting wiggles of delight, feeling her quiver with raptures of orgasmic bliss. My pondering postponement now ends, and I once again continue with my erotic course of alluring action. Move out of double jeopardy and go for a big score with a true daily double and bet everything in final jeopardy!!!

Life is full of risks, and now I trust myself enough, and my ever expanding awareness of her, to take the chance that lady luck will be smiling with me. Thinking, ever so briefly, about all the regrets of wasted opportunities that I lost along the way, because those gifts of offered moments weren't seized upon or just couldn't be acted upon, for whatever reason seemed to fit for not doing something joyful back then. All those calculated risks that were never taken, and those far too many *might have been's*, that never came into being. Never happened, only because I lacked the gumption to follow my gut feelings as they were for me at those very critical moments, missed moments of life experiences lost forever in the passing sands of time.

Yes, now is the time to bring her waking raptures of joy, while she slides smoothly free of her restful slumber to greet today smiling. She won't *go*—I know she won't *go*, but she sure will *cum*!!! And so will I, as I know she'll soon be joining in sharing our most becoming playfulness. My tongue reaches out as I fill my open mouth with her tender flesh, drinking in her delicious wetness—yes, I was sure she was wet, I just knew it. She wakes with a most euphoric, *"Ooooooh, yes, more please!!!"* Her first waking movements are in responsive sync with my kissing mouth, she craves deeper kisses, as she thrusts herself more fully to my mouth. Her beautiful bottom lips, once silently sleeping, are now very wide awake and broadly smiling with resounding purrrrs.

There's no voiding, nor any avoiding. My fear, which often is the way of fears biased by false assumptions made in haste, was totally and completely without any basis of supporting foundation. Too often, actions or inaction are the results of what we know, what we think we know, and what we don't know. Truthful first hand knowledge provides a firm basis for determining the choices for implementing actions—anything else is just guess-work. The intriguing seductiveness of the unknown has both the greatest risk, and also the highest potential for rewards. An anticipated return might be as about hoped for or totally unexpected in most positive ways, and that's what keeps life from being so dingingly dull and banally boring. Sometimes we know what's going to happen next, or we like to think we do. However, sometimes we don't know what's about to happen, because of the appearance of unexplainable variable aspects being tossed into play, or thrown out of play. So it is almost impossible to project what is likely to occur even when we think we know what we are doing, often we don't know nearly as much as we think we know. Life is always changing, and life goes on, even with changes that aren't at the time seen as being positive . . . eventually they become positive.

Frequently, we don't know that we should have been considering various ramifications until they're happening. And then, any given consideration is often misdirected as haunting afterthoughts, hind-sight is so insightful as long as you are looking backwards. At times life is frustrating not knowing what questions to ask or how to correctly evaluate the answers that you think you might have. An opportunity could be lost because we don't have all the necessary information or the where-with-all means to act upon what we know to be true. Therefore, nothing at all happens, even when it seems like a good idea at the time. Perhaps later, they'll both bewail and bemoan, in differing styles, about what they would have gained *if only* they had just gone ahead and *done it*—whatever the *"it"* might have been. Their ability to enjoy in the here and now of today is clouded over by lots of *if only's*, and a life empty of experiences except for the leftover clutter from dangling *might have beens*. Dinged away in an instant of not doing.

Nothing is as sorrowful as a person with talent, skills, and resources who does nothing with them. Or when a person gives up before achieving an attainable goal. They quickly throw in the towel when there's more fight remaining. Pulling out prematurely is indeed a major bummer. Instead of creating results, they produce bemoaning excuses and sling blaming stink all about, to cover their shortcomings. Truth is, they don't have enough true grit, the perseverance to stay with successfully solving the problem—rich in learning opportunities, until the quandary is successfully resolved, or until there is definite proof that the sought after goal is regretfully unachievable as envisioned. People with real tenacity regroup, rethink, replan, to try again, and again. They don't bother counting wooden rings, the only ones to count are the brass ones that produce the prizes. Nothing in the world can take the place of persistence. Persistence and determination are omnipotent.

Enjoy often . . . John

PRIDE

'Tis been said that *pride* goes before a fall. However, I do believe that in some ways pride has long ago fallen away through the cracks of society. But I wonder what kind of pride it was that has fallen away—more importantly what kind of pride has replaced the pride that seems to have fallen away with the grains of sand through the hour-glass. What variety of pride might still remain in the work ethics of humankind today???

I think one type of old fashioned pride, as the rush of good feelings an artist has when proudly signing a finished painting. Those old Masters worked with really crude paints and brushes way back when they were capturing the mood and the spirit of the time. The artists of old seemed to pay more attention to the details of subtleties expressed within each brush stroke. Today, some of the stuff that is being passed off as art is so bold and brassy, and at times very tacky, leaving lots of folks to wonder if these forms of non-expression are really works of art. Perhaps the tacky status is to mark off tasteless chunks of society in recent times. The artistic details have been lost in the boldness of broad stroking. The once careful blending and mingling of colors has been snapped into brazen crass contrasts shining like brass, now reflecting nothing more than shattered fragments of diluted emotions forever frozen in time—devoid of feelings.

Fashions are reduced to merely passing cash producing fads that are coming-in or going-out of style, as the *in-styles* of today are but passing seconds away from being quickly out of style tomorrow. Fashions remain in vogue until the tasteless reviewers of fashions discover a new rage to proclaim as being the *now* in thing!!! The smooth artistic passions of those old Masters have evolved into merely amassing harsh shock values to boldly grab—ever so briefly—the mass market's short and constantly changing attention span.

The once prideful signing of a creative work by the artist has been crassly converted into commanding big bucks just for affixing an identifiable designer's trademark to mass produced merchandise. The identifying trademark doesn't denote pride like it once did, and the manufactured product might not have been produced by the holder of the trademark. Most likely, it has been licensed out for assembly by the lowest bidder, often resulting in reduced quality at an ever increasing retail price. The once prideful essence of workmanship has slipped away in many areas of creativity, while the artificial values continue to be over inflated to even higher prices, being done by the whims of a buy almost anything public, with a foolish infatuation for overspending and a willingness to pay—regardless of price.

Often, the beancounters seem to be measuring the level of creativity, as it is applied to the anticipated market shares captured before the created fad loses public appeal. As long as the public is willing to peel off conned away bucks from a seemingly endless roll of dollars—the fabricated fad lives. Until the profit margin narrows away, then the falling fancy becomes part of the unmentioned history, only a brief notation on a spreadsheet as a profit or loss item. The pride of creativity has been sadly reduced to a *profit* or *perish* place. The fad produced product is now nothing more than a dust catcher, until time passages recycle the forgotten fad item back into born again public attention, as yet another over-priced collectable, now becoming part of someone's collection, and now collecting dust in a new location with an even much higher artificial value.

I wonder if the pride of creativity created its own demise, by creating the contrived wants for our instant gratification buying habits for disposable fad products. Every holiday season brings a new rash of fleeting fads for fleecing folks out of their hard-earned cash, paid out so quickly for only a passing fancy. Later, do people ever look upon the dusty remains of a purchased fad and marvel over the fact that they paid good money for *that???*

Perhaps the passing trend for disposable things came with the shift away from designing and producing products that would become heirlooms for future generations, to products being redesigned with planned obsolescence built in. A company producing a product that wears out from normal use, has an endless market for more of their products—or so it would seem. Tire manufacturers make all kinds of tires in different grades and sizes for motor vehicles and aircraft. Eventually, each of those billions of used tires have to be replaced, when a mere fraction of an inch of the tire tread wears away. Lots of people are employed to manufacture tires, and many more folks have the labor-intensive job of changing all those old worn out tires.

I don't know why—with all of the modern space-age synthetic materials that have been blended together to last forever—*why* tires still continue to wear out??? Now most likely, tire manufactures will cite they've made design and research advancements towards increasing the life span of a tire, and making them safer at higher speeds. Then they'd point to the rough composition of the paving materials used for highways that causes tires to wear out more quickly. Regardless of the reason, automobile tires must be replaced over and over again. The same is true for aircraft tires too, after so many landings those tires have to be replaced. Each year, vast profits are made on products that could be better designed and manufactured so they don't wear out as quickly as they always seem to do. Maybe the *wearing out factor* has helped to wear away the pride in quality products too.

I remember an old catch phrase, sort of a group of buzz-words from a time before *political correctness* happened, *'close enough for government work'*. It basically meant that a lower standard was applied to work being done for the government. Gee, where did the *we the people* part of the government go??? The feds have been into setting standards on all kinds of quality of life stuff from food to medicine to product safety and so on, with regards to what's acceptable and what isn't. Lots of standards to keep folks free of harm, but government employees and contractors were into believing if the job they do is sort of close to being right that's okay, or *close enough for government work*. However, some folks seem to think that working for the United States Government means that the bar for the acceptable quality job performance has been lowered. Where's the pride when the standards for the job you are expected to do has been lowered???

During my USAF years, I was fortunate to have played a part in creating the Strategic Air Command's PRIDE program. I recently learned that the PRIDE program was expanded to being used Air Force wide. When it was first introduced, it was a very basic SAC concept for encouraging Professional Results In Daily Efforts. An ongoing reminder for members of the command to take pride in the professional job they had to do, and to always strive in their efforts for zero defects in their assigned work. Those were the cold war years and the brief hot time of the Cuban missile crisis, when airborne B-52's and the newly operational ICBM's provided a nuclear deterrent maintaining world peace. This was possible because of a very quick response time for launching the heavy bombers within minutes and to start the countdown to launch missiles from isolated hard site silos. Crew readiness, mission planning, support services, and maintenance were critical to the mission. Operational Readiness Inspections (ORI's) were conducted to constantly test and evaluate combat readiness. There was a very high amount of professional pride in everyone doing their assignments to the best of their ability. Perhaps the pride came from everyone in the chain of command knowing how important their individual efforts were in doing their part to help to maintain the fragile balance of world peace.

Methinks the quagmire of the Vietnam sucked away lots of the pride from the military—partly because of all the string pulling done by the armchair politicians far from the battles. Those politicians kept on changing the military mission, and playing all kinds of costly games with tactics that were better left to the experienced on scene commanders. Another part, was the continuing question about trying to understand what we were doing fighting a war with so many lines drawn in the sand about what we could and couldn't do in battle, and also with so many hands in so many pockets. Seems the costly lessons learned about not crossing the 38th parallel in Korea were forgotten a decade later. Unlearned lessons are indeed repeated all over again. The pride of SAC that once kept the flows of peace in balance were now flying missions of doing *carpet bombing* with conventional iron bombs on Vietnam jungles. Some of the B-52 crews called their high-flying missions *knocking coconuts,* because without secondary explosions it appeared they were bombing empty jungles. 'Tis way difficult maintaining a sense of pride in being part of something that keeps changing at the whims of whoever is doing the deciding. Without a clear sense of direction and a positive purpose, there is little pride in doing assigned jobs—which were subject to change the next day.

The public outcry about Vietnam also took the pride away from the military, who had gallantly tried to do what they had been ordered to do. At the start of the United States involvement in Vietnam, most of the adult population of the United States had no idea where Vietnam was!!! This was the first time the American public watched the war on the nightly news and read about it in the press. Suddenly all kinds of public protests and support were being expressed about the fighting in Vietnam. Major splits of differing viewpoints were happening everywhere, and police were shown beating and dragging protesters off to jail. Lots of concerns were voiced about the war, and many in the military seemed to be fighting without the pride that had once been the cornerstone of our armed forces. The high price of lessons learned continue to be paid today, by many of the men and women involved in that mindless conflict that raged for so long and ended decades ago. 'Twas the false pride of believing the US had to be the *super power* that would make peace happen, that took the military might into Vietnam, and that's what got our asses into that horrible mess of a political cluster fuck!!!

Sadly, false pride takes away much of the real pride that there once was. It's as if we've transferred our pride into phony plastic values that usurp the realness of being really prideful about who we are and what we are doing to *the best of our abilities.* Now, some might be thinking that with *the best of our abilities,* I've cast a shadow of doubt over my belief that perfection is an unattainable myth. Perhaps you are missing the differences in being proud of a job well done, as it relates to doing *the best of our abilities,* and questing after the illusive perfection myth. The crew chief who is responsible for keeping an aircraft airworthy has a checklist to follow. The chief takes pride in knowing for certain that every item on that checklist has been properly attended to as part of the maintenance plan for aircraft safety. That is a tangible goal that is achievable when the skills, tools, and knowledge are all available to do the job perfectly and the performance of that job is within his abilities.

After years of doing an outstanding job maintaining his aircraft, the chief earned a promotion to be the maintenance manager of a squadron of 15 aircraft. The former crew chief wanted to maintain his outstanding record, so he personally ran from aircraft to aircraft double checking each maintenance item. He was trying in vain to do it all, thinking it was the way to maintain his perfect record. He told himself he was being a hands-on-manager, but his overbearing rechecking caused his crew chiefs to slack off, because he would always check over their work. The manager ran himself ragged, and maintenance suffered. The pride in an outstanding maintenance record started to slip away. Sadly, the overworked manager failed to establish trust in the efforts of his men, and a once attained goal of an outstanding record for flawless maintenance was lost as was his pride.

The quest for perfection frequently leaves people who are chasing after it, running ragged. They often have the misbelief that no one can do a task as well as they can. Instead of openly sharing the pride by combining efforts, they try to keep everything to themselves. There might have been contributions by others, but when the time comes for credit to be taken, the others are forgotten. Except when things don't go as planned, then the credit takers are quick to cast bogus blame for the failure on those unhelpful others who really fucked things up!!! They were the ones who were at fault, so say the perfect doers!!! Seems there isn't enough pride to go around, but there's always lots of blame to dump on others, when things get fucked up!!! The military has an award called a unit citation. The entire unit shares in the pride of a completed mission. Everyone assigned to the unit at the time, from the lowest rank to the commanding officer, is equally acknowledged for having played a part in the successful completion the assignment, and sharing in the credit increases the unit's pride and personal self-worth. Perhaps the pride that has fallen away, went elsewhere, along with the decreasing self-worth when others hog all the credit.

Kind of hard to develop pride in doing a job that you haven't done, like the crew chiefs slacking off because they knew the manager would be around to do it anyway, this is how a *why bother* attitude begins!!! Of course, there are some lazy slobs who don't have a bit of a problem not doing something because they're certain that someone else will come along and do it for them. That doesn't build self-esteem and there isn't any pride, unless they find some kind of warped conceit in having someone doing their jobs for them. Methinks that's a real phony kind of self-importance that will sooner or later befall those non-doers.

There are folks who do for themselves, only to have someone come along and find an endless list of faults with what has been done. They are nitpickers who will look at a piece of work, especially to find the most minute faults with what was done. Ugh, I had this problem with my father. No matter what I'd do, he'd have to look for something that he didn't like, a part he'd do differently or better!!! This was frustrating during my teenage years. The once in a lifetime thrill of my solo flight was a major achievement at my young age, but instead of my father sharing in my joy of having done it, he tossed a wet blanket on it by saying, *well it took you long enough to do it, you should have soloed weeks ago!!!* Ugh!!! Always with those *should have's!!!* 'Tis difficult feeling pride in self-worth when you live in the shadows of *should have's* cast by others.

You know, it's okay to learn from constructive criticism, but when there is nothing but criticism upon criticism that sure does hamper the ability to learn from what you tried to do, and ongoing faultfinding really does a negative number to lower your self-esteem. When I was teaching, I'd always try to look first for something positive to say about a student's completed assignment, and then focus on the areas where the student needed to improve upon. Too many folks seem to only be looking for what's wrong and pass over what's right. Methinks combining the right and the wrong in a constructive manner is what helps to make learning possible. Sometimes what might be seen as being wrong, is merely a judgment call that someone else might see differently. When you include the positive, you plant the mind seeds to help real pride to grow free of imposed shadows.

Once, when I was teaching an adult workshop in creative writing, a student handed in work that was totally off the mark from the assignment. Also, it was crude in flow and weak in content. I could tell the student was just trying to play upon her work as being *so creative!!!* But no matter how you dress it up, bullshit is still bullshit!!! My note to the student was, *you produced this bullshit in a timely fashion, now rewrite it one more time with feeling, and bullshit free!!!* Then I addressed specific sections and how she could have structured her wordsmithing, free of her failed attempts to lay bullshit on me. Indeed, a former bullshitter has the ability to recognize bullshit when he sees it, regardless of the creative window dressing!!!

At times, pride slips away by being taken for granted, as if once you have done something to take pride in, it somehow stays with you ever after. In my sophomore year of high school, I won a scholastic art contest on a regional level, and then, much to my surprise, I won at the national level too. This was thanks to the efforts of my marvelous high school art teacher, Pauline Stauffer, urging me to enter the art competition. During my junior year, I sort of felt as if I had my art courses aced, Miss Stauffer was giving me special projects to do, and I was involved in lots of the art things in various school activities. And then one day, she had heavy words for me, about how I was capable of doing more creative work than I was turning in. She went on to say how it was time for me to stop resting on my laurels and start bringing more of my creativity into the projects I was doing. It was very helpful how she laid that wake-up call on me. What she said was so true, I'd almost fallen right into that under achieving trap by resting on my previous achievements. Gee, it's so easy to fall into the place where past laurels are holding up what's *not* happening in the present.

What's most likely to happen when you rest on your laurels is you'll eventually get splinters in your ass!!! There have been lots of writers who write one best seller book that tops the *New York Time's Best Seller List,* and then they never publish again, at least not at that first high caliber of writing. There have been countless young promising artists who play all the ass-kissing games to secure a one-person-show in a gallery, and even after good sales and great reviews, they fall out of sight shortly after their show is over. Surely you remember the songs *In the year 2525,* by Zager and Evans, *Black is Black,* by Los Bravos, and *Play That Funky Music,* by Wild Cherry. They were all one hit wonders that made it once and then were never really heard from again in a major way. In 1968, the group called Iron Butterfly introduced a new style of music with their long cut of *In-A-Gadda-Da-Vida,* and then they fell out of sight, after opening the door for what would become known as *heavy metal.* I remember hearing it for the first time on my car radio as I was pulling into a client's parking lot. I was so taken by this unique arrangement of sounds, I thought I'd just sit there and hear the entire song. You know, *In-A-Gadda-Da-Vida* goes on for over 17 minutes!!!

Sure, there is a story behind each of these rising stars that seem to reach a peak, and then flutter off into obscurity. Perhaps they found their sudden taste of fame to be bitter and not at all to their liking. The severe glare of the constant spotlight and the ongoing public attention strips those famous ones of their privacy, and could indeed plunder their pride away. Maybe they get into a place of believing that no matter what they do, they'll continue to get rave reviews and their fans will always love them, and then slowly, their onstage presence starts to diminish. It might not be all that noticeable at first, except to those fans who follow every appearance they make very closely, but soon others begin to detect that the magical pizzazz is less, and the smoke and mirrors seem to be more in play. Could be that those once famous folks played their pride away as their tuneful notes faded in the night—followed by the fading fans.

Sometimes we bask in the prideful achievements of famous folks, admiring them for the many accomplishments that brought them fame. They become modern day icons we put on a pedestal. Some people try to emulate their ways of dress and being, as if by doing so, some of the faithful feelings from their hero-worshipping will rub off on them. They plunge into following every aspect of their icon's rise to fame—with each newly acclaimed honoring, that pedestal grows higher. And then something happens to bump into the pedestal, and the dishonored icon tumbles, falls from that high graceful place, and shatters into thousands of broken pieces. Within those broken pieces of glitz and glitter, we discover there was just a regular kind of a—perhaps slightly above average—person inside, with all of the same kinds of stuff that makes up all of humankind. Too often, yesterday's shining heroes become only the dust of memories blown on the winds of change. In the know-all and tell-all society of today, heroes have no privacy. Mistakenly we believe that *their public* has a right to know about all of their doings, and their undoings too. Their once personal ways of being were surrendered long ago, as sacrifices on the high rise altar of becoming a public figure. We only want to see them as some kind of perfect being, worthy of our adoring admiration, and in our all-consuming prideful awe, we've forgotten about the real person inside.

Some folks fall into doing pride in a vicarious way of projecting themselves to align with the prideful doing of others. Parents are often inclined to project themselves into the proud achievements of their offspring. Frequently plotting a course in life they prod their offspring into following, and imposing upon them life changing decisions that might not be the path they want to follow. When I graduated from high school I was given two choices by my parents: factory work at the mighty Big A—Armstrong Cork Company, which at the time was seen by their many employees as a cradle-to-grave company; or go into the USAF. This was a no-brainer for me, with my love of flying, off I went to join the Air Force. But many kids back then, didn't have much of a choice in the path they were expected to follow. Lots of friends were pushed into the same kind of work their fathers were doing, or sent off to the same college, same courses, same professors, same frat house, etc. And thusly, the very same set of frustrations gets transferred onto the offspring, along with the support that's there because they were doing what was expected and according to the plan made for them to follow.

Then comes the expectations of getting better, or the same grades, or doing well on the job. When that doesn't happen according to the plan, there's trouble in the making. Kids starts feeling like a failure so early in life, and the parents are disappointed at the ungrateful showing by their kids, who don't really appreciate all they have done to get them *there*, laying on guilt trips about all the sacrifices they've made for their uncaring kids. Regardless if *the there* is *the where* the kid wants to be, or if the kids were even aware of the unasked for sacrifices. The pushing parents want to take pride in the achievements they continue to expect, believing, and perhaps saying that their offspring will later thank them for all the choices they made for them. Besides, the kids are too young and immature to know what they want to do for the rest of their life. Frustration builds into resentment, and later in life they are frustrated adults who were locked into a course way back when by the prideful expectations of others. Instead of a burning desire to follow a direction of their choosing, they were herded into an appeasing place that wasn't pleasing to their often unexpressed wants and needs. Maybe they did express their desires and were told there would be time for that later, however, later never seems to come for them. All that seems to come later are more frustrations and unfulfilled expectations. The pride in their ability to make their own choices, and handle those outcomes as being positive or negative, is often handicapped by the well meaning undoings of others. 'Tis much nicer to share in the joys of the achievements of offspring—and to lend a listening ear when they need an older friend to talk problems through with—than deciding a path for them.

Pride gathers dust along the road of good intentions. Those efforts that start a new project or venture, only to see their fruitless efforts fall by the wayside. Of course they were all started with the best of hopeful intentions. The failed grand plan that once was in the works might have been just beyond the reach of what was being attempted, or maybe materials to do what was needed weren't available in a timely fashion. Regardless of the reasons, the efforts to drive onward to a successful completion were aborted before the project was finished. Pride gets draped in the tattered shrouds of *if only's* and *might have been's,* and self-esteem drops as the project is shelved away, never to be completed. Motivation slowly mopes off with all those endeavors that were left unfinished—joining other undones.

Some folks try to buy personal pride with the purchased skills of others, sadly believing that if enough time and money is tossed at a problem, the pending issue will be solved or eventually go away. This is a false kind of pride that's brought into being by others efforts, and that keeps the buyer far removed from solving the actual problem. They are separated from the task, until the time comes to take credit for successfully solving the dilemma. Then they are right there, basking in the glory of having done it all!!! Maybe one of those *shelved projects* was a book-in-progress, and they hire a ghostwriter to complete it and *polish up* the unfinished manuscript for publication. The odds are that the unmentioned ghost will be expected to fade away after collecting a fee for secretly rendered professional services.

Lots and lots of folks have a marvelous kind of silent pride in what they do every day. The postal workers and delivery service folks who make sure that each and every item reaches the addressee, and those who address the charitable needs of others in helpful ways to make it possible for them to help themselves. The trash collectors who have the thankless job of hauling away the spoils and throw-aways of society, and those who recycle what can be reclaimed and made useful again. Those who spin tunes on the radio, and those who tune-up vehicles. The maintenance clean-up crews who clean and polish by night, so all those areas are neat and clean for the endless traffic of workers the next day, and the folks who monitor and control the traffic flows inflight, afloat, and on the highways. The police forces who work tirelessly to protect and serve their communities in lots of ways. The folks in retail sales and services, who daily deal with the frustrating shopping demands of a constantly searching for a bargain public, and all the complaints fielded by those customer service folks who keep their cool. All the transportation people who move folks safety from here to there by various means, and then bring them back home again along with their luggage. The many behind the scene folks in offices, who provide vital administrative services that make something happen. The dedicated doctors, nurses, and techs, who care for the health needs of the many, and all those attendants who tend the needs of the impaired. Those imaginative teachers and professors who plant countless mind-seeds to expand upon our constantly growing knowledge base, and the assistants who help with parts of the learning. The news people and entertaining folks who work to keep us informed and amused every day. The many kinds of various builders, assemblers, and the folks who take things apart to fix-up repairable stuff. Those who conduct the sounds of music, and those who make musical sounds. The housekeepers, and innkeepers, providing lodging and resorts for playful relaxing. All the food service folks from the fast food places to the top dining places for fine feasting, and the folks who service and refill vending machines. Those who create and capture art forms as expressions of real life in passing, and those who form the designs for the greater enjoying of life. The many farmers, growers, livestock tenders, and harvesters of all kinds of seafood who produce a variety of food stuff for all of us. Those keepers of the fire, who keep the lights on, and those who quickly put out fires intent on burning things up. Those folks who work to keep buildings cool in the summer and cozy warm in the winter, and the fuel makers who make the fuels to keep things running. All of the members of the armed forces who are forever in a hurry-up and wait place, often far from home, always training for the next war that they hope they will never have to fight. Those who deal with matters of state, in stately ways of fairness. The clergy who bring aid and comfort to their flocks. Those elected political ones and hired government workers who remember that they work to serve the well being of, *we the people*. The folks who make channels of communications possible via phone, email, telegram, cable, internets, pagers, etc. Those folks who do all kinds of research and problem solving stuff on the land, sea, and air—in space too. The long and short haul drivers who cruise the highways and byways with their assorted cargo of freight. All those folks at the receiving end of a *911* call, who respond instantly in teamwork to pull others from the clutches of harm's way. The flower arrangers and the landscapers who help make the environment pleasing to the eye, and the groundskeepers who maintain playing fields. The security guards who keep watch to keep some mean people locked in, and guards elsewhere who stay alert to keep other nasty people out. Those painters, scrapers, and the people who remake things over, and those who rehab folks back to enjoying a healthy life. The professional sport players, who still play for the thrill of the game, and folks who make all kinds of fun games to play and entertain. Those who put signs and poles into place, and those who take public polls seeking a sign of consensus. The beancounters who keep track of what went where and what's coming from where, and the folks who make bean and other kinds of soups. The body shop workers who smooth out and paint over the dings and dents of life to make things right again. All the butchers, bakers, and candle stick makers who provide for consuming needs. Those who deal cards and spin gameful wheels of chance, and those folks who spin fabrics into a wearable reality. The folks who maintain and make places for swimming safe, and those folks who arrange for the pooling of resources. Those lawyers and judges who work to keep the balancing scales true and even for one and all under the law of the land. The people who make bearings to keep wheels turning, and those folks who help others find and stay the course of their bearings. The dentist who fixes and cleans teeth to keep aches from happening, and the ice cream and candy makers who make sweetnesses happen. The computer programmers who make the software that makes computers useful, and the folks who write all the manuals explaining how to use things properly, and those who write in novel ways. The sewage plant workers and the plumbers who help keep the flows happening, and those who treat water to be fresh and drinkable. The tool makers who craft the tools to make the manufacturing of all kinds of things possible, and those who sharpen and refurbish tools to keep them useful. Those who care for lost and stray animals, and those who groom and tend to ailing pets, and those who breed them and find them caring homes. The miners, steelmakers, and plastic mixers, who transform raw materials into useful forms, for others to fabricate with. The case managers who manage cases, and caseworkers who work cases. The timekeepers and foul callers. Those who operate and lay pipelines, and those who build bridges and carve highways into the countryside, and all those folks who patch and maintain them, and the folks who collect tolls from those who cross over them. The crews who sail ships, boats, and tug barges upon the waterways, and the longshoremen who load and unload cargo and the folks who store things safe. Those who cashier bucks and change, and those who count on changes in the weather and the market. The make-ready folks and printers who keep all kinds of presses running for the bindery folks to finish, and the paper-makers who make the paper for printing up all kinds of things. Those who dig up remains, and those who dig to hide remains away. The lumber Jacks and Jills who fall trees, and those who saw wood with their eyes open. The homemakers, who turn a house into a safe comfy home. Those parenting folks who help to grow offspring into being considerate and prideful adults, doing many of these kinds of things as being part of society.

Oh yes, that was a very long paragraph even in one of my rambles, but that's how it is with all these folks who work in silence, with pride in the jobs they do every day. Now, it is very possible that some might not really like the job they have to do, but they do what has to be done to get the job done. Too often you never hear about them and the thankless work they do, unless something nasty happens, and gets them thrown into the news for a brief 15 minutes of infamous fame. But mostly, everyone just does their job without really thinking very much about how important the work is that they do. Sure, everyone might slack off for a wee bit now and then, linger for a time on a coffee break, but when the call goes out to get the job done, they are right there to do what's needed to the best of their ability.

The problem with lots of jobs, is often times no one knows what you do until they need you, or until something isn't right, but most folks, just have no concept of the work others do, and they are always thinking about folks who seem to have an easy job. I have a friend Patrick who is a doctor. He has the vital job of restoring ailing folks to wellness—not an easy job. My high-flying friend Joe, the private pilot—soon to have his commercial ticket, works in the important area of water treatment. He works to assure the good taste and quality of water flowing out of a tap.

Unless there is a problem with the appearance and taste of water, we take water treatment for granted. Then there's Bill, and he has such a unique job and lots of folks have no idea what his profession is because it's unusual. No, he isn't some kind of rocket scientist. Bill is a highly skilled craftsman who does the demanding work of making minute corrections to fine engravings used on printing presses. When Patrick treats a patient, his efforts show in the patient's improving health. Joe's efforts to provide safe drinking water are seen in the sparkling clear drinking water. The result of Bill's skillful talents are hard to see, because he works from a set of engraving proofs. He carefully removes flaws and blemishes from the engraving set—his results are so successful they are unseen. All three of them have pride in their work. They each have special skills to take pride in, and they do their work to the best of their ability.

That's where the continuing pride of society is today. With all the common folks who have the pride to do the best they can with their individual jobs, and to continue to feel a true growing sense of pride in the ongoing results from their daily efforts. They don't look for the acclaim or glory, they just try to get their job done and collect their earned pay, and then come back and do it all over again the next day. So often in the hustle and bustle of the busy day, their efforts aren't even noticed, so easy to overlook things that get done in the background and are taken for granted, and still their pride remains. Perhaps they feel some pride with a few expressed *thank you's* in passing, or a nod and friendly smile, maybe even a seasonal greeting of good cheer. The kind consideration conveyed in sincere appreciation helps to keep pride alive, and well, and growing. The prideful rush of good feelings that flow from deep within you, when you know that today you did your job to the best of your abilities as you drift into contented slumber. Methinks the best kind of pride is homegrown—that self-esteem that grows pride within us all.

Take care and enjoy often . . . John

K-SCOPING...

Lots of folks in the here and now of today are forever wondering about what tomorrow will hold. Will the next day be sunny and bright, or will gloomy and rainy rule the day??? Is the path they follow going to take a sudden turn, or be straight and true for them??? What will tomorrow be??? Breaking into tuneful song and singing way off-key, *Whatever will be, will be, the future is not mine to see . . .* Yes, a very slight variation on the words to the song.

Ah, much of our endless quest in pondering the meaning of life is mistakenly invested in ways of foretelling the future. Some look to the Tarot card readers, *fortune-telling* in a mystical seeing the reader reads what *your future* will be. Others go with the allure of remaining tea leaves, because within the cup's remains are said to be lingering glances into *your future.* The magical casting of old worn bones, sticks, stones, and other castable things, are employed by some cunning folks to cast their viewpoints into *your future.* Oh, I almost forgot the merry hand-job doers, those fortune-tellers who are seers in hand line wrinkles of *your future.* I once knew a lady who was a marvelous reader of navels!!! She was so on target, and all she asked for in return—but, then that's another story!!! Alas, the many olden ways to craft about a supposedly seeing look into the unknown future, so many have become fortune makers for the tellers who have distorted the craft to fit their own bidding for bucks.

Back in ancient times, when druids walked about the land, they were said to be superior tellers of the future. They were known to speak the truth to one and all, and thusly, when druids spoke of the future, the flows of fate often brought forth just about the same future as the druids said would come to be. Druids were especially attuned to sensing the changing flows of the weather. Now remember, this was back before discovering the weather changing influences of the *butterfly factor* in regards to *chaos theory*!!! However, 'tis worthy to note, that the enjoyment of *Venus-butterflies* fluttering about was wide spread back then. The druids had an edge with the weather, because they were well known for attuning with the changing flows producing weather patterns. Their natural skills for knowing the differences and significance within pattern structures gave them above average foretelling insight. Druids could tell when the rains would come, when the sun would blink out for an instant in midday, when the earth was ready to receive sowed seeds, and when to harvest what mother earth was ready to fruitfully yield. Those early druids just seemed to have a bit of a knack for finding patterns capable of forecasting changes in the universal flows, that would, more often than not, come to be. With good crop planting info, the druids helped folks to learn seasonal cycles, and ways of doing caring kindness for mother earth. Some say druids could feel the coming changes, others said mother earth spoke to druids in mystical sounds of silence.

Methinks the druids stayed clear of telling about the futures of folks who wanted to know what the future held for them personally. The druids followed the *do no harm* rule, and it seems that there would be all kinds of potential for harm to be done, by telling folks about their future that could lead them astray. Folks knowing what *might* come to be, could indeed change how they are behaving in the here and now. Therefore, those deviating in the here and now, do change the direction of the future that they believed would come to be as the future was had been foretold—if the future had indeed been said for them. Also, methinks the druids believed that for all of life's happenings there was a reason. Mess around with what's happening, and that messing about could change in very different ways what was fatefully flowing into being.

Some folks are said to have *the gift*, or perhaps more correctly, *the curse* of being able to tell the futures of others. I've always wondered if this foreseeing was a blessed gift, then why do the *gifted fortune tellers* charge to *share* their *gifted insight* with others??? Could their readings be sort of milking the future to bring them a flow of bucks now, that only brightens the reader's golden future??? The bucks that they get come from the *fortune* part of the telling—ah, but 'tis only a donation. They get the fortune and you hear them telling!!!

Once upon a time when I was just getting into some of those druid type of flows, I did a very unique reading for a card reader. My long time friend Cathy had taken me out for a birthday lunch, and then surprised me with a visit to a card reader!!! The reader was wrong about all that she saw of my future, starting with her assumption that Cathy was my wife and we'd have lots of smart children!!! At the time, I was married to Jane, my son's mother, who wasn't able to join us for my B-day lunch. After she did a totally wrong reading of me, I did a reading for her—from her spread of cards. The *reader* thought it was a joke, and figured she'd let me make a fool of myself. Indeed a *mark* doing a reading—what a joke!!! I quickly went through each of the ten cards she had laid out face down—usually card reading spreads are done with the cards face-up. I only told her the meaning of each card, as it related to the earliest Tarot deck and her, flipping over the cards one-by-one, only after I told her what the unseen cards were. I was right on about which cards were what for all ten of the hidden cards. Indeed, the reader was very freaked by the whole thing and wouldn't accept Cathy's donation—she was rather anxious for us to leave. Oh my, lots of bad karma happens when people try to benefit from fooling around with the fate of others. Ugh, major bummer when that bad karma comes back at them!!! Alas, 'tis not at all nice to try to do harm to a druid.

We propel ourselves into our own fate. Follow along if you will, and I'll tell you of ways to know what your future might come to be. Now just because this works for some, that doesn't mean that this will do the same for everyone. What makes it work is sort of like what makes life work, or not work, and that's all a matter of attitude!!! The attitude that has some folks seeing a cup half full, and others seeing the cup being half empty--and with some folks seeing their cups running over, might mean they need a bra with a larger cup size!!! Hehehehee And even other folks are still looking for the cup!!! *I'm sure there's a cup around here somewhere!!!* So very much of your doing of life in the future, depends greatly on the perspective you bring to the doing of *your* life now. When you concern yourself with focusing on what's happening and needing doing today, then tomorrow is going to be a better day.

I try my best to look for the positive, and look for the odds being in my favor. A couple of decades ago, I was rudely awakened in the middle of the night by loud drinking partying sounds coming from the driveway next to my house!!! Half-awake, I put on a robe, and made my way outside to the source of the noise. Six college senior football type jocks were having an early graduation beer party alongside my house!!! Ugh, major bummer. I asked them to please move their noisy party elsewhere, because if my neighbors called the cops, I'd be the one the police would hassle and fine for allowing their disturbing the peace to be happening, so it would be good for all, if they'd move their party away from my driveway right away.

The biggest jock came up to me getting in my face, and then poked me in the chest, as he boldly explained the mathematics of the situation—that being that there were six of them who were very big, and only one of little old me. I was impressed he could count!!! I said that was indeed very true, but the only one of me, only knew one way to fight, and that's a very dirty serious kind of fighting. I told him the certain fact that I could take him totally out in a fraction of a second without thinking about it, and then I'd surely guarantee that two of his buddies would be knowing lots of pain before the other three jocks stomped the shit out of me. I told him in a calm even voice that I really didn't believe his life was worth his party macho act, and he shouldn't have a bit of doubt that he was going down very painfully, and the overwhelming odds were that he wouldn't be getting up again. Indeed, it was a life or death matter of their making, because that's often what's decided in the instant passing of a mere split second. Strange how so many meaningless things become an either or situation, such a bummer.

Much to my relief, he agreed that moving their party was the best thing to do, and sorry to have bothered me. I was very grateful that it was dark and they couldn't see how scared I was. Oh, have no doubt about it, I was prepared to act in an instant to take him out of the fight at the slightest hint of an aggressive move from him, but I was glad he saw the logic of moving away from the fight that they had unknowingly brought into my driveway. Having the shit stomped out of you is almost as painful as surviving an unexpected kick in the balls from a once upon a time trusted friend!!! Oh my, big time hurt!!! Besides, those jocks didn't know that I'm usually like an angry bear first thing in the morning, or when I'm pulled out of bed in the middle of the night, then I'm in my slowly awakening BC phase—that's *Before Coffee!!!* My attitude wasn't coming from a put-on macho act, all I did was let him know what was sure to happen in a way that left no doubt about what the outcome of his fate would be. Some might say how *un-druid* like of me, but I hadn't yet started to follow those *do no harm* ways of being—and in fact, *no harm* was done. Also, my plan of action was purely defensive, protective of hearth and home. Indeed, I did have a positive attitude, and I sort of played the odds!!!

I often wonder what might have changed in the course of history, if the ancient druids had been defensive when the Holy Roman Legions marched in to slash and slay them away because of the druid's un-christian like ways. The druids could have *helped* the weather flows to rain on their cute parade. Perhaps a freezing blizzard to slow their line of march with some frostbite. Maybe a hot scorching sun to fry their mindless brains inside those neat shiny metal helmets, an army all passed out from heat exhaustion isn't able to come a killing!!! Methinks those druids wouldn't be really *doing harm*, they'd just be allowing the elements to do the deed of heeding harm with a wee bit of druid like adjustments being made in natural flows.

Recently, a rat had been making nightly visits into the house to feast and make a mess with left-over food scraps. This unwelcomed visitor was upsetting to my wife Linda who keeps a clean house. I tried to block his ways of getting in, but to no avail. Linda was urging me to please *do something* about the nasty rat. So I bought a large industrial strength rat trap, that I set all baited with peanut butter for the rat to easily find. That night, with the fast zap from the sprung trap and a bloody splat, the rat's karma was recycled. Now I might be slightly pushing the druid belief of *do no harm* with my enticed *recycling,* but the rat was doing harm, and his harmful greedy actions sprung the trap. I'm not real sure how the druids of old would view my *recycling karma* concept. Since the druids were recycled away—perhaps to Iceland—because of imposed heavy religious happenings in the first century AD. Thusly, we have only bits and pieces of knowledge about the natural druid ways, and that's mostly from the hand-me down telling of folk tales. We know how folk tales being retold can change all kinds of things about.

Nowadays, folks have a yucky attitude about some kinds of hand-me-downs. The lore of old is . . . ah . . . so old and seems so out of place, in the polished shine of a new plastic craving society. Unless the hand-me has glitz and glitter of real money value, the hand-me on downs seems to be so lacking in something—perhaps it seems dirty!!! My father had an old army field jacket he wore in WWII, and that olive-drab jacket hung unworn in the closet for years. I'd try it on from time to time, although it was always too big—but a closer fit than the last time. Finally came the time when it fit me just right, and I needed a winter jacket, so I asked my father if I could have it. A nod and a shrug was all the fanfare there was in the transfer of this slightly tattered garment my father had once worn into battles.

I wondered what his feelings had been wearing this jacket, when the fighting foe was dead set on a course of killing him dead in a war. I wanted to ask how he felt then and now, about fighting another war for freedom in a far away land. But he never talked much about the war, not until years later in his life when we were both older. And then, with mere mentions in passing about the stupid ways of warfare, and how it is a wonder that the world survived all the dumb-ass mistakes that were made in the worldwide struggle. It was only in the final months of his life that he told me about putting his gun aside to help a young German woman deliver her baby, in a shelled out farm house in the middle of a battlefield—the magical moment of birthing while deadly fighting raged all around. Life continues on, even in the horrible face of war, birthings happen.

My father saved my life too, thanks to the war. He was off fighting the war when I was born, but he was with me that fateful afternoon when I almost lost my head!!! One of the things we did together was to fly model airplanes, or more correctly, we'd build them together and I'd fly them solo. He got dizzy going around in circles—as the control line model flew around and around in circles. I tried to teach him a focus point trick to abate his dizziness, but he'd never try it—methinks he had this old school belief that fathers only teach sons, sons don't teach fathers—oh, how wrong he was about that. In some ways, I'm writing this book to share with my son a few views of my life learnings that my father never shared with me about his life—I regret he never took the time to do this kind of sharing with me.

I was rather a hot combat pilot at flying slick looking control-line models—good eye hand synchronizing, with having the balls to push the plane's performance envelope to the max limit. Zapping the tail streamers off the planes of opposing pilots, we flew the model planes around in airborne circles, reaching speeds of over 100mph, while still on the ground. The rules of the game were that you flew as long as you had tail left—no tail and you're done. Landing to make fast pit-stops to refuel was allowed, and then quickly back into the air where several flying bandits awaited to do a pretend dog-fight. When your plane's tail streamer was cut-off, you had to leave the overhead combat flying, and fly low and level until you ran out of fuel.

I was doing some way good flying, chopping up pieces of tails for points and was way ahead in the combat kills scored. Then I ran out of gas and the engine stopped!!! Ugh, bummer when that happens--unless of course you're out on a date. I did a dead-stick landing for a fast pit-stop, refueling very quickly. Now my father is holding the model plane while I'm getting ready to flip the propeller, hoping for a quick start from my Fox 35 engine. All of a sudden my father is ducking and leaping over the model airplane and pushing me backwards yelling, "DOWN!!!" Falling backward from his shoving me, I was whacked hard on the head with a big time hurt hit, and my eyes were covered with gushing red blood!!! My blood!!!???

Fractions of seconds seemed so prolonged--as if hanging in suspended time, and everyone around me looked like they were moving in very slow motion. Another member of the Flying Dutchmen Model Airplane Club, who was watching the combat match, came running toward me pulling his tee-shirt off on the run. He bunched it up and pressed it to my bloody head. Two other guys were lifting me up and carrying me to my father's car. My father already had the car started while they put me into the front seat of the car. The guy holding the tee-shirt to my head kept applying pressure to what I figure must be a serious scalp wound and he was holding my brains in my head!!! With my father driving, we were off to the hospital in a flash—and I do mean a very fast flash!!! I was still trying to figure out what had happened. I was also being freaked with my father's driving—the time that had seemed to be standing still, now accelerated into a fast-forwarding blur. He was wheeling like a bat out of hell—long before *Meatloaf!!!* The ride to the hospital was a fright, he ran lights, wove in and out of—and bucked traffic on the wrong side of the road, at times riding all the way over on the shoulder of the road, and all the while laying on the horn. The guy holding the make-shift bandage to my head, was talking to me non-stop, asking me dumb questions like what's my name!!! He knew my name!!! He said my father pushed me out of the way of an airplane that was flying low and fast, and if I hadn't been pushed at that very instant the fast moving model airplane's propeller would have hit me square in the face!!! Methinks that would have been a real face-off with sudden death!!! What a bummer, a combat ace zapped dead on the ground!!!

Later, my father said that in a fraction of an instant, his mind had snapped back to the war, and he heard German 88 artillery shells coming in on his position, and his first reaction was to push me out of the way of the exploding shell fragments. Same with the guy holding his tee-shirt on my head, he had been a Marine corpsman during WWII in the Pacific, and he snapped back to running to save a Marine who had gotten a mean head wound from a sniper's bullet. From the way my father was driving, I wondered if he had even been a moonshine driver—and had snapped back to running away from revenue agents!!!

In the hospital ER, there was no waiting. The corpsman started giving the nurse a condition report as he carried me to an open operating table. Stat, the ER team went into action. All three of us were answering questions!!! The doctors were asking me if I could feel *this*, as I replied with a, *feel what???* The corpsman was being asked by a nurse if I had lost consciousness??? And two policemen were asking my father if that was his blue Ford parked in front of the hospital ER entrance???

Bunches of stitches later, they said I'd be okay, and they didn't think any of my brains had fallen out!!! However, my head was shaved as bald as a . . . ah . . . a baby's butt—good thing I had been wearing my hair in a real short crew-cut back then. They gave me some pills for the throbbing headache I'd have for a while, and I was able to go home. The police said they could have charged my father with at least a dozen moving violations, but in view of what was happening they didn't cite him. The doctor explained that I had been very lucky several times over. My skull bone was fractured slightly, this confirms the belief of some that I have a crack in my head, and I had two very serious lacerations, without the compress bandage being instantly and correctly applied, I would have most likely bled to death on the way to the hospital. Also, I'd escaped certain decapitation by being pushed out of the way of the incoming airplane!!! I really lucked out again by surviving my father's wild speed-racer run to the hospital, and all the red lights he went barreling right through, that seemed like accidents waiting to happen. The model airplane that hit me was a total wreck, so was the kid who flew it into my head—my hard head bent the nylon prop!!! That evening, calls were made to concerned friends to explain that I had a major bonging headache, not the light-weight ding dinking kind, and I'd be fine and flying again in a few days. Guess that was sort of like getting tossed off a horse thing, only very bloody!!!

Now, before you go off getting frustrated that I'm off on a tangent again, let me pull this tangent into the relativity of my ramble. The foretelling of our future grows from the seeds of our past mingling in the present, making our fateful futures to be as they will be. My almost being beheaded, and not the enjoyable kind of beheading, brought some very heavy dynamics into play. The young kid flying the ill-fated model airplane, watching the ensuing—that ensuing stuff can be so distracting—air-to-air combat being waged overhead with the pull of controlling strings. His lack of focus on the flight path of his model aircraft, placed me unknowingly in harms way. My father's suppressed memories of WWII, pulling him back to that harsh and hurtful period of his life—all in an instant—to hear the shrill scream of the approaching model airplane as an incoming German 88 shell, and then reacting as if he were back on the battle field with the quick and the dead, quickly ducking down while pushing me from the quickness of approaching death. The pull of the Marine medic flashing back to being under a sniper attack, and rushing to the aid of a fallen comrade. My father opening up the power of the Ford's big ass V-8 to race me against death to get me to the hospital before time and my blood ran out.

I'm in the middle of all these flows of fate, focused at that instant of time, on getting my plane back into make-believe aerial combat being fought with flying toys!!! Toys can kill folks just as dead, and that's a sad fact I came too close to knowing!!! Reflecting back on these bizarre flows of fate, I find myself acknowledging that there just ain't no way a soothsayer of today can really foretell the fated future of another—far too many variables are possible, and way too many lessons to learn, and too many questions waiting to be stripped down to the bare essence, for them to speak knowingly of another's fate.

The lingering karma from the war came into play and saved my life, about 15 years after that horrible world conflict finally ended. From the wrongs of harmful war came some good happenings at a high price. What's interesting to me, is that both of their conditioned reactions were rooted in basic survival skills, honed keen in long ago battles. Those fateful mind seeds of survival, sowed in a time of mortal combat, blossomed in an instant when their fruit was needed. Drawing from negative warring shit that they had both found themselves tossed into, and much later in peacetime, to apply those hard earned life experiences in positive life saving ways. Yes, I do feel having my life saved as being way positive, and thankfully, lots of good karma was indeed happening in positive ways of balancing.

The thing with this future telling stuff, is that in the mere fraction of a fraction of a second, the fateful future can change. No matter how smart we like to think we've evolved into being, we still do dumb fateful things!!! Dumb to have poked a hole in the ozone bubble!!! Even wise people do stupid things that change the futures of many people!!! Like ending the '90's, with a President being tried in the Senate for possible impeachment is way dumb—all things considered!!! Lots of fates got changed all about with that silly political fuss over who is doing what to whom in gratifying ways, with the ungrateful dead making a huffing and puffing thing about the whole yucky mess!!! Bill might win the top prize for being a wise-dumb-ass president!!! Such a big huff over such a wee bit of blowing!!!

Also, how come those computer dudes putting together the early operating systems identifying the current date, didn't count ahead to the year 2000 and discover they didn't have enough numbers working, and then hired the right number of numbers to do the job right??? At least when those old time wise guys invented the Hindu-Arabic Numbers, they worked out the numbers to match up with fingers and toes!!! Would Roman Numbers have worked for the computers to figure out the correct date??? I don't think so!!! In the year 999 AD, did they make the discovery that for the year 1000 AD they needed larger tablets??? Will the year 2000 do away with the AD, and then maybe become 2000 WWW??? World Wide Wonderfulness??? I believe we'll fix this KY2 dumbness, or is it YK2??? Or maybe they already have the designation down to a simple K2, in playing the problem identification reduction game.

The thing is, we've identified time frames and affixed measuring labels as very fine timeline indicators. With the speed of computers processing information, time has been sliced and diced finely into nano-seconds—which is like a billionth of a second!!! That's even faster than a New York half second.

However, it was the mass of time on the long end of the timeline that caused the YK2 problem. Partly because the daily date had been reduced to a six digit number, when eight is the magic number. The fact that the symbol for infinity is '8' might have been a major clue if they'd been thinking more and making less haste. At least those eight digits will work until the end of the year 9999, and that's a long, long time from now.

The other end of the calendar is also a mystery. When did those prehistoric folks make the transition into starting with recording time as a passing of marked history??? Did they wake up one morning and say this is when the year 1 starts??? I don't think so!!! There was no 'C' so they couldn't have known it was 'BC'!!! Historians have attached labels on large spans of times, classifying them as *ages*. Some cultures have affixed the measuring of time to fit their own unique *timestamp* to mark the sands of time with the beginning of their recorded political footprints. The early bureaucratic people were big on adjusting the calendar to provide a lasting memory by naming months of the year after them, and 'twas also a way of juggling the books back then, by adding a day to a month here and there as needed!!! Seems like those early politicians got a head start on messing things up, by playing with the calendar and causing the leap year thing too!!!

All this dawning of a new millennium hoopla is all well and good—well, the good remains to be seen, but in the eternal flows of the universe, a thousand years is barely a wink and a blink and a nod. The fears of disasters befalling humankind at the changing of this millennium are mostly problems of our own creating, like the YK2 computer dilemma and the holy ozone cap. Our dumbness in doing some piss poor planning is slowly catching up with us. Lazy slobby ways and inconsiderate interactions are starting to leave shitty stains on the sands of time. In greedy ways we try to capture an all seeing look into a future, when often a mere peep will do to learn what we need to know, and that's to stop leaving stains in the sands, and drawing limiting lines with *can't's, shouldn't's, and don't's.* Our collective dumbness is shaping the pitiful plight of our future, while we painfully play away natural resources.

We do indeed make our own future, just as what we do each day, or don't do, marks our passage across the sand. We also fall into doing those fateful self-fulfilling prophecy things. Sadly, the looking for doom and gloom has a weird way of bringing those looked for bummers into being. Tell a person often enough that they can't achieve a goal, and they turn away from doing what they might have attained. Start a new day believing it isn't going to be a good day for you and most likely it will be a yucky day. However, when you look for a UPS truck to come with an expected package, it never does!!!

At times, I've felt that the universe just sort of waits for me to be on the verge of enjoying something positive and good happening in my life, and then, in the 11th hour, have what had been looked forward to and worked toward, suddenly taken away. Be it promised venture funding drying up and going away; or a proposal that appeared to be moving forward, and then it is blown dead in the water by game players of nasty corporate politics; or a long anticipated arranged meeting dinged away at the last minute; or a sweet business deal that turns quickly sour; or an awaited visit that doesn't happen because of changes in plans, changes in interests, changes in shades of truths, changes changing!!! You know the feeling of having the rug pulled out from under you!!! But, regardless of the wrong done unto you, life goes on. Perhaps with a wee bit less of a smile, and certainly being more cautious and more guarded with extended and accepted trusts. Changes are the only constant truth that are always happening, even when you can't see them, or you don't want to see them, or won't accept them. Those changes making and marking fates are as endless as the universe. Raging out at those changing flows of fate is like raging out at the coming of the night. No amount of outrage will hold back the night. The clockwork wheels of fate continue to turn around and around, and what's bound to happen is what's happening—and one's fate changes in a nano-sec.

The way of the wheel is forever turning forward, leaving only traces of trackings behind. Nano-seconds of mingled fates merging into many tangled trails of our leavings—lingering with us as earned life learnings, slowly building up an inventory of life experiences as grist for what's ahead of the turning wheel. Alas, 'tis the blood, sweat, and toil that greases the ever moving wheel. Those who chart the future by the aligning of birth stars, plot but one course based on the magic of their ways, in grasping what the stars seem to say to them. The truthful flow of your future course is influenced by all those others with plotted courses that discourse and intercourse upon your destined course—fateful mixes and minglings experienced along the way into your unfolding future. Some of those many tracks may merely transgress slightly, a few might just be cosmic kisses in brief passings, and others will overlap in ways that almost cover your fateful trail, because those influences were so intense with life experiences to learn from, but not overwhelmed by.

The sum of all those experiences, large and small, have influences upon your momentous course. This smallest influence also has the power to change your course as major and minor happenings, at times, bring about the same outcome. Alas, 'tis like the *butterfly factor* in the chaos theory being transposed to sway the course—ever so slightly—of fateful flows, a mere instant of a second has the power to change a river of fateful flows. A small thing like the soldier on an advance across a battlefield, bending down to pick a lone colorful flower, just as a sniper's bullet zips harmlessly by where his head had just been a moment before; or maybe in his moments of being distracted by the lonesome flower, he fails to see the enemy repositioning an awaiting ambush. Indeed, the fluttering of a single butterfly has the power to minutely change the course of a raging storm. The fewest moments of an attraction or distraction have the power to change our fates evermore.

The pull of a single flower changed the soldier's fate. Those decisive pulls influencing our actions or inactions often come from within our ever increasing collection of all of our life experiences. Each and every awareness has the ability to *color* the pulls we respond to. The intensity of those colors aligning, often determine the strength of those coloring pulls, but the balance of those *colors* are ever changing as the wheel continues to turn and influences change—just like colorful patterns in a kaleidoscope are constantly changing with the slightest turn. Only your eye can fit the peep hole to see what the kaleidoscopic patterns of color will show about you. All those different colors of attitudes do indeed pull you this way or that way in the flows of fate. You make the choices about some of those colorful pulls, and at other times you don't have any choice at all—the colors pull you!!!

At times you may see a variety of rainbow colors through the peep hole to your inner self. The flows of life appear to be balancing in agreeable alignments of beautiful colors. Perhaps at times, the hues are heavy with jaded greens of jealous greedy attitudes ready to play upon your course in negative ways. Or maybe your colors are filled with bright glowing colors, propelling you into a positive flow that is so joyful. Then too, they could change to the darker shades of mystery, lurking as the unknown, when the sum of all your awarenesses only brings you a brief ambiguous picture and nothing more.

The only thing that's certain, is that the ever changing turns of the kaleidoscope will bring new changing patterns constantly coming into being. Each picturesque pattern is unique, ever so slightly different than the previous one, because the wealth of your accumulated life learnings are always increasing your inventory—from both the positive and the negative lessons of life. Also, the colorful picture grows clearer as the gray shroud of imposed guilt and shame are lifted away.

Your knowings of others are also part of the colorful array. With some, their colorful conditions sparkle brightly, as the truthfulness of their interactions with you; and some are tainted by the dinging dishonoring of friendships from lies that were told to you. With dishonesty happening in relationships, the colors that were once crystal clear, now become muddy from the shitty deceit dumbly dumped on the relating that isn't happening. Indeed, the wrongs that were done do taint the karma colors in your kaleidoscope. The staining taints bleed into other colors and make a mess, until fresh awarenesses flow truthfully with yourself and from others, and help flush the murkiness away.

You're the only one who knows the composition of the colors in your kaleidoscope. Only your eye can look inside to see your ever changing patterns jelling together. Only you know the scope of influences others bring to tint the mixtures of colorful awarenesses you have of those folks. Only you know if you'll bend to enjoy the beauty of a flower in the rough, or pass on by without as much as a passing notice. Your meditations upon the composition of the patterns, aligned ever so briefly in the kaleidoscope view of your life, hold the pulls of your fate, how well you see the truth within you makes your fate.

Your moods help to select the flavors of colors on the palette of your kaleidoscope. Will your colors today be sunny and bright, or rainy and gloomy??? The truthfulness of your path only comes into focus when you are truthful with yourself, and look through the transparency of the sparkles of others playing their influences of hues upon you. No one can foretell your future because they don't have your perspective of the kaleidoscope, and a slight turn will change whatever is seen there.

Methinks lots of folks haven't looked into their inner kaleidoscope in a very long time, perhaps they spend way too much time in front of a mirror only looking at fleeting surface appearances of outward changes. I wonder what colors will be found when they go K-Scoping, and what will they see their future to be??? *Whatever you see, will be, the future is you, you see, whatever you see will be . . .*

Take care, my friends, and do enjoy often . . . John

FATHER'S DAY 1998...

Honor thy father on this day when honoring is due, and when there is a father to bestow honors upon, for far too many fathers are gone from the scene, driven away from involvement with their offspring by strife that happens when mothers and fathers split apart and siblings get stuck in between.

Honor thy father with loving expressions and recalled cherished memories of shared learning's, of tender bonds forged from links of life's experiences, that are uniquely father and child gentle life knowings, about ways of trekking along life's path, being honest with one and all, truthful in relating and respectful of self by honoring promises made, doing no harm as thy will be done.

Honor thy father in the here and now, for with time passages he could become lost in the ever shifting sands of time. Changes do keep on happening. What is here today is sadly gone tomorrow. While some memories linger endlessly, other memories might need refreshing from time to time, like the fires of love that wax and wane with the flows of life.

Honor thy father as a caring person, who might not have always found the words to fully express the inner feelings of love in his heart, but knows vicariously your joys of exploration and your sorrows from life's disappointments. Also knowing your zestful sparkles of delight as you learn and we share the discovery of your newly found life awarenesses.

Honor thy father for life experiences shared, his offered efforts to convert his knowing of life into the weave of your life's flowing fibers. To learn from the wisdom of his ways of wrongs that he paid the price to learn from, for the fruit of mistakes hold the benefits of teaching about what doesn't work out in the form that was anticipated. The seeds of the trees he planted in his distant yesteryears have grown into tall spreading trees, now bringing you cooling shade from a glaring sun.

Honor thy father with the truth which rings with the clear chimes of freedom. To truthfully be yourself is a gift of self. Being truthful with friends is a debt of honor and increases esteem in respectfulness of self, far different than the dinging dong of entrapment lurking in the flatness of lies and falsehoods.

Deceitful doings reverberate in dings of haunting echoes as you learn that some people fear the truth they seek or know truths differently than you know truthful values. The truth of the here and now is the realness of you. Tomorrow, and tomorrows are nothing more than the allure of a promise made today. Promises are so fragile and do get broken, forgiveness is for giving when forgiving is due.

Honor thy father in thankful ways that betell of your undying gratitude, for the ways he helped you to learn of life and about being yourself in your life, about the freedom to truly be free, and of being trustful in growing friendships. Forgive him for ways that he never learned from his forefather's long ago.

Smile knowing that there comes a time when the spunky young offspring springs beyond the circle of the coiled spring, bouncing off to abound with your own ways in your ever expanding world.

See his smile for you spreading across his face, while you overlook the tears just forming in the corners of his eyes, for they are the special prideful flows shed only by fathers, as their offspring grow beyond the circle, but stays forever with growing precious love in the magical garden of the heart.

Happy Father's Day, my son, my friend, families we get born into, and get stuck with, for better or for worse. Families of friends are those special godsparks we select to grow always and in all ways as loving friends in the garden of our heart.

I love you my son, take care and enjoy often...Dad

THANK YOU MUCHLY...

. . . for taking the time to read my wordsmithing efforts,

. . . for allowing my thoughts to mix and mingle with your thoughts and feelings about the various topics touched upon,

. . . for hopefully keeping your mind open even when you had no idea where the tangents of my mind-flows were going,

. . . for your understanding that I don't profess to have the answers to your questions—I'm trying to figure out my own,

. . . for perhaps knowing some bursts of joyful laughter and maybe a silent tear or two with my gentle heart tugs,

. . . for being daring enough to maybe see a few things differently than you might have always thought of them,

. . . for giving consideration to perhaps returning to a few selections to harvest some more mind seeds,

. . . for finding words to be the links of friendship that's worthy of sharing and enjoying with your friends.

This concludes my collection of sharings here, but this really isn't an ending—hopefully this is a springboard for the beginning of another collection of my works for your future enjoyment. I invite you to play a part by suggesting topics for me to ramble about—just like several of these pieces came into being at the request of my friends. You may email me at: EnjoyOften@aol.com or via regular mail care of BBOTW. The potential for timely feedback from readers and the marvel of instant connectivity via the internet is opening wonderful channels of communication authors wouldn't have dreamed about twenty years ago. I'd really appreciate hearing from you.

BBOTW is a trend setter in self-publishing because they do cost effective, on-demand publishing, and handle order fulfillment for authors—while authors retain all copyrights and creative freedom. BBOTW also has the means of digitally storing the books they publish on computer disks, so their selection of books are always in stock and never have to be listed as being "out of print." They can promptly print a single copy at any time in the future at a reasonable price. I'd encourage authors to check out the unique publishing services offered by BBOTW as a means of getting your work-in-progress book into print quickly.

BBOTW maintains an online bookstore of their published titles at: www.buybooksontheweb.com or telephone them *Toll Free* at: 877-BUY BOOK.

Thusly, I draw this ramble to a close with my sincere gratitude for your interest, and with hopes of hearing from you.

Take care and enjoy often . . . John

John F. Harnish continues to enjoy a life long love affair with the creative process. Writing this book marks his return to the joys of creative writing for publication after an absence of almost 2 decades. John has successfully completed a wide range of consulting assignments in advertising and marketing a variety of new products and services. Frustrated by incomplete market analysis reports, he embarked on an independent course into doing primary research to design and develop more accurate forecasting methodologies based on pattern recognition analysis generated by the differing pattern structures from a single variable. He is a USAF veteran of SAC, and has been both a student and teacher in many of the areas of creativity—but he is always a student of life. John lives with his wife Linda in the greater Philadelphia area.